Full, Conscious and Active Participation

Celebrating Twenty-Five Years of *Today's Liturgy*

Michael R. Prendergast, Editor

PASTORAL PRESS

PORTLAND · OREGON

Full, Concious and Active Participation Celebrating Twenty-Five Years of *Today's Liturgy*.

ISBN 1-579992-115-9

© 2003 Pastoral Press

Pastoral Press
A division of OCP Publications
5536 NE Hassalo
Portland, OR 97213
Phone 1-800-LITURGY (548-8749)
E-mail: liturgy@ocp.org
Website: www.ocp.org
Managing Editor: Glenn CJ Byer
Assistant Editor: Melissa C. Phong
Editorial Assistance: Bari Colombari, Geri Ethen, Michael Kasner, Nancy Wolf

Publisher: John J. Limb
Editorial Director: Paulette McCoy
Book Design: Le Vu
Cover Design: Le Vu
Art Director: Jean Germano
Cover Art: Sheila Keefe

(EB 04/06)

Table of Contents

Introduction

This book contains a number of stellar articles that have appeared in the journal *Today's Liturgy* over the past twenty-five years. These articles feature the writings of some of the nation's most well-respected pastoral liturgists. New reflections by the authors introduce and expand on the original writing, with insights into the evolution of pastoral practice. The book celebrates the twenty-fifth anniversary of *Today's Liturgy* and the fortieth anniversary of the Second Vatican Council (1962–1965).

The book's title helps to underscore the promotion of liturgical instruction and active participation called for in paragraph 14 of *Sancroanctum concilium* (SC):

> Mother Church earnestly desires that all the faithful should be led to that full, conscious and active participation in liturgical celebrations which is demanded by the very nature of the liturgy. Such participation by the Christian people as "a chosen race, a royal priesthood, a holy nation, a redeemed people" (1 Peter. 2:9; cf. 2:4–5), is their right and duty by reason of their baptism.
>
> In the restoration and promotion of the sacred liturgy, this full and active participation by all the people is the aim to be considered before all else; for it is the primary and indispensable source from which the faithful are to derive the true Christian spirit; and therefore pastors of souls must zealously strive to achieve it, by means of the necessary instruction, in all their pastoral work.
>
> Yet it would be futile to entertain any hopes of realizing this unless the pastors themselves, in the first place, become thoroughly imbued with the spirit and power of the liturgy, and undertake to give instruction about it. A prime need, therefore, is that attention be directed, first of all, to the liturgical instruction of the clergy.

Since the Second Vatican Council the church has striven to implement this mandate of the council. Pastoral commentaries on the documents, the liturgical weeks, conferences, workshops and liturgical catechesis together with the oversight of bishops and offices of worship in the local churches have worked to make the mandate a reality. But here we are forty years after the council and there is an even greater need to provide liturgical catechesis and formation of both clergy and laity.

On this feast of manifestations the church celebrates three "epiphanies": the visit of the magi, the baptism of Jesus by John in the river Jordan, and the wedding feast of Cana. The articles and vignettes in this book are manifestations for the entire body of Christ calling them to embrace the aim to be considered before all else: "full, conscious and active participation."

—Michael R. Prendergast
Solemnity of the Epiphany 2003

Abbreviations

AGD   *Ad gentes divinitus:*
The Decree on the Church's Missionary Activity, 1965

BCL   Bishops' Committee on the Liturgy

CDW   Congregation for Divine Worship

CDWDS   Congregation for Divine Worship and
the Disciple of the Sacraments

CE   *Certiores effecti*: Benedict XIV's Encyclical
on Frequent Communion, 1742

DD   *Dies domini:* On Keeping the Lord's Day Holy,
Pope John Paul II's Apostolic Letter, 1998

DMC   *Directory for Masses with Children*, 1973 (CDW)

EA   *Environment and Art in Catholic Worship*, 1978 (BCL)

EM   *Eucharisticum mysterium*:
Instruction on the Worship of the Eucharistic Mystery,
1967

FDLC   Federation of Diocesan Liturgical Commissions

FYH   *Fulfilled in Your Hearing:*
The Homily in the Sunday Assembly, 1982
(Bishops' Committee on Priestly Life and Ministry)

GILOH   *General Instruction of the Liturgy of the Hours*, 1971 (CDW)

GIRM   *General Instruction of the Roman Missal*, 1985 (CDW)

GNLY   *General Norms for the Liturgical Year and the Calendar*, 1969

GS   *Gaudium et spes*: The Pastoral Constitution
on the Church in the Modern World, 1965

ICEL   International Commission on English in the Liturgy

IGRM 2000   *Institutio Generalis Missalis Romani,*
General Instruction on the Roman Missal, 2000
(CDWDS)

IGRM 2002	*Institutio Generalis Missalis Romani,* General Instruction on the Roman Missal, 2002 (CDWDS)
LG	*Lumen gentium*: The Dogmatic Constitution on the Church, 1964
LMC	*Lectionary for Masses with Children*, 1991 (USCCB)
LMT	*Liturgical Music Today*, 1982 (BCL)
LTP	Liturgy Training Publications (Chicago, IL)
MCW	*Music in Catholic Worship*, 1972, 1983 (BCL)
MS	*Musicae sacrae*: Pope Pius XII's Encyclical on Sacred Music, 1955
NPM	National Association of Pastoral Musicians (Silver Spring, MD)
OCF	*Order of Christian Funerals*, 1989 (USCCB)
RCIA	*Rite of Christian Initiation of Adults*, 1988 (ICEL & BCL)
RMarr	*Rite of Marriage*, 1969 (SCR)
RTV	*Renewing the Vision: A Framework for* *Catholic Youth Ministry*, 1976 (USCCB)
SCAP	*Sunday Celebrations in the Absence of a Priest*, 1993 (BCL)
SC	*Sancrosanctum concilium*: The Constitution on the Sacred Liturgy, 1963
SCR	Sacred Congregation of Rites
TL	*Today's Liturgy* (OCP)
UR	*Unitatis redintergratio*: Decree on Ecumenism, 1964
USCCB	United States Conference of Catholic Bishops (formerly the USCC & NCCB)

PART 1

Pastoral Liturgy

1

Three-Fold Mandate to Participate

I draw immense enjoyment out of preparing liturgies. I delight in imagining how every detail, when painstakingly considered, can lead the faithful to deeper moments of prayer. However, my experience has taught me a very important lesson: attending to every detail before a liturgy does not insure that unexpected things won't happen. Bear with me as I illustrate an example of how careful preparation and fore-thought were subjected to Murphy's Law.

Imagine, if you will, a song leader directing a music rehearsal of a new, bilingual Mass setting. Add to that scene a visibly frustrated presider standing in the back of the church signaling the musician to stop the rehearsal. Although his response was not surprising, it was jar-ring and disconcerting to the musician. Within a few seconds of seeing the presider's response, the song leader was forced to choose between two options: 1) stop in the middle of the rehearsal and let the English-speaking assembly figure out the *Cordero de Dios* on their own, or 2) continue the rehearsal, teach the assembly the new melody with the foreign text, and watch the presider's face change to a darker shade of crimson.

This incident touches on several issues posited in the following article. It involves the assembly, ordained ministers and liturgy directors. First, the article addresses the role of the assembly and the three-fold mandate to participate fully, consciously and actively. This mandate summarizes some of the most crucial components vital to the church's liturgical life. In the scenario above, the purpose of the rehearsal was not simply to acquaint the assembly with new music or to assist them with Spanish pronunciation. Instead, it was to further form them in their unique role in actively proclaiming the eucharistic acclamations. By inviting the acclamations to be sung in a language shared by the fastest-growing segment of U.S. Catholics, awareness of the ever-diverse body of Christ is consciously raised, thus impacting worship as well as daily life.

Second, the article resurrects a rarely referenced paragraph found in the first universal liturgical document of Vatican II. Although not explicitly, it correlates the level of commitment by the parish priest and/or the diocesan bishop with the liturgical participation of the faithful. In a very clear and direct way, it summons priests to possess a zealous attitude. Ideally, this active posture by the church's clergy was and still is a primary source of potent energy that generates and promotes the liturgical reforms. The word "zealous," however, should not be interpreted as the enthusiasm necessary to thwart a catechetical moment so as to start Mass on time. That type of energy may, in fact, be detrimental to the liturgical life of a community.

Lastly, the article offers a very bold proposal regarding the appropriate title and role of the "liturgy director/coordinator." The United States Conference of Catholic Bishops' pastoral letter regarding adult faith formation obliquely supports the proposal. This pastoral titled "Our Hearts Were Burning" upholds faith formation as the most essential component to the development of the Catholic Christian. Liturgical formation is one such component within faith formation. Regarding the previous illustration, one can only imagine what might have transpired if a liturgist (or someone with that role) had consulted with the presider prior to the liturgy. Certainly the issue was not limited to agreeing upon the correct time to start Mass. Rather, it was about respecting the faith community's need for liturgical catechesis. The liturgist, as proposed in the following article, would serve as the advocate for consistent and ongoing liturgical formation for adults and children.

The following article seeks to stimulate new ways of looking at the liturgy—not the details, but the fundamental principles. Hopefully, it will engage conversation among every member of the faithful, i.e., people in the pews, priests/bishops and directors of parish or diocesan worship. In doing so, ideally, it will lead Catholic Christians to consider their unique role in worshiping our Creator within the church's communal celebrations.

—Clara Dina Hinojosa

Full, Conscious and Active Participation

Clara Dina Hinojosa

"Engaged" but not in the liturgy

As a member of a cathedral parish situated in the city's urban core, I regularly sit beside out-of-town guests. On one particular morning I sat beside a visitor, a woman at least thirty years my senior. During the silence prior to the liturgy, my attention was drawn to this woman as she dug through her purse. She took out a devotional book and slowly passed through its pages, moving from one prayer to another. When it came time to stand and sing the gathering song, I saw that she did not reach for the hymnal. I assumed that she was still immersed in her prayerbook. However, throughout the rest of the service, she rarely lifted her eyes from her book. She never once opened the hymnal. Her responses to the common acclamations were weak, at best. It was obvious that her devotional book was the focus of her prayer.

In frustration, I wondered what I could say to this woman. I considered whether it was my right to say anything at all. Was I justified in my frustration, or was I just acting like an over-sensitive liturgist? "Ma'am," I imagined myself saying, "are you unaware that the liturgy is the primary and indispensable source from which you, the faithful, can derive the true Christian spirit? Did you not know that it is your right and duty to fully, consciously and actively participate in the liturgy?" Reciting liturgical documents helped me attain a graduate degree, but it has yet to serve me well when addressing or persuading the average person in the pew. Confused and disappointed, I bit my tongue and pondered why nearly forty years of liturgical reform had not apparently touched this woman.

What does it mean to be engaged in prayer?

This episode prompted me to consider the meaning of liturgical participation. It led me to review a quote that I have frequently recited but have never deeply discerned until only recently:

> The Church earnestly desires that all the
> faithful be led to that full, conscious, and
> active participation in liturgical celebrations

5

called for by the very nature of the liturgy.
Such participation...is their right and duty by
reason of their baptism. (SC 14)

Further reflection upon the woman led me to this conclusion: in reality, she was engaged in prayer in the midst of the Sunday assembly. But there is a clear distinction between her prayer and the prayer called for by the *Sacrosanctum concilium* and the numerous other documents that followed the Second Vatican Council. Although she was present at the liturgy, she was not present *to* the liturgy.

What an indictment! How is it possible that four decades' worth of liturgical renewal has left this woman and countless other Catholics unaware of their authentic participation in the liturgy? How did this occur? As we approach the promulgation of the church's new *Sacramentary* and *Instruction on the Roman Missal*, we have the opportunity, or to put it more strongly, the duty to catechize the faithful so that they may be active in and enriched by the church's liturgical prayer. How, then, shall we embrace this teachable moment?

To explore this situation in greater depth and consider possible options, let us, first, reflect on the phrase "full, conscious and active participation" and consider what it is and what it is not. Second, let us return to the *Constitution on the Sacred Liturgy* and reread other selected paragraphs. There we will find how the council envisioned liturgical catechesis to occur. Lastly, let us ponder what steps we might follow so as to truly embrace our newly refined Order of Mass and its supplementary resources.

Without a doubt, "full, conscious and active participation" is one of the most frequently quoted phrases in all of the liturgical documents. Indeed, it is a guiding and fundamental principle of the Constitution on the Sacred Liturgy, the first document promulgated by the Second Vatican Council. After nearly forty years of attempting to live out this reality, these words continue to inspire and intrigue us.

As a simple yet unconventional way of shedding light on these words, I'd like to compare liturgical participation with two forms of traveling. First, consider what it involves to drive a car. To get anywhere in a vehicle, the driver must get in the car, turn on the ignition and put the automobile in gear. Another form of transportation is taking the subway. In the subway station, the passenger boards the train, lets someone else drive, tunes out others around them and stays alert so as to know when they have reached their stop.

Comparing these two modes of travel brings a different perspective on liturgical prayer. I liken full participation to the very first act of placing one's body into the driver's seat. Conscious participation is that deliberate act of starting the engine. Active participation is similar to putting the automobile in gear, making it possible for the car's movement. Traveling on the subway is an experience which doesn't warrant being actively engaged in directing the train toward its destination. It is a relatively passive experience which warrants only that one know how to get on and when to get off.

To further our understanding of liturgical participation, permit me to use more conventional imagery. In order to fully, consciously and actively participate in the liturgy, the worshiper must desire three things: 1) to offer one's self, 2) to be awake and alert to the Spirit, and 3) to be open to transformation. Bringing to the liturgy an attitude of willingness, attentiveness and receptivity permits the Christian to become engaged in the work of building up the body of Christ.

Full participation

Being fully engaged in the liturgy involves more than being present at the liturgy. It requires offering one's entire self to the service of worship. It is sheer self-offering which reflects an alignment of one's self with the continual self-offering of Jesus to the Father. Although a prevailing and consumeristic attitude is "What do I get out of the liturgy?" the critical questions must be "What do I give to the liturgy? How is my self-offering a sign of worship?"

There are countless moments in life when one's body is present to a place but when one's mind is distant and removed. Other times emotional stress or spiritual anxiety can keep one from being fully present to an event or another person. In the liturgy, true and authentic self-offering begins with being fully present to God, one's self and to the faith community. Personally, there have been numerous occasions when I arrived to Sunday Eucharist or to the celebration of the Liturgy of the Hours with many distractions in my head. At times, a swollen knee or a broken heart have kept me from being fully present to the liturgy and to the people gathered there. Instead of considering how my wounded knee or heart could draw me closer to the paschal mystery, I ignored the connection and left the liturgy wondering why it was so ineffectual. In those situations, I eventually realized that I gave nothing to the liturgy, not even my fractured self. I was not fully present; my participation was marginal, at best.

Full participation requires a willingness to be present. As in gift giving, it involves placing one's entire self fully and completely before the Lord. Truly, it is a gift of one's body, mind and spirit. The degree to which one offers one's self is in direct relation to what one gains back from the liturgy.

Conscious participation

If the first step to ritual participation is total self-offering, the second is being awake and alert. This experience of being attentive and consciously participating involves the deliberate act of engagement. The opposite experience of conscious participation is what I call "liturgical sleepwalking." This is demonstrated (with regularity!) by those who enact the ritual gestures, speak and sing the words, and see or touch the liturgical objects but who remain disengaged as though on auto-pilot. I, for one, have fallen prey to liturgical sleepwalking. Often I have caught myself belting the music to a glorious hymn and later asking, "What was the meaning of the words that I just sang?" From my own experience, I have heartily recited the Nicene Creed but have sometimes reached the end wondering what I had just professed.

It takes a great deal of effort to be attentive to the liturgy. Rather than being mindful to its subtleties and nuances, those bored by the repetitiveness of the liturgy often express a need for more festive and upbeat worship. Instead of battling our culture's growing dependence upon a variety of constant stimuli, many desire the equivalent of electrical prods to keep them engaged. Members of the assembly need to deliberately stay awake, rather than tacitly involving themselves in seemingly "routine" gestures.

Conscious participation in the liturgy necessitates an attitude that is alert to the connections between liturgy and life. It warrants that one be deeply aware of God's presence in one's self and in the community.

Active participation

Of the three adjectives that are being explored, "active" participation appears to be the most discussed but most misunderstood. Active participation is commonly evaluated by the external engagement visible to another.

Undoubtedly, participation in any ritual involves external actions; these rituals form us as well as communicate intangible feelings and experiences. Kissing one's mother, holding one's partner, caressing the face of one's child are all external acts which speak of a deeper and invisible reality. Venerating the altar with a kiss, sharing the sign of peace with an embrace, signing an infant's forehead with a gentle touch are sacramental actions, ones that communicate God's unconditional love to another. Enacting gestures and verbally participating in the liturgical rites indicate a level of activity.

Regardless of what is externally manifested, the potential for internal transformation is what determines whether one was active or not. I am reminded of a personal example where lack of action does not mean lack of transformation. There are moments in the liturgy when I am so moved by the Spirit that I cannot sing the hymn. I sit quietly and listen to the words flow over me and into me. Although I am not actively moving my mouth, I am being transformed by the message.

Active participation, internal and external, gives the promise of transformation by offering one's self and being aware of how the Spirit leads, by having a desire to be engaged/transformed through words, gestures and objects that is mediated through God's presence by and through external or internal engagement.

Ultimately, a person's full, conscious and active participation in life is directly related to one's participation in the liturgy. One cannot truly be engaged in the liturgy if they are not engaged in life. One supports the other. Ideally, the purpose of liturgical catechesis is to establish connections between sacred rituals of the church and sacred rituals in our personal relationships. Appropriation of the liturgy to one's own life as a reflection of the paschal mystery is the goal of liturgical catechesis. In essence, liturgical participation is practice for living as a Catholic Christian outside the liturgy. In doing so, we build the reign of God, making God's grace operative throughout everything we encounter and for those whom we encounter.

The aim to be considered before all else...

The phrase on full, conscious and active participation spoke to what was to be the goal of liturgical catechesis. What was also clearly stated in the documents was how the catechesis was to occur. Consider the following quotes. Pay attention to who is being addressed and what expectations are implied (italics added for emphasis).

> In the reform and promotion of the liturgy, this full and active participation by all the people *is the aim to be considered before all else...Pastors must zealously strive in all their pastoral work to achieve such participation by means of necessary instruction.* (SC 14)

9

> Pastors themselves [must] become thoroughly imbued with the spirit and power of the liturgy and *make themselves its teachers*. (SC 14)
>
> With zeal and patience pastors must *promote the liturgical instruction of the faithful and also their active participation in the liturgy both internally and externally*. (SC 19)

It is unmistakable that the council members wrote these instructions directed to clergy. Without a doubt, ordained priests are expected to develop their own understanding and love of the liturgy as well as to promote the liturgical formation of the faithful. Although there are parishes and dioceses where liturgical leadership of clergy has been evident, for the most part these directives have not been realized.

Missed opportunities

One recent example gives evidence to the lack or total absence of proper catechesis. While teaching a course on prayer and worship, I was confronted by a woman who vividly recalled her initial and continued confusion regarding the liturgical reforms that followed the council. She spoke of how disoriented she was when they "turned the altar around and started saying the Mass in English." Others in the class talked about how very little explanation was offered after those radical changes were put into effect. In actuality, all of these people support the liturgical reforms. They were just not offered suitable instructions on why these liturgical reforms were important to the life of the church.

Regrettably, nearly forty years have passed and countless Catholics still have not had the leadership that was requested in the three quotes stated above. With little or no formation, many have been and continue to be left behind in the wake of the liturgical renewal. As the church draws closer toward the acceptance of significant liturgical changes, two things must be addressed: why has liturgical catechesis been neglected and what must be done so that the next forty years will see a greater commitment to liturgical formation? Although history is instructive, we would be better served by considering solutions to future possibilities than in finding fault in why liturgical catechesis has, in many ways, failed.

If I were to offer one solution to the future of liturgical catechesis, I would suggest that each parish (and most definitely each diocese) should call forth the services and gifts of a liturgist. I would even go so far as to recommend a specific title: director of liturgical formation. This specified role would be distinctly different from what most parishes presently experience.

The director of liturgical formation should be concerned with increasing the full, active and conscious participation of all members of their faith community. In contrast, in most parish settings with which I am familiar, I have noted that the "director of liturgy" is most aptly called the "coordinator of liturgical ministers." Given the multitude of ministers that most parishes utilize on any given weekend, the role of liturgy coordinator is critical. However, I would maintain that a director of liturgical formation would develop programs to catechize children, youth and adults into a deeper understanding of liturgical participation. This involves more than just training people to execute ministerial functions. It demands forming the assembly as persons who engage more deeply in liturgy and life. It involves discerning and calling forth the gifts of members within the assembly for the service of liturgy and great service of the community.

Conclusion

The success of the implementation of the newest editions of the *Sacramentary* and the Instruction on the Roman Missal will be directly related to the parish liturgical leadership, in particular the director of liturgical formation. Otherwise, forty years hence, the woman sitting beside me at the cathedral will reappear. She will not be fully, consciously and actively involved in devotional prayers. More than likely, she will not be participating in either devotional or liturgical prayer. Perhaps, without adequate liturgical formation, she and others won't find a need to be at the celebration of the Eucharist at all. For the future life and vitality of the church, parish and diocesan leaders must commit to forming the faithful into fully, consciously and actively participating in the liturgy and in life.

2

We Are Not Responsible for God

I was in Gene Walsh's choir in 1958 when he was first working through the issues in this essay—but be assured, they are issues for a lifetime.

Gene was always striving for holiness, but he was never pious. He was earthy; he loved the arts, especially music making. I remember his comments about *Shaharazad*: "When I was young," he said, " I thought that *Shaharazad* was the greatest piece of music ever written. Now I'm not so sure." I knew Gene until his death and he often changed in his lifetime.

Gene posed the question: how can I love God totally and direct the choir—do my work and pay attention to God at the same time? This essay is his answer, but the full answer was in the way he lived his life.

> I gave all my attention to the choir during rehearsal. I devoted myself entirely to God during prayer. I opened my doors wide to nature, to art, to music, to people and to the Holy Spirit. It worked for me.

But in the process of working out the answer to the dilemma of how to attend to God and everyday life, he also began to shape the basis of his fundamental philosophy of life: be open and be totally involved.

> I find openness the key—openness to different personalities, diversity in culture, variety of experience, nature, the earth, the world, all creation...We grow by relating.

> We open ourselves to the Spirit of God
> when we open ourselves to the world and to
> people...We make ourselves as open as we
> can in every way we can. Where do we stand
> on the scale from closed to openness?
>
> If we close ourselves to the world in
> which we live and to the people with whom
> we live, we close ourselves to God. There is
> no other way.

Gene understood "full, conscious and active participation" as something that everyone was invited to do at every moment of their life—it was not reserved to church, and it certainly was not reserved to praying to God. Total involvement was central to everything Gene said and did.

> We love people—we **seek them out**,
> pay them attention, respect them, love them,
> because they have their own worth and beauty.
>
> We **involve ourselves** actively in loving
> ourselves. God made us that way: loveable.
> Failure to love ourselves insults the God who
> created us.
>
> We **involve ourselves** in our work, job,
> study or time off.

But central to Gene's philosophy of life was that *we are not responsible* for God—God is.

> God is always close to us—God makes
> promises of faithful love and keeps those
> promises. God is always there, even when
> we don't have warm feelings.
>
> By giving ourselves to the task, we sur-
> render to God directly and immediately.

Gene's words still carry power—his life was even more powerful. This essay contains the essence of Gene's thought, and is well worth reading and re-reading again and again. But more important, it is a guide for how he lived his life. We could do no better.

—Virgil C. Funk

Renew the Face of the Earth

Eugene Walsh, SS

For years I directed choirs at the seminary and cathedral in Baltimore. When I began in the early forties, the theme "God's presence" echoed through the writings of our spiritual leaders. They helped us ask, "How can we keep God constantly before us throughout the work day?" What a big question! What a big achievement—if we could pull it off. These writers offered assorted techniques to help us make it work. Some even guaranteed their methods. It all grew complicated and called for tricky spiritual acrobatics.

From the very start, that approach caused me no little problem in working with choirs. My problem was simple. How could I give all my attention to doing my work with the choir and at the same time keep a door open for remaining in God's presence? It frustrated me. If I got in God's corner, I lost hold of the choir. And if I paid attention to the choir, I forgot about God. I had a dilemma that stayed with me for years. I felt divided. So I got some help.

Then I also got some sense. I realized finally that I couldn't play the division game any longer. I could not give my full attention to the choir's needs and to God's presence at the same time. So I stopped trying and started doing one thing at a time.

I gave all my attention to the choir during rehearsal. I devoted myself entirely to God during prayer. I opened my doors wide to nature, to art, to music, to people and to the Holy Spirit. It worked for me.

Openness to creation

We grow to adulthood by opening ourselves to creation and to people. In fact, it's the only way. Nothing substitutes for it. Without initial openness, there will be no beginnings, middles or endings. Closed people don't grow. They remain children throughout their adult life. This comes as no surprise. At times it seems that child-adults even outnumber grown-up adults. We need to take a closer look at the correlation between openness and growth.

I find openness the key—openness to different personalities, diversity in culture, variety of experience, nature, the earth, the world and all creation. We grow to fullness as persons when we realize, insofar as we can, all the gifts God gives us. We realize this potential by connecting to all that is within us and without us. We relate to God, neighbors, creation, ideas, arts, science, history and ourselves. If we do not connect and relate, we shrivel up and die. We grow by relating.

Openness to the Spirit

Openness to creation leads us to the Spirit of God. Life in the world can open us to life in faith: to the life we sum up in the word *spirituality*.

The basic rule is simple. We open ourselves to the Spirit of God when we open ourselves to the world and to people. The Spirit comes to us through the world in which we live and through the people with whom we relate. The Spirit already works in the world and in us, seeking to be released into our lives, into others' lives and into all creation. That is what we mean when we pray to the Holy Spirit, "Renew the face of the earth."

We have priorities in living according to the Spirit who renews the earth. The top priority is this: we make ourselves as open as we can in every way we can. To do that, we have to find out just how open we are. It's not easy. We cannot always get an accurate reading by ourselves. We may need others to let us know how they see us. That may be hard and may take a lot of courage. How does our family see us? The neighbors? Colleagues? Anything we can discover about ourselves in this way will be of great value.

Where do we stand on the scale that extends from closed to open? If we get an accurate reading on how open we are, we can do something about it, should we choose. If we never find out, we remain slaves of ignorance and captives of fantasy. We stay closed. I find particularly tragic on the human stage the great number of people who close themselves to change but don't know it.

A genuine life-giving freedom in the Spirit comes about as we consciously open ourselves to the circumstances of our lives, especially to the people around us. If we leave them to go off in another direction, we wind up doing busy, unproductive things or walking down dead-end streets. We describe here an important principle of Christian life: we open doors that keep us from each other and break down barriers that alienate us from creation. We open ourselves to the Spirit. There is no other way.

If we close ourselves to the world in which we live and to the people with whom we live, we close ourselves to God. In other words, we grow in the life of faith to the degree that we work with the Holy Spirit to "renew the face of the earth."

Involvement and excellence

Another principle of Christian life flows from this openness: we live life as thoroughly as we can. We get involved. We do well what we do—at whatever time.

A. We involve ourselves in each value for its own sake. That's our best reason for doing anything: because it is worthwhile in itself. We respect every part of creation because it deserves our respect. We love people for their own sake, not for God's sake. To love people primarily for God's sake in truth insults them. Are they not lovable in themselves? We seek them out, pay them attention, respect them, love them, because they have their own worth and beauty.

B. We involve ourselves actively in the business of loving ourselves. We seek to love ourselves more and more, because we are lovable. God made us that way: lovable. We deserve all the love we give ourselves. Failure to love ourselves insults the God who created us. Guilt—imposed by others and increased by us—constitutes the greatest barrier to love of self and love of God. Guilt results from human weakness and sin. God has nothing to do with it. We need to break through the guilt barrier in loving ourselves enough to open up to the Spirit.

C. We involve ourselves in our work, job, study or time off. We do this in every possible way. We put ourselves into whatever we do. We give it all our energy. We don't hold back. When we immerse ourselves in a task, we move closer to the Spirit of God. Is not that the goal? Also, by the same wholehearted attention, we turn out a more excellent work. In the process, we do not need to be aware of God at all. All we need is to be involved as completely as possible.

Total involvement lays the foundation. If we skip this step, how will God provide the growth, the increase and the fruit? To involve ourselves less than completely is to put a coating of sugar on our cereal. It may taste all right for a while, but it bores us quickly. Our enthusiasm wanes. The momentum collapses.

Such built-in failure characterizes the programs of many "schools of spirituality." They fail through superficiality. Their programs fail because they come from outside the self. They grow routine, mechanical, boring. We do not invest much in them. As a result, we end up worse off than when we began. And we blame the failure on ourselves rather than on the "school." The "school" with its programs is the real culprit. Now we need to learn from the big mistake.

Living in the presence of God

A final principle of Christian life could take this form: we do not take responsibility for God's loving presence. This insight runs counter to some prevailing notions of spirituality. In the good old days, what counted was our intention or our good will. Now we are saying that thorough involvement in our task is even more important. Our desire to do the most excellent job we can counts most. We don't even have to be conscious of God in the process. And that may need further explanation.

God is always close to us. It's a simple fact. God makes promises of faithful love and keeps those promises. God's business is to draw near. Nothing we do can change that, nor does our consciousness or lack of consciousness of God's presence make it more or less so. A sense of God's loving closeness feels good. Such feelings affirm and help us. God offers them at important times. But they really do not provide the only evidence of God's closeness to us. God is always there, even when we don't have warm feelings.

We frustrate ourselves by trying to accomplish two important things at the same time: an awareness of God's presence and a job well done. We can't divide our mind or our heart. And if our job has importance and requires care, do we have a right to give it less? To do a mediocre job is to betray God's purpose.

Teilhard de Chardin helps us understand this. Throughout his writings, a refreshing theme echoes: by giving ourselves totally to the task, we surrender to God directly and immediately.

Personal reflections

Reading Teilhard was a high point in my life. What a moment of conversion God gave! With dazzling clarity I realized God's closeness to us—and our nearness to God, even when we don't think about it or feel it. This was a great moment, a powerful insight and a wonderful discovery.

As a result, I started to live with an abiding sense of God's and our presence to each other—precisely in our work. I didn't have to be thinking about it all the time. What a relief! No more acrobatics!

I got excited about the insight and shared it with others. With this awareness came another discernment, no less worthy. It concerns liturgical music.

By giving our undivided attention to music, we enable the assembly to tap into the full power and life-giving energy that flow from making

18

beautiful music together. The gift we offer members of the assembly through music is encouragement to open themselves to the work of the Spirit at that moment. Music helps the great symbols come to life: gathering, reconciling, responding, declaiming, acclaiming, petitioning, remembering, thanking, praising, celebrating, sending forth. Music helps open our hearts to become receptive or vulnerable to the Spirit's work.

Now I look back with delight, knowing that the music we made all those years performed a needed service for God's people. For some it occasioned conversion. To others it gave comfort and reassurance. Still others it drew more fully into the celebration.

Those of us who did the hard and happy work of ministering music received something else: a deep, lasting satisfaction. We all knew that we were doing something good. That realization prompted efforts to do even better. Liturgical ministers, including musicians, need to derive regular satisfaction from our work. If we don't, we burn out and quit. We give up and start the restless search for something else. Why look further? What we seek is right here.

We rejoiced mightily in our work. How wonderful! We knew what we were doing, understood why, enjoyed it and took pleasure in our enjoyment. We suspected that it pleased and delighted God a great deal, too.

3

A Sacrament of Unity
for the Whole World

After the Institution Narrative in Eucharistic Prayer III, we pray to the Father in these words: "Look with favor on your church's offering, and see the victim whose death has reconciled us to yourself. Grant that we, who are nourished by his body and blood, may be filled with his Holy Spirit, and become one body, one spirit in Christ."

Are we, nourished with the body and blood of Christ, becoming "one body, one spirit in Christ" through the power of the Holy Spirit?

If so, how do we account for what some have called a growing polarization within the church, a polarization which the late Joseph Cardinal Bernardin said "had bred the kind of distrust among good people that obscures their more basic shared commitment to Christ, the church and the demands of pastoral care"?

If the Eucharist is to be a credible and visible sign of our ever-deepening unity as church, as the body of Christ, which itself is to be a sign of unity for the whole world, then we need good celebrations of the Eucharist more than ever.

By good celebrations I don't mean good music, good singing, good hospitality, good preaching and so on, as essential as these externals are for good celebrations. I mean coming to the Eucharist with proper internal dispositions.

As Vatican II's *Sacrosanctum concilium* (SC) says, "In order that the sacred liturgy may produce its full effect, it is necessary that the faithful come to it with proper dispositions, that their thoughts match their words, and that they cooperate with divine grace lest they receive it in vain" (cf. 2 Corinthians. 6:1). (SC 11)

In other words, coming to the Eucharist with polarized hearts, hearts lacking civility and a generous willingness to dialogue sincerely, defeats the ultimate goal of liturgy: our sanctification and God's glorification. (SC 10)

We must assume as we gather for the Eucharist that we are all there ready to "cooperate with divine grace," grace that will unite us by breaking down all those harsh, bitter, distrustful and unforgiving attitudes that polarize us.

We must assume that we all want Jesus' prayer for unity to be fulfilled in us as we gather around the table of his word and body: "I pray not only for them [the apostles], but also for those who will believe in me through their word, so that they may all be one, as you, Father, are in me, and I in you, that they also may be [one] in us, that the world may believe that you sent me" (John 17:20).

Then, and only then, can we say that we are open to ourselves as church, as Christ's body, to be a sacrament of unity for the whole world.

—Victor H. Balke

Sacrament of Unity
Catholic Common Ground

Victor H. Balke

Introduction

> Will the Catholic Church in the United States enter the new millennium as a church of promise, augmented by the faith of rising generations and able to be a leavening force in our culture? Or will it become a church on the defensive, torn by dissension and weakened in its core structures?

This is how the statement *Called to Be Catholic* begins. *Called to Be Catholic* (1996) "was prepared by the National Pastoral Life Center in consultation with Catholic men and women serving the church and society in a variety of callings and sensitive to the diversity of Catholicism in the United States."

Called to Be Catholic was enclosed with a letter from the late Joseph Cardinal Bernardin in which he explained that he had accepted a role of leadership in a project called the Catholic Common Ground Project. His letter indicated that "the project grew out of a series of discussions over the past few years among people dedicated to the church's pastoral ministry and dismayed by the apparently growing polarization in the church," a polarization that, he wrote, "had bred the kind of distrust among good people that obscures their more basic shared commitment to Christ, the church and the demands of pastoral care."

The Church: the Sacrament of Unity

Dissension, polarization, distrust: how ironic that these relatively strong, negative words should be applied to the church, whether in the United States or elsewhere! How ironic, because the Second Vatican Council, in its *Sacrosanctum concilium*, refers to the church as the "sacrament of unity."

> Liturgical services are not private functions, but are celebrations of the church, which is the "sacrament of unity," namely a holy people united and organized under their

bishops. Therefore liturgical services pertain to the whole body of the church; they manifest it and have effects upon it; but they concern individual members of the church in different ways, according to the diversity of holy orders, functions and degrees of participation. (SC 26)

In other words, since the church is the sacrament of unity, and since sacraments bring about or effect what they sign or signify, the church at worship is not only to sign or manifest the unity that belongs to God's people as God's gift, but through its very worship is to experience a deepening and strengthening of that unity. The church at worship is where we should most profoundly "profess the truth in love and grow to the full maturity of Christ the head. Through him the whole body grows, and with the proper functioning of the members joined firmly together by each supporting ligament, builds itself up in love" (Ephesians 4:16).

It is worth noting that number 26 of *Sacrosanctum concilium* appears under a major heading, "The Reform of the Sacred Liturgy." The liturgy, we read, "is made up of unchangeable elements divinely instituted, and elements subject to change." These latter elements "not only may but ought to be changed with the passing of time if features have by chance crept in which are less harmonious with the intimate nature of the liturgy, or if existing elements have grown less functional."

Ecclesia semper reformanda: the church is always in need of reform. As the Dogmatic Constitution on the Church (*Lumen Gentium* 8) said: "The church, embracing sinners in her bosom, is at the same time holy and always in need of being purified, and incessantly pursues the path of penance and renewal." Within this ecclesial context we may say with equal force *liturgia semper reformanda*: the liturgy is always in need of reform.

The church with its liturgy, always in need of reform, is called to be the "sacrament of unity." Indeed, the church through its liturgy, which is always in need of reform, is called to be the "sacrament of unity."

Is this really possible? Given the human proclivity to resist change, is it possible for a changing or reforming church to be the "sacrament of unity" through a changing liturgy?

Importance of catechesis

Not only is it possible for the church in and through its liturgy to be the "sacrament of unity," it is imperative that it be so; this is our calling as the church. But this takes work, lots of work, lots of prayerful work. It takes careful and extensive catechesis.

To be convinced of the need for thorough catechesis, we should remember how "each of us has been touched by the serious consequences of a lack of catechesis when some thirty years ago the *Sacramentary* was first published in the United States" (from a communication of the Bishops' Committee on Liturgy dated September 2000). We are still suffering from those serious consequences.

Is there not still some anger about statues being de-emphasized, and about the removal of the American and even the papal flags from the sanctuary? Is there not some residual suspicion about priests who were thought to be autocratic and "doing their own thing" right after the Second Vatican Council? Isn't there still some disappointment over the loss of what is described as the "mystery" of liturgy, and over the apparent loss of the "sense of the sacred," reflected in informal behavior and casual dress at liturgy?

How many communities suffered serious division resulting from differences over liturgy, especially over the renovation of old churches or the construction of new ones! How many people were divided over the placement of the tabernacle or the altar (center or off-center)! Proper catechesis might not have prevented all the anger and hurts that many people experienced shortly after the Second Vatican Council, but it would surely have helped a great deal.

Now we face the implementation of the *Institutio Generalis Missalis Romani*, to become the universal law of the Church upon its publication as part of the *Missale Romanum*. If we want to avoid the pain of the past, we must spend the time and energy on effective catechesis.

Perhaps the most fundamental matter that catechesis should address is the distinction noted above: the distinction between those "unchangeable elements" of the liturgy which are "divinely instituted" and those elements "subject to change." As one would expect, the *Institutio* affirms those "unchangeable elements" of the liturgy which are "divinely instituted." But it also contains certain modifications within the celebration of the eucharistic liturgy which touch on those liturgical elements "subject to change." Unless these changes are explained, and explained well, before they are implemented, they could well be the occasion for confusion and even division within the eucharistic community.

These changes should be explained within the framework of addressing deeper questions. For example, what does it mean to be "church"? Do we really know what we are singing when we sing of ourselves as "a pilgrim people," "the Church of God," "a family of believers, disciples of the Lord, united in one spirit, ignited by the fire, still burning through the ages" (from the hymn "One Spirit, One Church" by Kevin Keil)?

What does it mean to be a *communio*, a *koinonia*, and how do we measure up to the idealized Christian community described in the Acts of the Apostles (2: 42–47; 4: 32–37; 5:12–16)? Or how do we measure up to (or down from) the Corinthian community which Saint Paul could not possibly praise (1 Corinthians. 17–34)?

Other questions that should be the subject of catechesis are those that were spelled out in the communication mentioned above from the Bishops' Committee on Liturgy. For example, what does it mean "to join ourselves to the sacrifice of Christ who calls us to the sacred mysteries"? Do we appreciate the "essential and indispensable role of the priest," without whom neither Eucharist nor liturgical ministry is possible?

What does it mean "to worship as members of Christ and his church, rather than as individuals who happen to be in the same space at the same time"? Do we see the necessity of participating very actively through song and responses? Do we understand the need for common texts, common posture, common activity, unity of mind and heart (Acts 4:32), in order to have communal worship, as distinct from private worship and prayer?

If these fundamental questions can be adequately dealt with through proper liturgical catechesis, then the individual changes in the *Institutio*, which will still need explanation, may not lead to the confusion and resistance that many fear.

A rite for "liturgical reconciliation"?

Perhaps after the necessary catechesis and before implementation of the *Institutio Generalis Missalis Romani*, some kind of rite of liturgical reconciliation might be celebrated in each parish. The whole assembly could be invited to come together as the body of Christ to forgive and be forgiven for past offenses and insensitivities touching on liturgical issues.

Called to Be Catholic said that one of the urgent questions which the church in the United States knows "it must air openly and honestly" is "the eucharistic liturgy as most Catholics experience it." An appropriate venue in which Catholics could "air openly and honestly" their thoughts and feelings about their experience of the eucharistic liturgy might well be a parish rite of reconciliation.

This kind of rite at the end of one millennium and at the beginning of another seems to flow logically from Pope John Paul II's stress on conversion, penance and reconciliation. "It is appropriate that, as the Second Millennium of Christianity draws to a close, the church should become more fully conscious of the sinfulness of her children, recalling all those times in history when they departed from the spirit of Christ and his Gospel and, instead of offering to the world the witness of a life inspired by the values of faith, indulged in ways of thinking and acting which were truly forms of *counter-witness and scandal.*" (*Tertio Millennio Adveniente* 33)

In recalling the great events of the Jubilee Year, the pope recalled that the year had been "strongly marked by the request for forgiveness" (*Novo Millennio Ineunte* 6). "How could we forget," he asked, "the moving liturgy of 12 March 2000 in St. Peter's Basilica, at which, looking upon our crucified Lord, I asked forgiveness in the name of the church for the sins of all her children?"

John Paul II referred to this as a "purification of memory" which "has strengthened our steps for the journey toward the future." As we begin to take the next steps on our liturgical journey into the future through the implementation of the *Institutio*, could we not profit by first having a "purification of memory" in regard to our past "liturgical sins" against one another?

Conclusion

Yes, the church is the "sacrament of unity" and can be such a sacrament more and more clearly, even though it must be constantly renewed and reformed. And yes, the church can be the sacrament of unity through the liturgy—liturgy rightly understood and approached, even though it too needs timely reform.

For this to be, we need "Catholic common ground" in our approach to the meaning of church and the purpose of liturgy. If we don't find common ground in these fundamental matters, will we ever be—in the words of *Called to Be Catholic*—"a church of promise, augmented by the faith of rising generations and able to be a leavening force in our culture?" Surely no Catholic who truly loves the church wants it to be "a church on the defensive, torn by dissension," and thereby losing in great measure its credibility as a constructive and positive critic of our culture.

We must remember that the Second Vatican Council closed over 35 years ago. It is highly likely that many Catholics under 50 have not been deeply immersed in the council's teachings, at least not through a close reading of the major documents. Perhaps this is why Pope John Paul II said, "The best preparation for the new millennium, therefore, can only be expressed in a renewed commitment to *apply*, as faithfully as possible, *the teachings of Vatican II to the life of every individual and of the whole church*" (*Tertio Adveniente Millennio* 20).

For Catholic common ground in the meaning of church and its liturgy, we must return to the "Dogmatic Constitution on the Church" and the "Constitution on the Sacred Liturgy." These documents present the faith of the church in her understanding of her very self and of her worship. They are the work of the Holy Spirit within the holy church and represent Catholic common ground at its best.

I conclude with *Sacrosanctum concilium*, which gives us Catholic common ground in regard to the importance of liturgy within the church. After the statement that the "sacred liturgy does not exhaust the entire activity of the church," the document continues:

> Nevertheless the liturgy is the summit toward which the activity of the church is directed; at the same time it is the fountain from which all her power flows. For the goal of apostolic works is that all who are made [children] of God by faith and baptism should come together to praise God in the midst of his church, to take part in her sacrifice, and to eat the Lord's supper.
>
> The liturgy in its turn inspires the faithful to become "of one heart in love" when they have tasted to their full of the paschal mysteries; it prays that "they may grasp by deed what they hold by creed." The renewal in the Eucharist of the covenant between the Lord and [humankind] draws the faithful into the compelling love of Christ and sets them afire. From the liturgy, therefore, and especially from the Eucharist, as from a fountain, grace is channeled into us; and the sanctification of

men [and women] in Christ and the glorification of God, to which all other activities of the church are directed as toward their goal, are most powerfully achieved. (SC 10)

At the Last Supper, on the night when he was betrayed, our savior instituted the eucharistic sacrifice of his body and blood. He did this in order to perpetuate the sacrifice of the cross throughout the centuries until he should come again, and so to entrust to his beloved spouse, the church, a memorial of his death and resurrection: a sacrament of love, a sign of unity, a bond of charity, a paschal banquet in which Christ is consumed, the mind is filled with grace and a pledge of future glory is given to us. (SC 47)

4

The Church Is about Communion

Communion was and remains the spirit and legacy of Vatican Council II. It springs up regularly in all the major texts of the council. If we take *Lumen gentium* (LG) (Dogmatic Constitution on the Church) first, we read there that the church is "the sacrament of union with God, and of the union of all people among themselves" (LG1). In brief, the church is about communion. What brings the communion of the church into existence is the sacred liturgy, and so we read in *Sacrosanctum concilium* (SC) that the liturgy is "the summit toward which the activity of the church is directed and the fount from which all her power flows." (SC10)

Our union with God and among ourselves is founded in the liturgy, and in the Eucharist *par excellence. Unitatis redintergratio* (UR), (Decree on Ecumenism), urges Catholics to work and to pray for the fullness of the communion that has been so tragically lost in our two millennia of Christianity. *Ad gentes divinitus* (AGD), (Decree on the Church's Missionary Activity), urges all Catholics to be missionaries, working for and contributing to the final and eschatological communion of all people in Christ. *Gaudium et spes* (GS), (Pastoral Constitution on the Church in the Modern World), invites us to see the church serving humankind by promoting a world marked by unity, love and peace. One could go on, but even these few examples serve to illustrate the "communion ecclesiology" that Pope John Paul II and the bishops of the world see as the self-understanding of Vatican II.

The agonizing question is: how can this vision become a genuine, living reality for us, if we remain divided over that which unites, that is, the liturgy? Disputes over ICEL, conflicting positions on liturgical performance, mediocre and poorly prepared celebrations, vapid preaching—these issues divide us not just in general, in the church at large, but in our local eucharistic communities. It is not only tragic, but sinful. Our liturgical divisions and in-fighting hinder the mission of the church and our own growth in holiness.

Today's Liturgy works to enflesh liturgically the dynamic and corporate vision of Vatican II. As we join and congratulate Oregon Catholic Press in celebrating twenty-five years of *Today's Liturgy*, let us also take the opportunity to examine our liturgical divisions and re-commit ourselves, with hope and under grace, to making Vatican II's vision of communion a glorious reality in the world-wide church, in our local parishes and in our own hearts.

—Owen F. Cummings

Sacrament of Unity
Community of Christian Faithful
Unity in the Parish

Owen F. Cummings

One of the most obvious things about the church in the United States today is the extent of disagreement, sometimes quite acerbic and acrimonious, about all sorts of issues—doctrinal and moral and liturgical. Catholics are all too quick to describe (and condemn) one another as conservative or liberal or radical. Such descriptions and condemnations often turn up in complaints to the pastor or to the bishop's office, and have the potential to make life in the church very difficult indeed. That the liturgy should be embroiled in this in-house divisiveness is very sad.

The liturgy is, in the words of the Second Vatican Council, "the sacrament of unity...the holy people arranged and united under their bishops" (*Sacrosanctum concilium* SC 26). When the liturgy becomes a battleground, it fails to effect and express believers' unity in Christ; it also undermines their witness to the world. The same council's Dogmatic Constitution on the Church (*Lumen gentium* LG) states, "The church is in the nature of sacrament—a sign and instrument, that is, of communion with God and of unity of the entire human race..." (LG 1). How can the church be an effective "sign and instrument" of the unity of all humankind if those who gather for the sacred liturgy that is the source and summit of Christian life are at odds among themselves? Divisiveness over the liturgy deconstructs the mission and witness of the Catholic Church. Divisiveness arises out of failure to be the Catholic Church.

The seventeenth century priest-poet John Donne wrote:

> The church is Catholic, universal, and so are all her actions. All that she does belongs to all. When she baptizes a child, that action concerns me; for that child is thereby connected to that Head which is my Head too, and engrafted into that body, whereof I am a member. And when she buries a man, that action concerns me. All mankind is of one Author and is one volume; when one man

> dies, one chapter is not torn out of the book,
> but translated into a better language; and
> every chapter must be so translated.

Donne's "Catholic sense" says very clearly that through the sacraments, especially baptism, believers are connected to Christ, the head of the body, engrafted into his body, the church; their identity does not reside in what differentiates one from another—parents, education, social security numbers—though these are all things of great importance and necessary to our lives. However, from a Catholic point of view, their identity resides in their membership in the body of Christ, whose beating heart is the Eucharist. For Christians to be at loggerheads over the liturgy—which is absolutely essential to the community's health at the local parish level—is to lose something of their corporate identity in Christ and to become excessively individualistic, perhaps even narcissistic, when it comes to that which is most sacred.

Monsignor Kevin Irwin, in a recent article ("Getting Past the Liturgy Wars," *Church*, Fall, 2000, p. 5), made the point that in respect of the liturgy the heady days after the council were often marked by excitement, challenge and satisfaction—positive reception of the council's reforms—but in the years that followed, there was rapid movement to acrimony:

> We have moved from the "liturgist as ter-
> rorist" phase (with both humor and invective
> hidden beneath this barb) to the present
> "liturgy wars." By this I mean that some today
> are indeed warring about such symptomatic
> issues as whether Mass celebrated *ad orientem*
> is theologically and liturgically preferable to
> Mass celebrated facing the people. They
> debate whether the Roman Canon is the only
> normative and traditional text for the Roman
> Rite to use as opposed to the eucharistic
> prayers approved for use with the publication
> of the revised Roman Missal and since...

Anyone could probably add to these illustrations from local experience. The question and challenge is, "How do people at the parish level get past the liturgy wars so that the liturgy may be both a rich, positive, creative experience and may enhance their witness and mission to the world?"

I propose that a parish engage for five months in a program of liturgical renewal characterized by five steps, one step per month. Step one is to take up Bishop Victor Balke's invitation to a "Rite for Liturgical Reconciliation" (see page 32). Bishop Balke describes this rite as "coming together as the body of Christ to forgive and be forgiven for past offenses and insensitivities touching on liturgical issues." Leaving aside liturgical denunciation and condemnation, community members would seek forgiveness of one another, and of Christ, for their failures regarding the liturgy. Genuine reconciliation would demand active listening to one another, without premature contradiction or closure. While there should be no facile covering over of differences about the liturgy, it needs to be emphasized that "difference" and "division" are not synonymous. All who have liturgical responsibilities need to be heard; each has something to offer. The Holy Spirit animates the entire body of Christ, not just those associated with a particular point of view. Finding a liturgically knowledgeable facilitator with good "people skills" to take part in the listening and sharing needed for such a Rite of Liturgical Reconciliation would not be easy, but would be immensely worthwhile.

Step two involves a deepening of parish liturgical spirituality. This sounds rather grandiose but actually I mean something quite straightforward: slowly reading the prayers of the rites, as well as the introductions to the various rites; offering one another insight and wisdom from this careful reading; and praying the prayers together as a source and expression of personal prayer. What I am describing is essentially the Benedictine practice of *Lectio Divina*. This practice of careful reading of liturgical prayers would involve *lectio*, slow reading aloud of agreed-upon texts/prayers; *meditatio*, thinking, ruminating, questioning, sharing of personal appreciation of and reaction to those texts/prayers with the direct consequence of multilateral enrichment; *oratio*, praying the actual text/prayer together; and *contemplatio*, silence before the mystery of God. If the habit of *Lectio Divina* were cultivated with regard to all the prayers of the liturgy, participation in the liturgy would be profoundly deepened, and parish unity intensified, with a growing recognition of the power of the liturgy.

The third step has to do with careful attention to liturgical style, gesture and posture. If the liturgy is heaven drawing earth to itself, the Divine Communion effecting and strengthening Communion vertically and horizontally, then how the liturgy is conducted becomes very important—how we walk, how we talk, how we come to

Communion, how we respect quiet in the worship space and so forth. How liturgical ministers and assembly members dispose themselves physically in liturgical celebration says much about what they are doing. Further, how they conduct themselves as an adult community during the liturgy is more effective catechesis than volumes of lesson plans about liturgical meaning. So, in this third step, clergy, liturgical ministers and people are invited to an examination of conscience in this area, including also a purpose of amendment.

As Irwin says in the article mentioned earlier, "In studying the documents that govern the liturgical reform, I do not recall coming across the terms 'tone' or 'style.' Yet what many people notice about liturgy is precisely its tone and style...Whatever shape one gives to the liturgy, an overall tone of reverence and care should be apparent. Such things cannot be mandated by a reformed liturgical book." This makes such good sense, yet perhaps this is an area for immediate personal renewal. If there are things that may be done appropriately to make the style of celebration more dignified, more mystagogic, then each has the obligation to attend to them with great care. Those involved with the sacred liturgy could examine their own performance and invite comment that would render the tone and style of the celebration more suasive of God's presence and action.

Step four is the proper implementation of the liturgical books. Regarding the new *General Instruction on the Roman Missal* (GIRM) there has been much talk, and rightly so, of the Mass, but there are six other sacraments, each with its own liturgical protocol. Are the liturgical books being observed and implemented with due care? A parish might well sit down with the *praenotanda*, the introductions to the various rites, and the rites themselves, read carefully through them, and examine the community's practice regarding the rites. What is being done well? What is not being done? What is being done poorly? What needs to be done for the celebration to improve?

Having said that, the fifth and most important step is the recognition that we are not doing the liturgy—rather, the liturgy is doing us. The liturgy is the pattern of speech and action by means of which the Divine Communion of the Trinity "trinifies" us. It is the way through which we receive a share in God's own divine life. Gathered, reaffirmed and restored as body of Christ in and through the Eucharist, surrounded by the other sacraments, we are then called to act as that body in the world. (See Owen F. Cummings, *Eucharistic Soundings*, Dublin: Veritas Publications, 1999, p. 125.)

If a parish were to spend time over a period of five months or so dealing with each of these five steps, the unity of the parish would be enhanced and its mission furthered. Combatants over the liturgy who come together in Communion, for Communion, would feel encouraged to set aside their liturgical swords for plowshares and their spears for liturgical pruning hooks, as in Isaiah 2:4. I don't imagine for a moment that this five-step process of liturgical renewal would engage the majority of people in the parish. But if pastors, members of liturgy committees, music ministers, altar ministers, communion ministers— all those formally involved with the liturgy on behalf of the entire parish—made the unity of the parish a priority, wonderful things could happen.

5

Silence Allows Us to Listen to the Universe

Men and women during the ages have needed silence and made use of it to listen to themselves, to know themselves and to understand the importance of all that has transpired in their lives. Humanity, even more so in our day and age, needs silence to come to a deeper self-knowledge and to understand the world in which we live, a world that is often tormented and whose pace is often frenzied. We need to enter into our very own interior to listen to the song intoned by nature itself, the gently flowing water of rivers, the crashing waves of the sea, the whisper of a refreshing breeze, the mother singing a lullaby to her child, and above all we need to enter our own interior to calm our self and to calm our own home (life), as the great Spanish mystic St. John of the Cross wrote:

> One dark night,
> fired with love's urgent longings
> —ah, the sheer grace!—
> I went out unseen,
> my house being now all stilled.
> (St. John of the Cross, "The Dark Night," 1578)

A restful and calm silence will allow us to listen to the universe that is populated by voices, and at the same time will free us from so many worries, so much stress, all that "senselessness" suffered by our brothers and sisters in the din of the large cities, amidst the traffic and the noise of the city, and why not? Silence frees us from so many liturgies that seem like overburdened programs of readings and prayers needing to be finished in as little time as possible!

Romano Guardini said, "Silence is the ultimate expression of music." How true his words are. If we listen to the "Hallelujah Chorus" from G.F. Handel's *Messiah,* the silence accented by tympani, prior to the final "Alleluia," is a silence charged with tension, with loveliness and beauty, filled with reverberations and vibrations before the final chord.

Henri Davenson, in his commentary on *On Music* by St. Augustine, writes, "All music is the seed of silence." Ludwig Van Beethoven noted in a largo on his symphonies, "The more water a river carries, the less noise it makes." In the same vein, our life being much deeper, the more interior silence we have in our life, the less noise we will make and the more effective we will be; we will be able to hear the song that God has placed in the hearts of each of our brothers and sisters in our world.

Imitating Jesus

Silence quiets our individualism, it silences our disagreements and it subjects our opinion and our prejudices to the word of God and opens us up to the perfect gift from the Father. Jesus entered his own interior life by observing silence, thereby making his own life a song of eternal praise to the Father.

As Christians, we make silence in our lives by imitating Jesus, whose voice was reduced to silence: "Like a lamb led to the slaughter or a sheep before his shearers, he was silent and opened not his mouth" (Isaiah 53:7). Silent before Caiaphas; silent before Pilate; silent on Calvary; silent on Golgotha before the ridicule and jeers of the crowd. In the reign of the silence of God only one melody is heard with two refrains: "It is finished" and "Into your hands I commend my spirit."

Before this silence of God, we are left with the empty tomb, merely a reverberating space, hewn from the rock awaiting a future voice, the voice of the Risen One that sings a new song: "You will be my witnesses in Jerusalem...and to the ends of the earth."

—Antonio Alcalde Fernández

Silence: The Sonority of God

Antonio Alcalde Fernández

An environment of attentiveness

In order to create an environment of attentiveness, brief silence is needed. A word spoken amid general distraction is a word lost. So that God's word can resound in the members of a liturgical assembly, an environment of attentiveness is constructed through which they welcome that word.

In truth silence is not the only way to create this environment of attentiveness, but we Christians gather not only to savor a perfect silence. Clearly, although silence is not of central importance it nevertheless merits a central place in liturgy. Silence does not make celebration, but it enhances celebration with rhythm and intensity.

When we gather to celebrate the liturgy, silence helps attune us to another dimension, another atmosphere. It helps us assimilate what we celebrate. After all the preparation, and when everything—microphones, orders of worship, lectors, greeters, altar servers—is ready, we need silence in order to present ourselves openly before God, ready to celebrate.

As silence marks the rhythm of the music and brings forth a new movement, so also does silence regulate action during a celebration. A celebrative silence will be weighed and valued more for its intensity than its length.

Silence can be a special moment of fullness or resonance: a personal and inner welcome of the word. It can also be an empty space, an absence of communication, an indifference to the other, like the silence we experience in a waiting room or elevator when we find ourselves with strangers. In order for silence to be resonant, it needs to be an active presence in each individual toward all others present—and in all together toward the mysterious reality we call "God."

Music for an environment of silence

Music can help to create a state of attentiveness and to synchronize the focus of all assembly members. But music can also distract people. When it becomes the object of attention, it changes the assembly into a concert audience. Music for an environment of silence is a means rather than an end.

Music played as a "background" for certain rites—such as the institution narrative of the Eucharist—distorts the action rather than encourages contemplation of the mystery. As the memory of the Lord's Supper is recounted, all need simply listen without the camouflage of music. After all, would we consider using instrumental music to back up the homily?

A song also can help create a climate of attentiveness and resonance with the mystery, especially if we are reconciled with ourselves and with others in the assembly. But it can also impede authentic resonance, especially when we are under stress or not in communication with others present, even though we are listening and singing.

Out of this silence, laden with attentiveness and therefore with expectation, we hear God's word resound. Sister Juana Inés of the Cross said, "In silence there are voices."

The need for silence in liturgy

Silence is one of the most valuable elements of a liturgical celebration, which involves actions, gestures, words…and silence. One needs always to be aware of it, especially when readings need to be heard clearly and understood well. The lector needs an environment of silence in order to prepare well and to proclaim the readings with full understanding of what the words mean. Punctuation marks do not all have the same length of silence. Lectors need to know how to vary them intelligently—between phrases, sentences and paragraphs—being sensitive to the density of content. The intelligent use of silences or pauses helps hearers understand ideas and offers opportunity for these ideas to develop their evocative power. Hearers do not always know the texts read in liturgy; hearers need to hear, to understand and then to assimilate them.

Long ago, people felt awkward in a moment of silence. Few knew what to do. It seemed that something had gone wrong, was not being provided, was poorly planned or simply had been forgotten. Such negative, empty silences needed to be filled with announcements, songs, organ music or improvised prayer—anything.

Now, however, liturgy again integrates silence as a positive element of celebration. In other words, silence is affirmative; it enters areas words do not reach. There are eloquent silences and profound communicative silences. There are silences worth a thousand words rising from the inability of words to express the fullness of God: the silence of worship and prayer. This silence is ineffable, beyond words.

It is the profundity of words and their possibilities, not their empti-
ness. This silence is not hearing and saying nothing. Rather, this silence
is hearing and saying in another dimension.

More than ever our busy, nervous Western society needs oases of
silence, and our urban churches can easily provide such places of
peace. Just like the rest of society, liturgy needs this silence too. First,
silence becomes indispensable as a means of transition. Silence allows
us to move with grace from asphalt to church, from chronological time
to the sacred time of a celebration, from the noise of traffic to the
awareness of God in the "tiny whisper" that comes right after the great
fire (1Kings 19:12). Crossing through the vestibule and entering the
holy space allows us to put ourselves in the presence of God and relive
the experience of Moses: "Take off your sandals, because the ground
on which you stand is holy" (Exodus 3:5). We discover in the gathered
assembly someone beyond us. We meet the Holy One who gathers
together those who were separated. We meet God who calls and summons us from every corner of the land so that we form one people.
"Where two or three gather together in my name, there I am in their
midst" (Matthew 18:20).

Silence needed for celebration

Silence has a place in liturgical celebration for different reasons:
before and during the liturgy silence is an integral element in the general dynamic—it links ritual actions together. In the general dynamic of
the celebration and its parts, silence may depend in some measure on
the liturgical sensitivity of the presiding minister, in much the same
way that the tempo in the performance of a musical composition
depends on the sensitivity of the director.

The *General Instruction of the Roman Missal* (GIRM) affirms the value
and necessity of silence in every liturgical celebration, especially the
Eucharist, for which moments of silence are needed to enable the
fullest participation.

> Silence should be observed at the desig-
> nated times as part of the celebration. Its
> function depends on the time it occurs in
> each part of the celebration. At the penitential
> rite and at the invitation to prayer, all recol-
> lect themselves; after a reading or the homily,
> all meditate briefly on what they have heard;
> after communion, all praise God in silent prayer.
> (GIRM 23)

In the *Directory of Masses with Children* this statement appears:

> Silence should be observed at the desig-
> nated times as part of the celebration lest too
> great a place be given to external action. In
> their own way children are genuinely capable
> of reflection. They need some guidance, how-
> ever, so that they will learn how, in keeping
> with the different moments of the Mass (for
> example, after the homily or after commun-
> ion), to recollect themselves, meditate, pray
> and praise God in their hearts. (DMC 37)

A celebration without silence—whether with children, young people or adults—becomes suffocating, impoverishing and deafening.

An authentic, intimate participation in the Eucharist requires from
time to time that assembly members observe moments of silence in
order to focus inwardly on their personal, conscious activity and to
avoid routine or mechanical participation. We must explain to the
faithful the reasons for this liturgical silence, which does not oppose
but rather greatly enhances prayer. There is a pedagogy of silence, just
as there is a springtime silence in liturgy. For the beauty of the whole
work, silences in music are spaced out. Consider George Frideric
Handel's "Hallelujah" chorus from *Messiah*: the great silence before the
last "hallelujah" is laden with tension, resonance and sonorous
vibrance before the final chord. So also in the liturgy, silence has positive power to evoke fuller participation, active worship of God and
conscious involvement of the faithful.

Moments of silence in the eucharistic celebration

According to the Second Vatican Council, "At the proper times all
should observe a reverent silence." (SC 30) Likewise, *The Roman Missal*
proposes four periods of silence as *proper*, that is, *obligatory*. These
moments involve the entire assembly's participation in the eucharistic
celebration.

1. Liturgy of the Word

In liturgy we do not just read God's word; we celebrate it. In liturgy
the word is not the object of study, interpretation, discussion or scien-
tific explanation. In order to be more than information or indoctrina-
tion, the word is "wrapped up" in silence. Only outer silence and,
above all, inner silence will permit us to listen openly and welcome

God's word into the temple that we are. Only in silence can we examine well enough what we have heard and allow it to transform us. Ultimately, the actions of hearing and welcoming that take place in the Liturgy of the Word depend on the inner silence of the listener and the faith and skill of the lector. For the lector, this includes solid preparation, pauses for sense, good rhythm and clear intonation, with brief moments of silence between readings. These elements help set the stage for the word of God to penetrate well and resound fully in each assembly member.

2. Invitation to prayer

When prayer leaders invite assembly members to pray, they must pause for a moment of silence before saying the prayer to encourage an inner focus. After we say "Let us pray," "We acknowledge our sin" or "We pray," we must allow for a short silence and articulate the actual prayer or intention. If we do not cherish such silences, the celebration becomes just words, sentences and rites heaped upon one another, and we find ourselves enveloped in rote mumbling, mindless distraction, divided attention, noise and, above all, lack of participation.

3. Preparation of the gifts

We carry the bread and wine to the altar, an action that befits the celebration of the Eucharist; we can also carry other gifts suitable for worship or gifts for the poor. But sometimes we change the preparation of the gifts into a processional exhibition of arts and crafts that has nothing to do with the liturgy. These casual extras distract people and divide the attention of everyone. Such elements steal strength from the intense transitional moments of the liturgical celebration.

This is the moment of the preparation of the altar and the gifts, when we have finished worshiping at the table of the Word and move to begin worshiping at the table of the Eucharist. This is the moment for a good climate of welcome, rest, assimilation and change of pace. Assembly members do not need to be singing: instrumental music, a choral anthem or silence suffices to help create a precious moment for the transition from one table to the other.

For the preparation of the altar and the gifts, *The Roman Missal* permits the presiding celebrant to say the prayers of divine praise "audibly" as he receives the bread and wine; and the people respond. But it also permits those prayers to be said "inaudibly," favoring silence and actually directing that two of them are always to be "inaudible." When the action reaches the "Pray, my brothers and sisters," the rites and words of the preparation are complete, and attention is drawn entirely to the eucharistic prayer.

4. After Communion

We observe silence after communion so that all can "spend some time in silent prayer." (GIRM 56j) The time is specifically for the praise of God. *The Roman Missal* considers appropriate a hymn or song of praise sung by the entire assembly. The silence prepares for this praise.

The presiding minister and other ministers give a poor signal to other assembly members if they purify the sacred vessels, put things away or prepare the *Sacramentary* for the final prayer during the period of silent prayer after communion. These can be done later (see GIRM 120).

Conclusion: The silence of worship and praise

Silence enhances the personal prayer of praise to the God who has given us Christ Jesus as food.

> Adoring silence is indispensable to liturgical celebration, and each community has to discover the right moment for it...At this point we experience the inadequacy of our words, the awkwardness of our gestures and the smallness of our thoughts before the majestic presence, the splendor and beauty, and the august holiness of our God. We all experience at one time or another—although unfortunately it may be rare—intense moments of silence in which, after many words, songs and actions, God passes through the assembly in the "tiny whisper." (Juan Martín Velasco, *Misa Dominical*, 36.)

In the hushed, divine music of silence and in the echoing solitude, God sings an unending melody of love for every creature, and God's sonority echoes through the inner harmony of each one.

6

Are the Children any Closer?

When I wrote "The Liturgical Life of Children" in 1992, I hoped to illustrate the profound impact that liturgy has on the formation and transformation of our children. With this goal in mind, I stressed the need to work toward inclusivity, not separateness; harmony, not fragmentation; unity, not divisiveness in the preparation and celebration, especially of the Sunday celebration of the Eucharist. Yet the concerns that I had then about the full, conscious and active participation of children in the liturgy remain as true today as they did then, if not more so.

As I look back over ten years, I see that while much has changed, sadly much has also remained the same. The plight of children in the world and in the church is still a source of major concern. We need only look at recent societal and ecclesial events to know this is true. The ways we discriminate against children in the liturgy listed under "Where Have All Our Children Gone?" not only remain but in some cases have been extended to older youth as well.

As is often the case, the issue of the place of children in the liturgical assembly reflects the larger issue of the unity of the body of Christ at the Eucharist. We need to evaluate practices that have subtly crept into our liturgy that divide the community: on Sunday we offer a "cafeteria" model of church where you can select a Mass for children or avoid it; a Mass for family or avoid it; a Mass with no music, if you prefer not to sing; a Mass for youth or avoid it; a Mass for a special language group or avoid it; a Mass with baptisms or avoid it and so on. We need to begin to focus on how we can start to deepen the understanding of what it means to be a true liturgical assembly, to pray with one voice as the body of Christ, and where all delight in the presence of infants, children, youth and adults, men and women, poor and rich, healthy and sick, young and old, the various colors of our skin, and where all delight in the music and language of other cultures.

Since 1992 this vision of the liturgical assembly has been promoted in a variety of ecclesial documents. The place of children in the Sunday celebration of the Eucharist is heralded in the introduction to the *Lectionary for Masses with Children*:

> The fullest reality of the liturgical assembly
> is children and adults together—not separate
> celebrations which run the risk of diminishing
> the place of children in the liturgical assembly.
> It should be noted that the same thing can
> happen if inadequate attention is given to
> their presence in the full assembly. (LMC 54)

The United States Conference of Catholic Bishops' document on youth ministry, *Renewing the Vision: A Framework for Catholic Youth Ministry*, "promotes the participation of youth in liturgy" and calls for the incorporation of "young people more fully into the sacramental life of the church, especially the Eucharist." (RTV, p. 44).

And in the 1998 apostolic letter of Pope John Paul II, entitled *Dies Domini*, it states that "the Sunday assembly is the privileged place of unity." Thus, while acknowledging that every parish community has different groups, it proclaims that "this is why on Sunday, the day of gathering, small group Masses are not to be encouraged" in order to ensure "that the life and unity of the church community are fully safe-guarded and promoted." (DD 36)

The full, conscious and active participation of children in the liturgy can be correctly understood and valued only if it is viewed within the larger context of the entire church worshiping together.

—Linda L. Gaupin, CDP

The Liturgical Life of Children

Linda L. Gaupin, CDP

As each new year begins, newspapers and magazines seize the opportunity to tell us what is *in* for the coming year and what is *out*; what's *hot* and what's *not*. Generally I find these lists amusing. I await them eagerly so that I can discover if I live on the cutting edge of new trends or if, as usual, I grew outdated. So when I received the January 1, 1992, *Washington Post,* I paged quickly to Martha Sherrill's "Ins and Outs" list. It may interest readers to find rosary beads definitely in this year and pearls out. (One point for me!) On television, *Studs* is in and *Jeopardy* out. (Alas, I love *Jeopardy*. What a sad sign of the moral decay in our country!) Recycling gifts is in; shopping for new ones is out. (Good for the vow of poverty!) As I pored over the list of sixty or so "Ins and Outs," one item in particular struck me: Martha Sherrill has pronounced children in. (In case it concerns you, the adult child of codependents is out.)

What piques my interest was not so much that Martha Sherrill deems children in but that children seem to be attracting more general attention in many sectors of our society. For example, the United Nations' Children's Fund holds up children as our hope and our legacy, to be protected as zealously as a farmer protects seed grain. That body's report, *The State of the World's Children, 1992,* resulting from the 1990 World Summit for Children, holds up several children's issues worth defending nationally and internationally. One of its basic principles, "first call for children," argues that the growing bodies and minds of the young deserve a society's best resources.

We need the children

Recent surveys agree. In January 1992, the National Association of Children's Hospitals and Related Institutions and the Coalition for America's Children reported that nearly two-thirds of U.S. voters put children's issues near the top of their personal political agenda. A survey of 6,200 registered voters indicated a preference for government action on behalf of children, and eighty-five percent of those voters considered political leaders "not doing enough" to help children.

The U.S. bishops, too, have added their voice to the growing concern for children in our society. At their national meeting in November 1992, they approved the statement "Putting Children and Families

First: A Challenge for our Church, Nation and World." Furthermore, many bishops personally helped launch the campaign in their writing and through press conferences. A recent Catholic News Service Report cites the following:[1]

"Children must be our priority." Bishop Howard J. Hubbard Albany, NY

"Children have soft voices, voices that other sounds in our society can easily drown out." Archbishop Pilarczyk, Cincinnati, OH

"Our children and families are hurting… they are undermined by poverty, hunger and homelessness…They are neglected by misplaced priorities." Cardinal James A. Hickey, Washington, D.C.

"Childhood should be a time of happiness, security and peaceful growth, and for many it is…but for a growing number of children at home and around the world this is not the case. For them, childhood is a time of danger and destruction…If we raise a generation of dysfunctional children today, our society will be dysfunctional tomorrow." Bishop Favalora, St. Petersburg, FL

What does this have to do with the liturgical life of children? It should have a profound impact on those who work at any level with the liturgical life of children. The concerns for children's dignity, rights and needs evidenced in church and state should give rise to serious questions about children's dignity, rights and needs in liturgy.

Why? Liturgy intimately connects all aspects of life and thereby has to face injustice too. God transforms those who gather into the body of Christ and through them transforms the world. Sometimes we forget this link between liturgy and life. If we look back, however, to the beginnings of the liturgical movement in the United States, we see that the pioneers of that movement saw liturgy as a source of power for social change. One of the greatest of those catalysts for the Canadian and U.S. liturgical movement, Virgil Michel, stated, "Pius X tells us that the liturgy is the indispensable source of the true Christian spirit; Pius XI says that the true Christian spirit is indispensable for

---

[1] *Catholic News Service,* January 8, 1992, 5–6.

social regeneration. Hence, the conclusion: the liturgy is the indispensable basis of Christian social regeneration."[2]

Where have all the children gone?

If liturgy is a source of power for social change, and if the plight of children is now acknowledged by both the church and the larger society, then is it not reasonable that we examine the role children play in the liturgy? Could children be suffering from discrimination in liturgy that parallels their discrimination in the larger society? No one says that we discriminate against children intentionally. But in our liturgy, could we nevertheless reflect more on the injustice of the larger society than we reflect on the justice of God on their behalf? For instance, do we discriminate against children when we do the following:

- neglect in our preparation for the weekly parish Sunday liturgy the children normally present?
- forget in our planning that these children, who represent several age groups, have some liturgical needs that possess great importance but that differ from those of adults?
- ignore their assistance even in the planning and preparation of our Sunday liturgical celebrations?
- succumb to the practice of introducing a "children's liturgy" or "family liturgy" occasionally in our Sunday schedule, as if children and families are not a particular concern at every Sunday celebration of the Eucharist?
- schedule a separate Liturgy of the Word for children at the Sunday gathering of the parish assembly?
- prefer to dismiss children from the assembly rather than to improve the quality of the liturgies of the word for all?
- overlook the suffering of adults and children alike because of poor celebrations of the liturgy of the word?
- pretend that children "vanish" during homilies?
- disregard the principle expressed in the introduction to the *Lectionary for Mass,* which "demands that the homily be truly the fruit of meditation, carefully prepared, neither too long nor too short, and suited to all those present, even *children* and the uneducated" (LM 24; emphasis mine)?
- fail regularly to include children in the liturgical ministries even if they are old enough and possess sufficient skill?

---

2 Virgil Michel, "The Liturgy as the Basis of Social Regneration," *Orate Fratres* 9 (1934) 545.

51

- fall down in our responsibility to provide liturgical catechesis for these children or to offer liturgical formation that prepares them for such ministries?
- give children a sense that they can get more out of liturgical celebrations with peers than they can out of liturgical celebrations with the whole parish on Sunday?
- offer children's liturgies that do not reflect the integrity of our ritual and sacramental tradition, thus "unforming" them liturgically?

These questions touch only the eucharistic liturgy. If we examine other sacramental areas, our inconsistent practices raise even more questions about children's participation in the liturgy of the church. For example, why are baptized children denied first communion until the age of reason? Why do children have the privilege of celebrating the Rite of Penance when they reach the age of reason but not the privilege of celebrating the Rite of Confirmation?

We do not resolve problems for children merely by listing ways that they are discriminated against in our liturgy. Nor do we resolve their liturgical plight even by changing some of the irregularities on our list. In some ways we are coping with an impossible situation in the best way we can. Real change will occur only when we come to grips with the root of the problem.

Liturgical conversion

The cure will not come by simply including children in more liturgical activities. It will take place only when we change our minds (*conversion*, in the biblical sense) about some basic realities of the church and its liturgy.

First, we need an honest theology of childhood. We don't celebrate with children or catechize them or minister with them because someday they too will be adults. We celebrate with children and catechize them and minister with them because we recognize the Holy Spirit of Christ Jesus in them. We accept their dignity. We know their privileged place in the church. We love them for themselves—now.

We appreciate children for being children. We place a high price on them because they minister to us from their very childhood. We do not "tolerate" their childhood. We do not give children "permission" to be children. We cherish their childhood.

Change will come when we acknowledge the child's breadth and depth of vision. Things will start moving when we recognize the child's special sense of the sacred, the child's unique feeling for the faith. Such sense, feeling and appreciation of spiritual realities can be denied at times even to more mature and intellectually advanced persons. Do we not read in the scriptures, "Whoever does not receive God's reign as a little child, shall not enter it"?

We need to value the child's very helplessness and dependence, the child's openness to the future, the child's ability to reckon the real with the unlikely or the unseen. These childlike qualities challenge adults in the basic mystery of faith. The rites of the church acknowledge that children can appreciate God's gift of new life, that they have the ability to change, that they can welcome and respond to God's word, and that as children they can grow well when they receive nourishment through these sacred realities (see *Rite of Christian Initiation of Adults*, 252–330).

Second, we need to learn how children grow through liturgy. Often we base our perception of growth on a person's ability to understand or explain things rationally, even things that reach far beyond rational understanding or explanation.

We forget that children worship naturally and have an acute sense of belonging (or not belonging). Eastern Orthodoxy can teach us much on this. Constance Tarasar states:

> The practice of integrating children into the life of worship in the Orthodox Church is simply one of *immersion into the experience of worship*. "Taste and see how good the Lord is" (Proverbs 34:8). Experience (taste), then understand (see; be illumined)—this is the methodology. Children who are introduced to worship from the time of infancy accept their role in worship naturally...Their common participation in the sacramental life of the church unites them as one family in the body of Christ. The child learns to worship through experience from the very first moments in the church. The child's first "understandings" come through the senses.[3]

The fullness of this reality comes about only when the assembly is ready to welcome children, embrace them and celebrate with them. No small matter! It involves fundamental Christian self-understanding. Louis Weil notes:

---

3 Constance Tarasar, "'Taste and See': Orthodox Children at Worship," in *The Sacred Play of Children* (New York: The Seabury Press, 1983) 51.

Children, by their human nature and baptism, are appropriate liturgical participants even in infancy. If they are not, then it is virtually impossible to justify the church's unbroken tradition of infant baptism. In fact, that tradition pleads for full participation by all members of the body...The authentic inclusion of children in the normative models of parish liturgy may work for the salvation of the adults...Children bring a naturalness to the liturgy which stands as a judgment upon our over-formalized routines...They bring a wonderful openness to the experience of word and gesture, touch and movement—the whole array of human elements which lies at the heart of the liturgical act. Their feelings find articulation in the corporate context, since they have not learned to put on a religious mask.[4]

Questions about children's participation in the liturgical life of the church are essentially questions about the church. By virtue of their baptism members of the church have been incorporated into Christ and formed into God's people. Because of their age or rational abilities, children are not just "as-if" members. Nor are young children the responsibility only of their parents. By virtue of their baptism they are the responsibility of all the faithful.

The issue comes down to the place of children in the church. Members of a community fail when they avoid liturgies at which children are baptized, build rooms to muffle children's noise, and prefer to send them off to nurseries, classrooms or separate liturgical activities. We need to welcome children into our midst with open arms. We need to incorporate them more fully into the full, active and conscious participation of the assembly at liturgy.

---

4 Louis Weil, "Children and Worship," in *The Sacred Play of Children* (New York, The Seabury Press, 1983) 55–57.

Liturgy, children and justice

Liturgy as a source of social regeneration for children means this: where the larger society

- shuns children, we embrace and welcome them;
- alienates children, we give them community;
- ignores them, we show them hospitality;
- turns a deaf ear to them, we see and hear them;
- offers them an empty hand, we share the bread of life;
- promises them gloom, we proclaim hopeful good news;
- scorns them, we affirm them with praise and thanks;
- starves them, we provide Christ's body and blood;
- isolates them, we give them union in Christ;
- deserts them, we walk with them, companions on the path, and help them live daily the prayer Jesus taught us.

If the Eucharist shapes our lives, it can truly transform and regenerate the social life of children too. The U.S. bishops noted in their pastoral letter, *Economic Justice for All,* that worship enlivens our reflection on the values of the world and that it challenges our way of life. Therefore, liturgy is the starting point in addressing the problem of the plight of our children.

We need to ponder the words of Archbishop Pilarczyk in the context of our liturgical activity:

> Children have soft voices,
> voices that other sounds
> in our society
> can easily drown out.

PART 2

Musical Liturgy

1

Musicians' Work Is Still Prophetic

When Michael Prendergast asked me to take part in this twenty-fifth anniversary celebration of *Today's Liturgy*, I couldn't believe it. Had I really been writing columns for twenty-five years? No, thank God. I started when John Limb, then editor of TL, envisioned an expanded version of *Today's Liturgy*. During one of my visits to Oregon Catholic Press, he asked me to write a short column for each week of the liturgical year. Who, me? Write text? In college, I was the student who began all creative writing papers with the equivalent of the very original opening sentence, "It was a dark and stormy night." But John is very persuasive and, as often happens, "it seemed like a good idea at the time."

John began to steer a course that would continue in the wake of his predecessors—providing music suggestions and planning forms for readers, and sailing as well as into uncharted waters with articles and liturgical suggestions by nationally known pastoral musicians and liturgists.

The expanded *Today's Liturgy* introduced us to new music and musical styles. From Latin to the vernacular, from strictly organ accompaniment at liturgy to a wide variety of folk and symphonic sounds, OCP met our musical needs and kept us abreast of what's available through *Today's Liturgy*. Hasn't it been an exciting time in the church, and certainly in church music?

Pastoral liturgists who shared a vision of a renewed church wrote articles that renewed us in our faith. Composers wrote new music that helped us implement the vernacular (and not merely the English language) in song. Music can add joy, solemnity, unity and beauty to liturgy, not as performance but as servant of the liturgy. The planning guide did much of the preliminary work of preparing the music for Sundays so we might have some free time to spend with our families and friends. (I am reminded of the organist who told me that she knew she was at church too much when she noticed her little daughter who accompanied her to funerals would bring along a Barbie doll and a little shoe box.)

Articles and columns attempted to give insight and practical suggestions for implementing the new rites. Authors wrote about weddings and funerals, about the seasons of the liturgical year, other sacraments such as first Eucharist, confirmation, sacrament of the sick, holy orders, music as prayer, and the role of musician within the assembly and in liturgical worship. Readers learned more and more about the evolving role of the assembly and why Catholics do what we do at Mass. Musicians grew attentive to the idea of pastoral music as a ministry. Many took the call very seriously. Nourished and reinforced (through TL) in understanding the difference between ministry and performance, musicians helped pass the word to other ministers how we are called to priesthood through our baptism and that ministry involves presence as well as task. We learned about liturgical texts and devotional texts, about song leaders and cantors and their differing roles. On a very practical level, experts made suggestions for the recruitment and retention of musicians and other ministers. We learned how to train ushers to be greeters as well as to manage the worship space. TL encouraged and challenged us to embrace inculturation. Prophetic articles enabled us to do liturgical catechesis before the term was fashionable. Children's needs received special attention, followed quickly by assistance for those working with teens and young adults. All these areas of interest in a parish were accommodated through the missal and hymnal programs at OCP, but it is *Today's Liturgy* that threaded the needle that helped us sew it all together. Know what? Much of what we have accomplished in ministry, we take for granted. But in reality, over the years many readers have taken on a lot of parish responsibilities. They now have not only one, but several areas of pastoral expertise. Although all are still seekers, all are not novices. It is not only *Today's Liturgy* that has matured.

In my very first article for *Today's Liturgy* (Ordinary Time/Assumption 1986), I mentioned that my colleague at the Georgetown Center for Liturgy, Paul Covino, suggested that some ministers felt like prophets because they seemed to be "a voice crying in the wilderness." (John the Baptist, pray for us.) I think music ministers have been truly at their prophetic best by helping form a holy people over the years through music. With sights set on making the kingdom of God on earth a reality, our assemblies continue to sing songs calling for the establishment of God's realm on earth. Musicians have helped the assembly reawaken their baptismal gifts. Music has pointed the way for people to live out that call. Traditional and contemporary texts helped teach about God and what God is like. Pastoral musicians help imprint music in the minds and hearts of the assembly, urging them to sing of God's son, Jesus.

Many of us grew up in a church during which the transcendent aspect of Christ reigned. Let's not discount the important role that composers have played in restoring a sense of the incarnational Christ. Some critics have railed against texts that speak about *us* at liturgy instead of God, but is it narcissism or is it the incarnational God of whom we speak? With few exceptions, most of the time when we have sung about ourselves or to one another in liturgy, the text has been based in Scripture, particularly the psalms. Poetic texts directed to the assembly sing of a church that roots itself once again in the incarnation of Jesus, that recalls the Pentecost event when we all received the Christ-light within us. If anything, this return to incarnational theology has prepared our people for this challenging time in church history. Knowingly or not, our texts have emphasized that God is in the community, in relationships, in people.

If our faith was focused only on the transcendent aspect of Christ and the institution as *persona Christi*, the faith of the people would be a lot worse off in these times. *"Somos el cuerpo de Cristo"* allows the church to be human as well as divine.

I am writing this from a hotel room several floors above where the United States Conference of Catholic Bishops is holding their annual meeting (for which I am the musician). While it is true that only males are making decisions, their collective wisdom should not be dismissed. It has been a powerful experience. Although the current liturgical legislation of the church comes as a personal disappointment to some, we can't forget that the Holy Spirit is leading us. As always, the Holy Spirit is leading in a totally unpredictable fashion. It gives me comfort to know that Mary may have had the same feelings in her own encounters with the Holy Spirit. Like Mary, with no knowledge of where the journey would lead, many of us said "yes" to the nudging of the Spirit. (Holy Mary, Mother of God, pray for us.)

Although I believe the Holy Spirit is leading us, the new legislation for liturgy (questioned by some) certainly has me putting my hope completely in the Spirit's creative and unpredictable meanderings.

Where can we go? Go the creative way of the Spirit. At liturgy, texts may not be inclusive any longer, but I will see to it that the women in the assembly sing a verse on their own as often as possible so that their voices might be heard in our assemblies. Also, there are other places to pray than at liturgy. Devotions have always been popular with Catholics. How about creating some that meet the needs of today's worshipers? Isn't that how novenas, missions and sodalities got started? We certainly are in need of healing and lamenting for starts.

Many of us have committed a lot of our life energy to liturgical reform because what we do at liturgy forms us as God's people.

At a time when war looms on the horizon and the mighty and self-righteous will be brought down sooner or later, we must ask ourselves—who are the mighty, really? Is the war myth the answer, really? Let us continue being prophetic! Sing songs that remind us of our place as Christians in the global village.

At a time when the faithful are disillusioned and distancing themselves from the church because of the abuse troubles, join in the song: "O healing light of Christ"…"Because of Jesus"…"There is a balm in Gilead"…"Healing river of the spirit."

I am proud of our work in God's vineyard. It's been a delicious time. I used to say that music ministry has framed my life in meaning…something that teens and young adults crave. But now I think that is not quite true. Better to say that this ministry has given me a place in life from which I can seek out meaning in my life. This ministry is filled with a lot of grace-filled moments, but also with a lot of craziness.

As I have said many times, we are still doing Vatican 1½ liturgy, not Vatican II. I want to be a part of what is to come. I am counting on *Today's Liturgy* to continue to keep all of us in touch with one another, to keep us up to date in this ever-changing field of liturgy, to challenge us to openness, to new music, to inculturation; to continue to give us information that is helpful not only to musicians, but also to pastors, liturgy committees, directors, catechists and educators.

A final word. For sanity and longevity in your ministry, don't forget to keep reminding yourself: *I didn't break it and I don't have to fix it.* I am intrigued by what Thomas Moore has to say about prophets in his latest book, *The Soul's Religion*:

62

The…annoying preoccupation with perfection may be a corruption of the proper spiritual calling to be a prophet. Certainly we can all stand up at times and complain about the state of things and try to inspire toward improvement. This is the calling to justice, which is a profound way to fulfill your spirituality. But the corruption of it is a mundane, misplaced expectation of personal perfection. It makes the spiritual life a burden to those who practice it and to anyone in the vicinity. It is unnecessary and can be transformed into the more convivial task of being exactly who you are—completely and imperfectly.

(Thomas Moore, *The Soul's Religion*. Harper Collins, NY, 2002 118)

Today's Liturgy has been a great source of inspiration in keeping all of us in contact with current musical and liturgical developments and also with one another. For the latter, I am extremely grateful and feel very privileged and humbled. Thank you and may the spirit of God bless us with another twenty-five years of grace.

Holy Spirit, pray for us.
Holy Mary, Mother of God, pray for us.
St. John the Baptist, pray for us.
St. Jude, pray for us.
Blessed John XXIII, be with us.

—Elaine Rendler

Musicians' Work Is Prophetic

Elaine Rendler

Are prophetic gifts reserved for only a few spectacular biblical personalities such as Isaiah or John the Baptist? Or are there prophetic roles in our era of Christianity?

The dictionary defines "prophecy" as the ability to foretell the future by supernatural means. This definition fits more the world of fortune telling than religion. Perhaps a prophet today is one who is a visionary...someone with a dream who helps shape the future through insight and wisdom.

If we apply this latter definition, we can see various prophetic roles in our contemporary Christianity. The role of the musician in the present day Catholic Church is indeed a prophetic one in its own way. Of the myriad dimensions of the ministry of music, two facets in particular seem to me prophetic: musician as lay minister and as teacher.

As the laity become more and more aware of our rightful place in the church, we are seeking out ways of becoming more actively involved in lay ministry. As we begin to answer the call to priesthood by baptism, we begin to recognize the serious implications of commitment. We can look to the ministry of music as one of the oldest ministries where lay people have served the people of God.

This is not to say that only the unordained may serve as music-makers, but that we lay people have been a vital part of liturgical celebrations in centuries past and will continue to do so probably until the Second Coming! But as recently as yesterday, we musicians tended to think of our ministry as a service we performed for others. To minister is to serve, but it is more than performing a service for others.

The prophetic insight for all ministries that musicians are discovering is that ministry involves who we are and how we look at the world. It is a way of life and commitment to the Savior and to people. William Bauman lends insight into a deeper and broader definition of ministry in his book *The Ministry of Music*:

> To bring joy, to bring relief from pain and
> sorrow, to end anxiety and fear, to share what
> enriches—this is ministry. Ministry is not an
> attempt to do someone over in some precon-
> ceived pattern. It uncritically respects the
> individuality, taste, and life choices of the

persons served, freeing them to create themselves anew. It urges, inspires, shares, supports;
it never forces.

And let us not forget the important contributions made by women in the ministry of music. Until ten years ago, it was virtually unheard of to have a professional musician as a full-time parish staff person. This is more and more becoming the norm.

When I grew up, most of the music in the average parish was played by women and taught to all of us by women. Because the foundation for this most liberal approach to women in ministry was based on economics, women could help supplement their husbands' incomes but hardly support a family as a church musician. This opportunity did, however, open a prophetic role for major contributions by women to key leadership in the church.

In remembering the church of our childhood days, many of us can call to mind the rituals, festivals and liturgies, with their richness of sight and sound, that have shaped our vision of the heavenly kingdom and of God. Music is a vital part of that remembering. Let us not underestimate the impact of the music of our faith upon us.

The musician either through care or carelessness shapes the spirituality and nourishes the vision of the assembly of today and tomorrow. My colleague, Paul Covino, has suggested that John the Baptist might be a good patron saint for music ministers. After all, we often feel like a "voice crying out in the wilderness" on Sunday mornings.

That is the scary reality of this prophetic dimension of music. Whether we like it or not, we will have created lifelong impressions on a generation of children who are the hope of the future and the moving forces in the church of tomorrow.

They, too, will remember the glorious sounds and images of their childhood faith. They will pray the psalms as their ancestors prayed them. And they will pray them with their children and grandchildren. Perhaps the next generation will love their prayers even more because some musicians helped enhance those prayers with melodies of beauty and inspiration.

God give us the wisdom and insight to choose well.

2

The Primary Musician of Every Liturgy Must Be the Assembly

As far back as 1973, *Music in Catholic Worship* made this startling assertion: "Good celebrations foster and nourish faith. Poor celebrations may weaken and destroy it." (MCW 6) This amazing document also gave us the three classical criteria that help us determine the place and value of a particular musical element used in the liturgy: the musical, pastoral and liturgical judgments. That statement and those judgments are the central assumptions that form the basis of this article. The other major influence for this piece is what I have listed as the tenth "right" of the assembly: *The assembly as primary agent and celebrant of the liturgy.* It is this fundamental principle coupled with the assumptions above which grounds and gives a solid theological basis to the other nine "rights" of the assembly included here.

Music has always enjoyed a certain preeminence as an art form in the liturgy, but when we read in *Sacrosanctum concilium* that "...full, conscious and active participation by all the people is the aim to be considered before all else" (SC 14) it becomes clear that music in worship cannot be the sole domain of the choir, the cantor, the organist or the music director. The primary musician of every liturgy must be the assembly, because, as Gabe Huck has stated, "liturgy is something sung." Therefore, if the assembly is the primary agent whose full participation is the most important consideration, then it is the assembly that must also be the primary singer!

After reading this article when it first appeared in *Today's Liturgy* one music director asked, "But what about the place of the choir? Do you think we should have them? How should it function?" Much has been written on the relationship of the choir to the assembly, and that topic could be an article (or a book!) in itself. By listing these ten "rights" of the assembly with regard to liturgical music, I do not intend to preclude the place or the use of choirs to enhance the church's worship and the assembly's songs. What is important, however, in whatever way the choir ministers in a particular liturgy, is that the fundamental primacy of the assembly and the assembly's musical participation be respected.

Because I have been a music teacher, a parish liturgical minister, a choir director and a director of an office of worship for two dioceses in the United States, I have had plenty of time and occasions to observe various liturgical celebrations in a wide variety of settings. Of course this experience has informed many of the observations included in this article. However, the most important experience, the one I treasure most and the one that has been most formative for me, flows from my lifelong participation as a member of the assembly. For me, and for all of us who value full, conscious and active participation in the church's liturgy, this is our first vocation and our most important ministry.

—Jeremy Gallet, SP

Whose Music Is It Anyway?
Assemblysong: Rites and Rights

Jeremy Gallet, SP

"Liturgy is something sung," writes Gabe Huck in a resource for liturgies with children. "We have gotten fairly accustomed to thinking that there are times at liturgy when we sing. It would be better if we thought that there are times at liturgy when we don't sing—but mostly, we sing. The assembly sings their liturgy. That is the way things are supposed to be. They don't sing during the liturgy. They sing the liturgy." [1]

The assembly sings their liturgy. That short statement has tremendous implications. There are two in particular that I would like to explore.

First, "the assembly sings *their* liturgy." "Their" is the operative word. It is not Father's liturgy, the children's liturgy, the choir's liturgy or the liturgy of the local planning committee. It is theirs. All of them. The gathered folks—a multi-faceted and diverse gathering of people with different spiritualities, worries, ages, abilities and needs. *Fulfilled in Your Hearing* puts it this way:

> The eucharistic assembly that gathers Sunday after Sunday is a rich and complex phenomenon. Even in parishes that are more or less uniform in ethnic, social or economic background, there is great diversity: men and women, old and young, the successes and the failures, the joyful and the bereaved, the fervent and the half-hearted, the strong and the weak. [2]

However, the document goes on to say, by reason of their baptism this gathering of persons, in all its diversity, is indeed the body of Christ. This gives the members their common identity, mission and ministry:

> The assembly has come together because its members have been baptized into the one body of Christ and share a common faith.

---

[1] Gabe Huck, ed., *Preparing Liturgy for Children and Children for Liturgy* (Chicago: Liturgy Training Publications, 1989), 17.

[2] *Fulfilled in Your Hearing: The Homily in the Sunday Assembly* (Washington, D.C.: United States Catholic Conference, 1982), 8.

> This faith, though rooted in a common bap-
> tismal identity, is expressed in ways that
> extend from the highest levels of personal
> approbation and intellectual understanding to
> the most immature forms of ritualism and
> routine. And yet, to a greater or lesser degree,
> it is faith in Jesus Christ that is common to all
> members of the assembly.[3]

The assembly as body of Christ has been part of the Christian community's self-understanding from the very beginning. It is a key concept in the writing of Paul and the gospel writers as well as the works of patristic writers and theologians throughout the church's long history. "Where two or three are gathered in my name, there I am..." Thus when the early Christians came together for table fellowship and prayer, they recognized this presence of Christ among them—indeed, they understood that they constituted the very body of Christ. As the body of Christ they were moved to do what Jesus did. It probably would be more accurate to say they were driven, under the power of the Spirit of Jesus, to do what he did; that is, to proclaim the Scriptures and to break the bread.[4] Thus, from the very beginning, the liturgy belongs to the entire assembly.

This understanding was weakened in the Middle Ages as Christ's presence in the eucharistic species received increased emphasis. However, the social dimension of Eucharist never really disappeared and the documents of the Second Vatican Council bear witness to the recovery of this image in the church.[5]

Second, "the assembly *sings* their liturgy." The gathered people of God don't recite, attend, assist at or listen to the liturgy. They sing it. As a (nearly) lifelong music minister, my first reaction to that statement was, "Yeah. Right. Saying it doesn't make it so." I am sure that many of you reading this can relate to my feelings. You might even want to stop here! Please don't. There are quite a few things we can do as music ministers and liturgy planners to help the assembly take hold of what is rightfully theirs.

---

[3] *Ibid.* 9.

[4] See Acts of the Apostles 2:43–47.

[5] See *Lumen Gentium*, 7, 8, 14, 15, in *Vatican II: The Conciliar and Post Conciliar Documents,* vol. I, rev. ed., Austin Flannery (Collegeville, MN: The Liturgical Press, 1975, 1984), *The Constitution on the Sacred Liturgy*, 7, 48, 59, 84; and *the General Instruction of the Roman Missal*, 56, in *The Liturgy Documents*, third edition (Chicago: Liturgy Training Publications, 1991).

The manner in which churches are built and renovated is critical to the ability of the members of the assembly to perceive themselves as the one body of Christ and to take hold of singing the liturgy well. Acoustics are extremely important, but some churches have all the ambiance of a living room, which is terrible for singing. The church in which you minister may be one of these. A church full of carpeting, padded pews, acoustical tile and low ceilings can make us feel like we're singing in a closet full of winter coats. Also, long narrow churches, or churches which give the impression that we're spectators at a play or a concert, do not contribute to full, conscious, active participation simply because of the very nature of their floor plans and environment. They lead, rather, to a sense of isolation and passivity. Solving these problems is something for the long term, involving a great deal of research and money.

In spite of this, we can take several immediate actions, as well as changing some aspects of our own attitudes and practices, that will improve the musical participation and ownership of the assembly in the liturgical celebration. I think of these in terms of the "rights" of the assembly. As the director of an archdiocesan office of worship, I do quite a bit of traveling and experience many different styles of liturgy. It is from my reflection upon these experiences that I derive the following "rights."

1. The assembly has the right to music that is both accessible and worthy.

This is the first "right" and may be the most difficult of them all. The music must be subject to the three judgments outlined in *Music in Catholic Worship*: the pastoral, the liturgical and the musical.[6] This means that the texts are strong and theologically correct, the music is beautiful, the piece is suited for the part of the liturgy for which it is used, and it is within the performance capabilities of the assembly. People recognize trivial and banal music and texts for what they are and, in spite of the fact that they may be easy to sing, they will not stand the test of time. Children, in particular, are very astute when it comes to this perception, and although they may sing such hymns in class or in church, they will leave them behind as "childish" as they mature in the faith.

---

[6] *Music in Catholic Worship* (Washington, D.C.: United States Catholic Conference, 1982), 25–41.

This became very clear to me when I was planning a graduation Mass with an eighth-grade class. I had no idea what they would consider appropriate music for this event, and I was prepared for a fight. To my amazement they requested "Bless the Lord My Soul," a Taizé psalm we had sung as a processional throughout the Lenten season, "I Am the Bread of Life" by Suzanne Toolan, and the Gelineau setting of the twenty-third psalm, "My Shepherd Is the Lord." In fact, all the music they picked was music that was sung with gusto by our parish. I had underestimated both the youth and the assembly's formative power. The assembly's ownership of these strong pieces witnessed to those eighth-graders that they were worthy and valuable.

Great care must be taken with unpublished liturgical music composed by the local pastoral musician or choir leader. Some of this music is quite good, but my experience is that much of it is not. As unpublished music, it has not undergone the scrutiny of a music editor so that texts are often poorly set in ways that do not respect the natural accents of the language, and melodies are frequently mediocre at best. Nor has it undergone the discipline of a liturgical editor, and this can result in some theological problems, as well as texts that are inappropriate for the part of the liturgy for which the piece was intended. I have sung (or attempted to sing) a setting of the *Our Father* written locally. I knew it was supposed to be the *Our Father* because that's where it came in the Mass. The text was a far cry from what I know that prayer ought to be. I have had the same experience with the *Holy, Holy, Holy* and psalms that were really hymns with vague references to the Scriptures.

Finally, choosing accessible music does not mean that liturgy planners and musicians never challenge the assembly to sing something that is difficult or demanding. With careful teaching, good support and enough repetition (see number 5 below), assemblies can accomplish amazing things musically!

2. The assembly has the right to hear itself when it sings.

This, of course, is directly affected by some of the issues I mentioned earlier: acoustics, carpeting, and so on. However, there are many aspects regarding this "right" over which musicians have a great deal of control. One of the most important is microphone volume and use. A case in point: I was traveling in the archdiocese and attended a church where the people seemed to have a good grasp of their role as a singing assembly. There were songbooks in the pews, the music was announced and posted, and people appeared very willing and able to sing. But as the music group played their introduction to the gathering hymn, I was stunned at the sheer volume of the sound. The instruments were all miked or electronic, and each member of the group also had his or her own microphone. There were several large amplifiers set up, as well as some things plugged directly into the sound system. The people around me seemed to be singing, but I couldn't tell for sure since I could see their mouths moving but couldn't hear myself singing, much less anyone around me. The man next to me was wearing a hearing aid and had a pained look on his face. I could feel the bass guitar notes in the pit of my stomach. All this might be fine at a parade, but was certainly not appropriate for the liturgy. I expected the music leaders to realize their mistake and adjust the volume for the *Gloria*, but it remained just as loud. The rest of the liturgy was the same, and as I was getting in my car, my ears were still ringing! This happened to be a contemporary group with mixed instruments, but I have experienced organists who make the same mistake. It is true the organ leads the assembly's song, but there are definitely times when it is much too loud for a particular space or liturgical assembly. This discourages, rather than enhances, the assembly's song and forces them into a spectator/listener mode.

Cantors and song leaders also need to respect the assembly's song—for that is truly what it is. Unless a cantor is singing verses to the gospel acclamation, the responsorial psalm, invocations for the *Lamb of God* litany, or perhaps verses of a communion hymn, he or she should not be at the microphone. The message that is sent to the assembly is that the song leader is singing for them, and a solo voice booming over the microphone will discourage assembly singing.

3. The assembly has the right to sing those parts of the liturgy that truly belong to it.

There are certain parts of the liturgy that must never be sung "on behalf of" the assembly or taken away from them. Foremost among these are all the acclamations of the Mass—psalm refrains, gospel acclamations and eucharistic acclamations. These belong to the entire gathered people of God. In regard to the eucharistic acclamations James Dallen has written, "The attitude of the presider and people, and the style with which the acclamations are done, should indicate clearly that these are parts of the [eucharistic] prayer, not interruptions, interventions or decorations."[7] I would add that this attitude is incumbent upon the musician also. These are part of the eucharistic prayer, which is greatly diminished if the whole gathered church does not sing them.

I experienced this first-hand when I was visiting a church one Thanksgiving Day. There was a large assembly gathered for the liturgy and about one-third of the community were visitors who had come from out of town or other parishes to celebrate the holiday with their families. We were given a worship aid listing all the hymns to be sung except the acclamations, and I assumed, after noticing that omission, the acclamations would be in the common repertoire—something that most parishes would use at one time or another. It turned out that the gospel and eucharistic acclamations had been written by the leader of the music group (see number 1 above). They had not been published, and unless you were a member of that parish and attended a particular celebration every Sunday, you had no way to participate. In other words, all the peripheral music was accessible to the assembly; the part that was most rightly theirs was not.

4. The assembly has the right to both words and music.

Many members of the assembly will tell you they don't read music. (Actually, most members of most choirs I have conducted have told me this also.) This is not, however, an excuse for not giving it to them. I know the words to the *Holy, Holy, Holy* but I could not sing them in the example of right number 3 because I did not know the tune. Many refrains have two endings. Frequently one goes up and the other goes down. Even if one does not read music well, the relative position of the notes in these instances can help one to remember the difference between the two endings. Thus, you do not have to be embarrassed as your voice rings out with something different from the rest of the assembly and musicians! People rely on the notes for melody direction more than they probably realize, and those of us who do read music well can strengthen and stabilize those around us if we have the music as well as the words. This is simply an act of hospitality and respect for the assembly.

---

[7] James Dallen, "Spirituality and the Eucharistic Prayer," *Worship* 58 (1984), 368.

5. The assembly has the right to be taught new music.

This is essential to helping the assembly "sing their liturgy." When the assembly is taught a new song, it becomes clear to them that they are expected to sing it. If it is a new song for the preparation of the gifts or a song of thanksgiving after Communion, it may not be clear to them that they, and not just the choir or music group, are expected to sing. Nor are they likely to. However, if a hymn is thoughtfully and well taught (which could be an entire article in itself) the assembly will know that the song is theirs, that they are invited to sing, and for the most part they will attempt to participate. No song rehearsal should last longer than two or three minutes and the members of the assembly should be treated with respect at all times. Phrases like "I can't hear you!" or "C'mon, you can do better than that!" have no place in respectful song rehearsal. If the song or hymn tune is difficult it would be better to rehearse it briefly over a few weeks, or even to teach parts of it, rather than to browbeat the assembly with long rehearsals and disparaging phrases. Another teaching technique that could be used more frequently is to repeat the refrain at the beginning so all get a "second chance" to sing it; and, of course, there should be some kind of inviting gesture to bring them in. (See number 6 in *Cantor Basics*, Revised Edition, published by Pastoral Press, OCP 9648PQ).

6. The assembly has the right to repetition.

Any ritual must be a repeated action. Nathan Mitchell, one of my professors at Notre Dame, used to say to us, "We think with our skin." Rituals are patterned actions and gestures we know by heart. Things we know how to do. They are rooted in our imaginations and our memories, which in turn are rooted in our very bodies. This means our bodies must "memorize" what we are doing. These repeated actions, done in community, are part of the interactive and dynamic experience of coming to faith, part of the common language of images, symbols and language used by a community to articulate religious meaning.

This is especially true for liturgical music (and implies that right number 1 has been observed). Eucharistic acclamations, Communion antiphons and psalm refrains must become part of an assembly's repertoire that they know "by heart." The implication for liturgical ministers is that often we must lay aside our preferences, our tedium with a certain set of acclamations or a particular song, for the sake of the community. We are there to serve the community and its prayer, and not to satisfy our individual need for new and "exciting" music. Admittedly, this is not always easy, especially if we participate in multiple Masses on a weekend. By the end of Lent, I had played and/or sung "Bless the Lord, My Soul" over twenty-five times, not counting rehearsals, because we used it as a processional song for all the Sundays of Lent except Palm Sunday of the Lord's Passion. However, the way the community responded to and "owned" the hymn, as well as the sense of prayer it engendered, made it all worthwhile.[8]

7. The assembly has the right to music played and performed with skill and accuracy.

As I travel from parish to parish, I am amazed at the various interpretations of particular hymns. Leaders of music often "edit" a piece of music, disregarding the composer's original score and intention. I am not referring to words, but to the actual music itself. I have heard music written in 4/4 time played in 3/4 and vice versa. Pieces like Dan Schutte's "Here I Am, Lord" and "City of God" or John Foley's "Come to the Water" have had measures added or dropped in the middle of the piece. Such incorrect idiosyncratic renditions of music make it impossible for a piece to be widely sung. If members of a parish where such "editing" has been done attend a parish in which the music is performed correctly, they may find it difficult to participate—or worse yet, be mightily embarrassed as their voices ring out alone during an interlude written in the original score, but omitted by their own parish music group. This lowers participation as members of the assembly begin to feel some loss of confidence and a sense of uncertainty about their ability to sing the hymn. Sometimes music leaders think they are improving a piece, making it more singable. Often, however, this is just poor and sloppy musicianship and has no place in the liturgy.

If competent accompanists cannot be found in a certain parish or for a certain service, it is better to sing *a cappella*. The human voice is the first (and sometimes best) instrument. Poor and inaccurate musical accompaniment discourages community participation more than no accompaniment at all.

---

[8] Each week we enhanced the chant a bit. The first week we sang in unison, so the folks would get a good grasp of the melody; the second week we added parts. After that the cantor began to add the verses (from Psalm 103) over the repeated refrain. We also varied the instrumental accompaniment; thus, we had both variety and repetition.

8. The assembly has the right to a worship aid that is thoughtfully and well put together.

Again, this is a matter of hospitality and respect for the assembly. Musicians who minister in a parish that prints a weekly—or even an occasional—worship aid have a serious obligation to see that it is worthy of the liturgy and the assembled body of Christ. It should contain everything the assembly needs to participate fully, it should contain proper copyright notices, and it should look professional, even beautiful. Today, with computers, sophisticated printers and multi-tasking copiers, there is no excuse for producing something that looks like it was done carelessly or hastily.

9. The assembly has the right not to be entertained.

Entertainment is not engagement. It does not foster full, conscious and active participation, and generally it does not demand anything from us. However, the liturgy must demand something from us. We need to ask the question, "What does it cost us to do the liturgy?" Indeed, what does it cost us when we pledge ourselves to be broken and poured out for the life of the world just as Jesus was? What does it cost us to drink from the common cup? What does it demand of us when we answer "Thanks be to God" to the mandate "Go in peace to love and serve the Lord"? We cannot respond to these challenges as a passive audience.

Unfortunately, music ministers are fighting the prevailing culture on this one. Entertainment is all-pervasive in our present milieu: hours of television watching, CDs, DVDs, movies, video games, computer games, even games and entertainment on our cell phones. When a community looks up and sees a music group in front of it, it expects to be entertained—especially if the music area is a stage-like setting.

By our demeanor, our presence and our attitude as ministers of the liturgy, we can either help or hinder this expectation. Our own attention to the liturgy is of utmost importance. With some music ministers it is clear that the only important part of the liturgy is what they are doing when they are performing. It's all about them. They don't attend to the rest of the service and can even become distracting as they shuffle music and tinker with their instruments. The placement of the pastoral musicians also affects the perception the assembly has of its role—as entertainer or true ministers. *Built of Living Stones* states it well:

> The placement and prayerful decorum of
> the choir members can help the rest of the

community to focus on the liturgical action
taking place at the ambo, the altar and the
chair. The ministers of music are most appropriately located in a place where they can be
part of the assembly and have the ability to
be heard. Occasions or physical situations
may necessitate that the choir be placed in or
near the sanctuary. In such circumstances, the
placement of the choir should never crowd or
overshadow the other ministers in the sanctuary nor should it distract from the liturgical
actions.[9]

Thus when the choir or instrumentalists are intensely engaged in
the liturgy itself and are clearly members of the worshiping community,
they become icons of what full, conscious and active participation can
be for the rest of us. The message will not be lost on the assembly.

10. The assembly has the right to claim its role as primary agent and celebrant of the liturgy.

Liturgical ministers, whatever their office, by their attitude and
presence can diminish or enhance the dignity and primacy of the community as celebrants of the liturgy. The celebration of Eucharist is an
activity of the whole body of Christ, head and members, for the
Eucharist is the center of ecclesial life and the common possession of
the whole church.[10] Alexander Schmemann states this beautifully and
clearly, in words that all liturgical ministers—not just musicians—
should heed carefully in their services:

Only the entire church, manifested and
actualized in the "assembly as the church,"
has the mind of Christ. Only in the church
gathering are all gifts, all ministries revealed
in their unity and indivisibility, as manifestations of the one Spirit, who fills the whole
body. And therefore, finally, each member of
the church, whatever his "rank" in the

---

[9] *Built of Living Stones: Art, Architecture and Worship* (Washington, D.C.: United States
Catholic Conference, 2000), 90.

[10] *This Holy Living Sacrifice* (Washington, D.C.: United States Catholic Conference, 1985),
6–10.

church, must be a witness before the world of
the entire fullness of the church.[11]

Musicians whose service is based on this principle are not only fine pastoral ministers and icons of service, but are first and foremost active and conscious members of their assemblies as well.

---

[11] Alexander Schmemann, *The Eucharist, Sacrament of the Kingdom*, trans. Paul Kachur (New York: St. Vladimir's Seminary Press, 1987), 80.

3
Before All Else

The aim to be considered before all else is the full, conscious and active participation of all in the assembly. We began the reform and renewal of the liturgy with those prophetic words forty years ago. This aim has formed and transformed our vision, worship, ministry, parish and our very identity as Catholics. That vision has shaped our understanding and experience of ministry and service in every aspect of our life as church. Full, conscious and active participation done well and with conviction in the eucharistic assembly naturally impels us to collaboration in every aspect of being the church in this age. Collaboration is a given, for as we pray so are we to live and act or our worship becomes hollow, lacking both depth and sincerity. We can no longer do the liturgy and can no longer do, become or envision the church outside the norm of full, conscious and active participation. This, as *Sacroscanctum concilium* still reminds us, is both the right and responsibility of all the baptized. We do this, both in the liturgy and in the life of the parish, each according to our own roles and ministries, needs and gifts, but we always do it together for the sake of all, for the building up of the body of Christ. The liturgy thus becomes the icon, the image or the model for how we are to live and act and be the church.

The collaboration between pastor and pastoral musician described in the following article ought not to be viewed as an exception to the rule, but rather seen as the ordinary way of doing the work of the liturgy—the work of the prayer of the people. The aim to be considered before all else requires a vigilant deliberateness, a conscious choice and a willingness to do the work—sometimes the hard work—of listening, learning, reflecting and sometimes, perhaps often, changing one's mind and heart! Such is the work of the liturgy and such is the work of belonging to the Lord and being the body of Christ!

—Mary Jo Quinn, SCL
—Edward J. Hislop

Sacrament of Unity
Ministry of Collaboration
Unity between Pastor and Musician

Mary Jo Quinn SCL and Edward J. Hislop

Mary Jo Quinn, a Sister of Charity of Leavenworth, Kansas, and Edward J. Hislop, a presbyter of the diocese of Helena, Montana, served together from 1985 to 2001 at Saint Mary Catholic community in Helena, Montana.

How do a pastor and a pastoral musician achieve unity? What does collaborative ministry mean?

The ministry of liturgical service is rooted in the real life of the parish. When collaboration is the style of ministry in every aspect of parish life—Christian formation, RCIA, youth ministry, pastoral care, social concerns, parish administration and, not least, liturgy—the whole staff shares in the entire ministry. Pastor and pastoral musician collaborate with one another because their work is about bringing life to the experience of the liturgy.

The staff, especially the pastor and musician, shares the vision of the eucharistic liturgy as central to the life and mission of the faith community. The liturgy must be taken seriously by everyone on the staff who shares commitment to the principle of the Sunday Eucharist as the "font and summit" of parish life and ministry. Regardless of how many Masses are scheduled each weekend, each celebration of Eucharist is seen as part of the entire celebration of the parish's Sunday liturgy.

Preparation for Sunday Mass involves sustained effort, evident care and quality time, so that the liturgy is experienced as the central and primary event of the week. This is reflected in the quality and "noble simplicity" of the environment, including the cleanliness and order of the worship space, the investment in qualified personnel, well-prepared liturgical ministers, the use of quality musical instruments, the abiding worth of the musical choices, and the sense of reverence and beauty exhibited. The primacy of the liturgy must also be reflected in parish stewardship and financial budget. It must be clear to the community—and to anyone who visits the parish—that its liturgical celebration is of preeminent importance and is the primary and indispensable experience of the week.

82

One of the marks of this preeminence is the investment of presider and assembly to the proclamation of the eucharistic prayer. In 1985, our first year of shared ministry, Marty Haugen's *Mass of Creation* served us well both as an accessible presider's setting of the eucharistic prayer and as an engaging setting of acclamations for the assembly.

Assembly members and choir singers learned the *Mass of Creation* that fall. At Christmas, when the presider sang the eucharistic prayer, it was as if the parish had never heard the prayer before. Assembly members' understanding of the prayer deepened; they began to experience "full, conscious and active participation" in the prayer as proclaimed by the presider in the name of the whole church. The assembly was actively attentive to the proclamation and sang their acclamations with full voice. As the experience unfolded at Christmas and Easter each year, the assembly grasped even more deeply the meaning of this great prayer of thanksgiving. This was affirmed in reflective sessions with parishioners following the Easter season.

In ensuing years, we examined additional settings of the eucharistic prayer. After agreeing that the new acclamations would be worthy additions to the parish repertoire, examining the presider's part always called forth the same question: "Will the assembly truly experience the prayer of thanksgiving as that of the whole church in which they fully participate?"

That process of examining the musical experience of the eucharistic prayer was one of the elements of the parish's transformation to a community of care and outreach. The preaching of the gospel was related to the community's life around the eucharistic table. Assembly members prayed the prayer, too; they did not simply listen to its proclamation.

Musicians especially can agree that, in most parishes, people do sing. The revised ritual books provide an opportunity for renewed catechesis. A mystagogical approach allows the community to reflect on what has been done in the renewal thus far. The following questions can shape that reflection: "What is a singing assembly? What is that assembly singing? How can that singing be refined, deepened, improved? How can we reaffirm our commitment to the singing assembly?"

As the parish grows in its experience of liturgy, continuing and ongoing formation of those engaged in the liturgical and music ministries are crucial to collaborative ministry, at both the parish and diocesan levels. A single workshop or experience is the beginning, not the end, of developing talent, gifts and insights. Liturgical catechesis continues and never ends for the assembly, the presider and the liturgical musician.

On a practical level the pastor or pastoral administrator must encourage and support this continuing formation. This means providing funds for both paid staff and volunteers to participate in continuing education—workshops, voice or organ lessons, attendance at NPM conventions, perhaps even financing a summer's tuition.

It is apparent that parish life, liturgy and ministry are vital, and alive in communities that for a number of years have taken seriously the reform of the liturgy. Where the reform has not been taken seriously, communities have suffered. Much of the consternation over the state of liturgy in this country and throughout the world flows out of the negative experiences of those parishes where the renewal has not been taken seriously. There are problems, yes, but the liturgical reform cannot be blamed for those problems. The fact is that in many places, the reform has not been done, or it has been done without conviction and consistency.

The clergy of a diocese must be open and willing to be formed in the liturgy and in the meaning and function of music within the liturgy. If the clergy and pastoral staff are not open to continuing formation, that spells a great deal of trouble for the pastoral musician, for anyone who cares about the liturgy and, most especially and sadly, for the assembly itself.

> The responsibility for effective pastoral celebration in a parish community falls upon all those who exercise major roles in the liturgy. The practical preparation for each liturgical celebration should be done in a spirit of cooperation by all parties concerned, under the guidance of the rector of the church, whether it be ritual, pastoral or musical matters. In practice this ordinarily means an organized "planning team" or committee which meets regularly to achieve creative and coordinated worship and a good use of the liturgical and musical options of a flexible liturgy. (*Music in Catholic Worship*, 10)

What is the practical role of the liturgy team? The committee brings the wisdom and experience of the parish and helps articulate the life of the parish. The liturgy team assists in the preparation of the liturgy, relying on the liturgical books. It is the role of the presiders, liturgy coordinators, pastoral musicians and other qualified personnel to carry out the "nuts and bolts" of the liturgy.

The mystagogical approach is again useful in this context. For example, the liturgy team, with invited members of the assembly, might reflect upon the experience of the Triduum by asking questions: "What did this mean for us this year? What did we feel, experience, see, touch, hear and smell? How were our hearts changed?" This opens a new dimension of how the liturgy is prepared and how it will continue to be prepared.

The liturgy team might invite people from the parish for an afternoon of reflection on their experience of the Sunday liturgy, or what happened through the Christmas season, or the effect of the Triduum. These kinds of insights are necessary in shaping the authentic liturgical life of the community. Where there are many music volunteers, they should be invited to meet together and begin to make some appropriate choices together; involving those who are involved in music preparation—cantors, choir members, organists—helps broaden the vision.

When we began to work together at St. Mary's we examined the musical needs of the parish. We believed that one of music's functions is to unite the liturgy and the parish. Together we developed the musician's job description, which initially centered around three specific tasks: to develop an instrumental/vocal music group consisting of piano, guitar and any other instruments appropriate to the musical style of the group; to recruit and develop a children's choir; and to assess the parish repertoire and set reasonable goals for repertoire development, in addition to the earlier-mentioned need for a full Mass setting. The parish was also inconsistent in singing a Communion processional. These became the first year's priorities.

A pattern for learning began that never changed. In the fall, pastor and musician in collaboration with the liturgy team discussed the needs and goals of parish music for the year to come. The "teaching Sundays" within Ordinary Time were scheduled. The presider respected the teaching moment, both by his own presence and by priority of time. (The "teaching time" always began at the set time for the beginning of the liturgy.) It was always apparent that the pastor fully supported the musical agenda; he could support it because it was mutually discussed and agreed upon. Both pastor and musician understood that neither the music nor the presider should dominate the liturgy but each should complement the other.

Presiders and musicians who work together must be energized by a common passion for the liturgy and its power, a passion for the prayer of the people, for the proclamation of the gospel, for the Eucharist and the eucharistic prayer. They must be passionate for the mission of the church that comes about because of the liturgy. If there is no passion, then much of what is done is not worth doing. If there is no passion about all that goes into and comes out of the Sunday assembly, then the parish loses both vision and direction.

The local church is the place where the church is the church—the place the church lives, gathers, breathes, sings, listens, eats, drinks and is sent forth on mission. Although the diocese is called the local church (and indeed it is), in reality—in the experience of the people—it is the parish. It is in the parish where life happens, where conversion occurs, where transformation is effected, where Christ is fully present. Pastor and musician working together must understand the significance and the importance of parish life and ministry in all of its diversity and in all of its demands. In that awareness, we know that from the liturgy flow all the other ministries within the parish. Then we can truly affirm Augustine's words as we journey to the table each week:

> If, then, you wish to understand the body
> of Christ, listen to the apostle as he says to
> the faithful, "You are the body of Christ, and
> his members" (1 Corinthians 12:27). If you
> are the body and members of Christ, then
> what is laid on the Lord's table is the sacra-
> ment (*mysterium*) of what you yourselves are,
> and it is the sacrament of what you are that
> you receive. It is to what you yourselves are
> that you answer "Amen," and this answer is
> your affidavit. Be a member of Christ's body,
> so that your "Amen" may be authentic. (St.
> Augustine, Sermon 272, PL 38:1247)

It is this experience and reality that evoke conversion—ongoing conversion and transformation of persons, assemblies, parishes, dioceses, presiders, pastoral staff, deacons, bishops, indeed the whole world. Sunday after Sunday, year after year, generation after generation, conversion is the language of liturgy, that entrance into the mystery of Christ's life, death and resurrection.

When the pastor and the musician are able to complement one another in skill and expertise, in passion and in love of the church, the experience is neither primarily musical nor centered in the presider; rather, the celebration of the liturgy is the "sacrament of unity" (*Sacrosanctum concilium*, 26) for the whole assembly. It is then that these words take on power and deeper meaning: "go in peace to love and serve the Lord!"

4

Collaboration Is a Way of Living

Part of our formation as liturgical ministers includes understanding how our particular ministry "works," whether it is proclaiming the word, ministering the Eucharist, leading sung prayer, greeting with a spirit of Christian anticipation, preparing the worship space or preparing the liturgy itself. However, another part of our formation includes understanding how our ministries "work" together, how all the parts fit into the whole.

In addition to considering how the parts fit together within a given liturgy, we are challenged to understand further how we work together throughout the whole of the liturgical year. One of the greatest challenges to music ministers, whether instrumentalists, members of the choir, cantors or choir directors, is gaining a profound sense of the liturgical rites of the church. Much is to be learned not only from the prayer texts of these liturgies and from their rubrics, but also from the introductions or general instructions of these rites.

One example is the Rite of Christian Initiation of Adults (RCIA). Most choirs "sing at" the rites of the RCIA, rather than "singing with" those who celebrate the rites of the RCIA. Those who are leaders in parish RCIA processes should be proactive in inviting those in parish music ministry to study and to pray the rites and prepare them together. RCIA directors are called to move beyond seeing music ministers as utilitarian adjuncts to the celebration of rites.

In his letter to the Romans, Chapter 12, St. Paul gives us an image of the body of Christ: one body with many parts. Though many, we are all part of one another, since we belong to the body.

He speaks a bit further about the gifts we have. "Since we have gifts that differ according to the grace given to us, let us exercise them: if prophecy, in proportion to the faith; if ministry, in ministering; if one is a teacher, in teaching; if one exhorts, in exhortation; if one contributes, in generosity; if one is over others, with diligence; if one does acts of mercy, with cheerfulness" (Romans 12: 6–8).

Collaboration is not just some "pie-in-the-sky" corporate concept of a way to work together to achieve a goal or complete a project. Collaboration is a way of living, of being church, of mutually regarding one another as persons, and of regarding one another's gifts.

In the first letter to the Corinthians, Chapter 12, St. Paul talks about the parts of the body needing one another, and not mutually dismissing one another as not being needed. It is precisely in needing one another, in being connected to one another, in empowering one another, in calling forth one another's gifts, that we show forth the presence of Christ alive in the world today.

In the letter to the Ephesians, St. Paul says, "Living the truth in love, we should grow in every way into him who is the head, Christ, from whom the whole body, joined and held together by every supporting ligament, with the proper functioning of each part, brings about the body's growth and builds itself up in love." May our work together be the example of love which draws people into the community and ultimately toward God.

—Dolores Martinez

Sacrament of Unity
The Singing Assembly

Dolores Martinez

This description of one parish's experience over the course of three years illustrates a move toward collaboration in a pastoral setting. A true spirit of collaboration can witness to the parish community that those who minister to them, and in turn inspire them to minister to others, are of one mind and one spirit: the church as the sacrament of unity.

In my first year as liturgist in one parish, the approach to the Easter Triduum seemed disjointed. Each of the choirs was assigned a different night of the Triduum, selecting its own repertoire. More often than not, those celebrating the Triduum in its entirety found it difficult to enter into prayer and music that were not part of their Sunday worship experience.

A second problem arose in the relationship of choir to the elect who had gone through the catechumenate and would be celebrating the sacraments of initiation. The elect normally attended Sunday Mass at the same time each week and were accustomed to the contemporary style of music of one particular choir, as well as their presence, their witness and their friendship. But a different choir was selected for the Vigil celebration, one accustomed to singing traditional hymnody set in four voice parts and unused to singing ritual music full of acclamations and litanies. The elect and the contemporary choir members felt a severe disconnect—some of the latter chose to attend the Vigil as members of the assembly. It was obvious that some were disappointed.

How could we give the best service to the body of Christ, to this parish community as well as to the elect on this most important night in their journey of initiation? How could we witness to them a fuller image of the church in the way that we worked together to support their journey?

Considering norms

I considered the following norms as the basis for an evaluation of our ministerial, liturgical attitudes. *General Norms for the Liturgical Year and the Calendar* (GNLY) states, "Once a year at Easter the church honors this resurrection and passion with the utmost solemnity" (GNLY 1) and continues, "Therefore the Easter Triduum of the passion and resurrection of Christ is the culmination of the entire liturgical year. Thus the solemnity of Easter has the same kind of preeminence in the liturgical year that Sunday has in the week"(18). Finally, GNLY states, "The Easter Triduum begins with the evening Mass of the Lord's Supper, reaches its high point in the Easter Vigil, and closes with evening prayer on Easter Sunday" (19). To merely talk about this seriously undermined our ability to communicate Triduum spirituality to the assembly. We could communicate the importance of these principles to the people of God far better by living them out. The present praxis would have to change.

A second norm was that found in *Sacrosanctum concilium*:

> Liturgical services are not private functions, but are celebrations belonging to the church, which is the "sacrament of unity," namely, the holy people united and ordered under their bishops.
>
> Therefore liturgical services involve the whole body of the church; they manifest it and have effects upon it; but they also concern the individual members of the church in different ways, according to their different orders, offices and actual participation. (SC 26)

How could we in fact involve the whole body of the church, even in this microcosm called parish? How could all musicians, as well as all the other liturgical ministers, really show forth "church" by celebrating the Triduum as a more united community?

I knew that I could not unilaterally legislate what I considered to be important changes just because I was the parish liturgist. I also knew that I would have to win the trust of the musicians, as well as the priests, deacons and other key ministers for this celebration.

While trying to make some changes, I was met with resistance. Choirs had "set their turf" about these parts of the Triduum: "We've always assigned these choirs to these liturgies." This is where, as Bishop Victor Balke put it in his article (page 23), we experienced "dissension, polarization and distrust." It was evident that there was little shared commitment to this celebration and thus to those of the faithful who experienced it in its totality. If, in fact, this celebration of the Triduum "pertained to the whole body of the church," why were these liturgies being experienced not so much as private functions but as divided ones that belied the "sacrament of unity" called for by *Sacrosanctum concilium*?

However, some changes were taking the music ministry in a new and positive direction. Catechumens and candidates began to attend different Sunday liturgies. The idea was to expose them to different styles of worship, so that they understood that they were joining the Catholic Church—all of it, not just the 8:30 a.m. Sunday community of the Catholic Church. This also exposed the catechumens and candidates to more members of the community, making them not abstract ideas prayed for in the General Intercessions, but real people whom assembly members had met and touched. All the rites of the catechumenate began to be rotated through the various Masses throughout the year and over subsequent years.

Since the 8:00 a.m. choir had embraced the RCIA process (and the whole concept of adult initiation), they "journeyed" along with the catechumens and candidates to the different Masses. One weekend they would sing at 8:00 a.m., the next weekend at 10:00 a.m., the next at 5:30 p.m. on Saturday and the next at the noon Mass. The choir regularly assigned to those time slots would rotate into the 8 a.m. slot for a given weekend. Stylistically this was not a challenge, at least for the choir, since the same style of music was sung throughout. While this approach had some positive results, it presented another set of challenges. One of those was the assembly members' unfamiliarity with the contemporary style of music, given their usual Sunday repertoire.

Integrating the celebration

In the course of my third year in the parish, the challenge was extended to all choirs to begin to understand the rites of the RCIA, to learn the ritual music that supported the rites and to embrace the people who were making this journey. This approach eventually superseded the "journey choir" approach. All the choirs were given a schedule indicating when the catechumens and candidates would be present at a particular Mass time. Each director planned music for the rites, which was taken from one common resource for music for the RCIA.

An explicit and direct invitation was extended, in person and in writing, to each choir member including cantors, to form one choir for the Triduum which would draw from all musical resources to fit the needs of the ritual at a given time. Approximately fifty people responded. They understood that their presence as ministers was expected all three days. They understood that this liturgy belonged to everyone, and that those who were to minister through music should celebrate it in its entirety. They understood that this would cost them time and energy and, yes, they would get tired. But what a great way to get tired!

A series of exclusive rehearsals was set for a time different from any choir's regular weekly rehearsal; Sunday night was selected, from 6–9 p.m. for six weeks, not counting Palm Sunday of the Lord's Passion. One of the biggest challenges was to help to move the music ministry members' hearts and minds to a new theological understanding of the meaning of Triduum as one celebration and to encourage their participation in this once-a-year opportunity to celebrate the paschal mystery.

A second challenge was to help them to understand that the elect and candidates were indeed the focus of the night: icons for the rest of the community of the paschal mystery as expressed through the waters of baptism, confirmation and joining the community in Christ's banquet and in his mission to the world.

One advantage was that several of the members of this Triduum choir were members of the former "journey choir." They already spoke the language of initiation and knew the meaning of the statement "initiation…is the responsibility of all the baptized." (*Rite of Christian Initiation of Adults*, Introduction, 9)

The third challenge was to bring the choirs with their respective repertoires together. While each choir in principle agreed on the assembly's vital singing role in worship, that differed greatly in practice from Sunday Mass to Sunday Mass. The different choirs' input regarding selection of repertoire was solicited as one way to build trust between musicians and liturgist, as well as among the musicians themselves. They also had to articulate why they thought a particular piece was the best selection for that part of the liturgy. The best repertoire from all styles was selected in a fair and balanced way based on the needs of the ritual, not on a *quid pro quo* approach.

Repertoire selection included an examination of the principles of participation found in the *Sacrosanctum concilium*, paragraphs 14 ("full, conscious, active participation by all present") and 48 ("they are not to be there as strangers or silent spectators"). What music best suits this part of the rite in order to engage the assembly and to facilitate their participation? Members of different choirs began to engage in more sincere conversations with one another, not just the perfunctory "hello" on the way into or out of Mass.

Deacon Owen Cummings asks, "How do people at the parish level get past the liturgy wars so that the liturgy may be both a rich, positive, creative experience and may enhance our witness and mission to the world?" (page 34). One way is through catechesis, also mentioned by Sr. Mary Jo Quinn and Fr. Ed Hislop (page 83). Another is through conversations around the dinner table, not the planning table. A third is to start with the sources, the liturgical books and documents themselves.

The beauty of the singing assembly

By beginning with the liturgical books themselves, reading the texts of the prayers and Scriptures as well as the rubrics, we could move more easily into an objective selection of music which would fill the needs of the ritual. One example is music for the *Mandatum*, the washing of the feet. The rite offers six antiphons, each from a different Scripture verse. What music could we find that would utilize one or more of those verses in order to express in song the theology of this rite? As overall coordinator, I had to give guidance, but I also had to trust their experience and opinion.

Since the parish engaged in an extended time of foot washing—men, women, young, old, abled, disabled, and so on—and all were invited to wash the feet of others, the music had to fill the extended ritual moment. Their choices included "*Ubi Caritas*" (Bob Hurd) and "*Ubi Caritas*" (Laurence Rosania) as well as "Jesus Took a Towel" by Chrysogonus Waddell, OSCO. The refrain of the latter song made sense if those singing it were engaged in either washing or being washed: "Then he washed my feet, yes, he washed my feet."

The ultimate test came on Holy Thursday when some members of the choir moved to wash and be washed. The experience was powerful. Besides trusting their judgment of music and their willingness to enter into the experience fully, I had to trust that the Holy Spirit would do the work of moving their hearts. The musicians had to trust that I was not setting them up for embarrassing moments with some new-fangled way of celebrating Holy Thursday, but that what I was asking them to be open to would indeed bring them a new sense of the entire paschal mystery.

Since one of our biggest challenges is the catechesis of the assembly (in addition to catechesis of those who minister liturgically to them, from bishop to sacristan), it bears repeating that the best catechesis in the liturgy is a liturgy that is celebrated well. To celebrate well, we made good use of symbol (basins, pitchers, towels, multiple stations for foot washing throughout the church); we sang well (involving the assembly in singing throughout the rite); we took time, not rushing or shortchanging the power of the rite to act on us.

Finally, one of the best practices that our community had embraced was a parish-wide "breaking open of the word" similar to that of the catechumens and candidates during their RCIA journey. Choirs looked at the readings for the following Sunday in preparation of the music they would be singing. It all began to make more sense to them. The sharing and the praying began to grow with each passing rehearsal. No longer was it just about notes and good vocal production but rather a real growth in their own spirituality, in caring for one another and in caring for the parish as a whole.

5

Please Try This at Home

As part of our observance of the "Nine Days to 9/11" at St. James Cathedral in Seattle, we established a place of prayer in the cathedral's north aisle. At the weekend Masses during the novena, we sang a hymn of praise as usual following Communion. Then, after the dismissal, the "go in the peace of Christ," we sang "Let There Be Light" together as the ministers led a procession to the place of prayer.

The exception proved the rule: people stayed to sing to the end of the hymn. And because we so rarely sing following the dismissal, the words of the hymn were not mumbled through or put away after a verse or two. Rather, the "sending forth" became a genuine call to action:

> Let there be light, Lord, God of hosts!
> Let there be wisdom on the earth!
> Let broad humanity have birth!
> Let there be deeds instead of boasts!

This experience brought home to us that the hymn of praise is not simply a transplanted "sending forth"; rather, the two hymns serve quite different liturgical purposes.

In the church's liturgy, what we *don't* sing is sometimes as important as what we *do*. The *Gloria* is omitted during Advent and Lent, and the *Alleluia* during Lent, not to shorten or simplify the Mass but to drive home a point. The return of the *Alleluia* at the Easter Vigil thereby becomes both sign and expression of the return of Easter joy. In the same way, the hymn of praise can open up possibilities for powerful liturgy.

Since this article was published in 2001, we have received a number of queries about the hymn of praise—how do you get started and how do you make it work? You *can* make it work, no matter the size of your parish or the size of your repertory, but there are two basic requirements:

1. Consistency. Even assemblies learn by practice. Make it work by following the same format week after week, giving people plenty of time to get comfortable with it.

2. Develop your non-vocal repertoire. Doing the hymn of praise effectively also means having instrumental music that truly helps to send the faithful forth to love and serve the Lord (and to get Father comfortably to the door). The procession, whether it be an organ toccata or the tolling of a single bell, can be a wonderful, wordless trope on the final prayer of the Mass. The church shows great wisdom, after all, in letting the people (not the cantor!) have the final word: "Thanks be to God!"

(NOTE: The new *General Instruction on the Roman Missal* reaffirms the role of the hymn of praise in the liturgy. "After communion, the priest and people may spend some time praying silently. If desired, either a psalm or other canticle of praise or a hymn may be sung by the entire congregation." IGRM 87–88)

—Corinna Laughlin
—James Savage

The Hymn of Praise

Corinna Laughlin

"After singing a hymn they went out" (Matthew 26:30).

In the early 1980s, the eucharistic liturgy at St. James Cathedral in Seattle ended with a closing hymn. "Week after week," says Dr. James Savage, director of liturgy and music, "from my station in the choir loft high above the cathedral's main aisle, I would witness the same distressing things. The cantor would announce the hymn and some would begin singing. Promptly at the end of the first verse, the presider would close his book, reverence the altar and leave the church with the servers and other ministers. People would run for the parking lots via every one of the cathedral's twelve doors while the cantor and choir struggled on through the hymn's remaining verses with musical forces now alarmingly diminished. We sang 'Hark! How the heavenly anthem drowns / All music but its own,' while our earthly voices were drowned out by the knocking of kneelers, the slamming of hymnals and the thunder of departing feet."

Thinking perhaps the problem rested with repertoire, we tried familiar and unfamiliar tunes, traditional and non-traditional texts; we tried more verses and fewer verses; but nothing induced the faithful to remain to the end. The only exceptions seemed to be certain great solemnities—Easter and Christmas—as well as the months of May and October, when, according to long cathedral tradition, a hymn to Mary was sung immediately following Mass.

The assembly had come to an unspoken, but definite, decision. They left, not because they didn't want to sing, but perhaps because they sensed something liturgically wrong. "Throughout the liturgy," Dr. Savage notes, "the people have been given their instructions by the priest or deacon ('Let us pray,' 'Lift up your hearts,' 'Join in their unending hymn of praise,' 'Offer to one another a sign of Christ's peace.'). At the end of the liturgy they're told to 'Go in the peace of Christ,' 'Go in peace to love and serve the Lord,' 'Go!' But suddenly the cantor intervenes: 'No! Don't go; stay and sing.' It's a direct contradiction. As a result, the singing of the closing hymn became a kind of organ- or choir-led paraliturgy imposed in order to give the presider a graceful exit." Our concern at the cathedral was that a sung prayer during which people depart sent a message that the people's singing at Eucharist had no value.

Singing the Mass

We looked into the origins of the closing hymn and into the church's teaching about the assembly's participation in the music of the Mass. The closing hymn was a recent concept developed in the years preceding the Second Vatican Council. In his 1955 encyclical *Musicae Sacrae*, Pope Pius XII spoke highly of traditional vernacular hymns, which "can be a powerful aid in keeping the faithful from attending the Holy Sacrifice like dumb and idle spectators" (64). He encouraged the use of such hymns in low Masses, provided that they never replace "the sacred words of the liturgy...sung in Latin during the Eucharistic sacrifice" (47). Hymns thus served a dual purpose: they involved the faithful and provided a place for the vernacular. This pre-Vatican II encyclical helped create what has been called the "four-hymn syndrome": because none of the liturgical texts could be sung in the language of the people, places were found for hymn-singing before the celebration (the entrance hymn), during the Mass (offertory and communion) and at the end of the celebration (the closing hymn).

By the time the Second Vatican Council convened, the four-hymn, low Mass model had been in place for several years. However, *Musicam sacram* (1967) took quite a different direction, indicating the eschatological purpose of music in the liturgy: "It raises the mind more readily to heavenly realities through the splendor of the rites. It makes the whole celebration a more striking symbol of the celebration to come in the heavenly Jerusalem." (5) It therefore becomes essential that the people take part in the liturgy itself, in keeping with the visions of the heavenly liturgy in Revelation, where countless voices join together in worship composed of song and dialogue. (Rev. 4) *Musicam sacram* insists that "the faithful should, as far as possible, have a part in singing the Proper of the Mass." (33)

A 1969 query in *Notitiae* asked whether, after *Musicam sacram*, the four-hymn low Mass model might be continued; the oft-quoted negative response was definitive.

> What must be sung is the Mass, its Ordinary and Proper, not something, no matter how consistent, that is imposed on the Mass. Liturgical song involves not mere melody, but words, text, thought and the sentiments that the poetry and music contain. Thus texts must be those of the Mass, not others, and singing means singing the Mass, not just singing during Mass. (*Not.* 5 [1969], 406).

100

Singing the Mass rather than singing at Mass means that no specific allowance is made for a closing hymn following the final blessing. The eschatological view of Mass as an earthly sharing in heavenly worship does not allow us to go out as we came in, but insists on the transformative power of the liturgy. If indeed "we gather for worship and scatter for mission," then we must go forth changed—and the way we celebrate the liturgy must reflect that change.

The *General Instruction on the Roman Missal* (rev. 1975), reflecting *Musicam sacram*, also moves the optional final song to just before the dismissal, rather than just after it: "After communion, the priest and people may spend some time in silent prayer. If desired, a hymn, psalm or other song of praise may be sung by the entire congregation." (56j; see also 121) The dismissal therefore retains its special function of "send[ing] each member back to doing good works, while praising and blessing the Lord," (57b) this instruction is retained in the 2000 revision, section 88. The main American commentaries on music in the liturgy—*Music in Catholic Worship* (1972) and *Liturgical Music Today* (1982)—combine old and new, incorporating some of the reforms suggested by *Musicam sacram*, but at the same time retaining older models, especially in terms of the issue of hymn-singing. The degrees proposed by *Musicam sacram* were rejected ("Almost unlimited combinations of sung and recited parts may be chosen. The important decision is whether or not this or that part may be or should be sung in this particular celebration and under these specific circumstances," [51]) and both the hymn of praise following communion and the recessional song are listed as options, with neither given preference.

The hymn of praise

And so, in the mid-1980s, we began to experiment with the hymn of praise. The response was immediate. "It felt inevitable," recalls Dr. Savage. "The church was wise to provide an opportunity for the people to celebrate their oneness by singing. Almost all the other music in the Mass accompanies a ritual action of one kind or another—a procession, for example—but the hymn of praise, like the *Glory to God*, gives us an opportunity to do nothing but stand as the body of Christ and sing a prayer together."

Singing a hymn of praise allows for many more options in the selection of texts and tunes than did the closing song. Choices are often suggested by the communion antiphons proper to each Sunday of the year. The antiphons, variously confident in public praise and quiet in interior meditation, can provide a needed link between the Liturgy of the Word and the Liturgy of the Eucharist.

We often use the hymn of praise to suggest unexpected connections with the readings. Here are some specific examples.

101

On the Fourth Sunday of Easter (Year B), the gospel of the good shepherd suggested a myriad of potential hymns. For the entrance hymn, we sang "All People That on Earth Do Dwell" (OLD HUNDREDTH), and for the hymn of praise "My Shepherd Will Supply My Need" (RESIGNATION). Both hymns recall the gospel, but in quite different ways. The first is voiced in the public and plural praise of the hundredth psalm: "We are his folk, he does us feed, / And for his sheep he does us take." The second uses the first-person, interior poetry of Psalm 23: "In pastures green you make me feed, / Beside the living stream. / You bring my wand'ring spirit back, / When I forsake your ways."

On the 22nd Sunday in Ordinary Time (also in Year B), Mark's gospel—"From within people, from their hearts, come evil thoughts, unchastity, theft, murder, adultery, greed, malice...(Mark 7)"—did not immediately suggest a hymn. Rather than focusing on the hypocrisy of the scribes and the Pharisees, we focused on the word "heart," singing Wesley's text "O for a Heart to Praise My God" (RICHMOND), which took on a new meaning in this context: "A humble, lowly, contrite heart, / Believing, true, and clean."

The hymn of praise is not always quiet and interior; it can offer another moment for celebration at great solemnities like Epiphany, Pentecost and Christ the King. Hymn texts may be related to the particular celebration, such as "giving" texts on stewardship Sundays or healing texts at anointing services.

Going in peace

Our experience at St. James Cathedral is that, paradoxically, without the "closing song," more people actually stay to experience the procession, the great symbol of our going forth.

Among the advantages in singing a hymn of praise rather than a closing song are these: the musical possibilities are much more varied, from quiet adoration to exuberant joy. The sung prayer is more closely tied to the Eucharist. The dismissal takes place after the shared singing. Not least, it works.

The author gratefully acknowledges the assistance of Father Michael G. Ryan, Pastor of St. James Cathedral, and Carolyn Lassek, director of the office of worship for the Archdiocese of Seattle, and indebtedness to Dr. Paul F. Ford, whose thoughtful introduction to *By Flowing Waters: Chant for the Liturgy* (The Liturgical Press, 1999) has helped shape these ideas about the assembly's participation in the liturgy.

PART 3

Rites/Liturgical Year

1

Revisiting Galilee Revisited

In the years since I first wrote about the healing ministry of the church and that article was published in *Today's Liturgy*, I have come to a broader understanding of what a healing ministry might be. While many writers today are looking to baptismal catechesis (especially the Rite of Christian Initiation of Adults [RCIA]) as the source of a model for all catechesis, I suggest that the church's healing ministry may provide a second model, one that may be truer to the situation in which most catechists and ministers of the church find themselves. In fact, the healing ministry of the church is a ministry to all believers, for in some sense we are all broken.

While RCIA sees us recruiting and welcoming all those who feel called, broadening the healing ministry of the church allows us to address this brokenness that we find in every Christian. It calls us to seek out and find each Christian, be they Roman Catholic or not, and work with what good is already there.

This overall model for ministry and catechesis based on the church's concern for the sick would begin with presence, actually knowing where all the people who need ministry (all Christians) are. The need for each Catholic parish to lead a concerted effort to identify all those who claim the name of Jesus, and especially all those who claim to be Roman Catholic, is not new, but if the healing mission of the church is our model for ministry, this first step takes on a special urgency. Not only are they out there, but they need healing.

Once we know who is out there, we need to identify their needs, working through the church's ordinary means of growth—which in this case is taken directly from our ministry to the sick: prayer, counsel, Communion and penance. If it is discerned that there is a real need for more extraordinary measures, they flow naturally from these efforts. In the ministry to the sick this takes the form of anointing and *viaticum*. In the case of a catechetical ministry to all Christians, this would probably take the form of personal instruction.

But beyond this, and crucial to this notion of ministry to the sick as a model of ministry to the wider church, is that every person deserves personal attention. We need to seek out all who claim Christian as their name and attend to their needs. No one can be left out. The demands that this type of commitment would place on parish life are not unlike the demands flowing from ministry to the sick—it makes a one-person show impossible. All need to see this as indispensable, and all need to hear the call.

As daunting as this is, it is also an opportunity to reinvigorate parish life and the life of faith, returning the focus to the whole people of God. Writing "Galilee Revisited" brought me face to face with the need for active ministry to all who are separated by illness from the body of the church; this return visit shows that this is true for all people of our parishes. The church and its people need this now more than ever.

—Glenn CJ Byer

Galilee Revisited: The Healing Ministry of the Church in the New Millennium

Glenn CJ Byer

> He went around the whole of Galilee teaching in their synagogues, proclaiming the Good News of the kingdom, and curing all kinds of diseases and sickness among the people. His fame spread throughout Syria, those who were suffering from diseases and painful complaints of one kind or another, the possessed, epileptics, the paralyzed, were all brought to him, and he cured them (Matt 4:23–24).

The title of this article refers to that time when Jesus returns to Galilee and begins his ministry, a ministry of healing, the word and repentance. His mission begins here, in the healing ministry, that showed those who lived in darkness a great light.

The light was, by analogy, heard in the words of Jesus, but the light was (of course) more clearly and properly to be seen in his works of healing. The repentance of the people was effected by words, but even more by the healing that he worked. I love the passage of Acts that talks about Paul's healing of the man who died when he fell from the window: they took the boy away alive, and were greatly encouraged (Acts 20:12). Such a marvelous understatement. An essential, and perhaps the most powerful, component of the Christian message of repentance is the healing of the sick.

To those who study Christian history, this states the obvious. The charisms of hospitality, of caring for those who are in a strange country; of healing, as found in the hospital orders of St. John and others during the crusades and since, and found in the many nursing orders of the church; of charity, especially as seen in the ministry to the sick and dying, as seen in the rites of the church—these charisms have been the heart of who we are as the body of Christ, as natural and miraculous for us as breathing is to the human body. While a hallmark of our times has been to see sickness, dying and death as more or less exclusively medical matters, the spiritual has not been totally lost. One example is in Missoula, Montana's St. Patrick Hospital where Therese Shroeder-Sheker has a ministry known as the Chalice of Repose (www.saintpatrick.org/chalice/). It is a ministry of music thanatology in which the person who lays dying is sung into eternity. The basis for this ministry is found among the medieval monastic practices, but it has been shown to be equally relevant today. The sick, the aged, the dying and all of us are, in fact, in a strange country; we are on a crusade; and we are in fact all seeking our way home, to be sung on our way by the angels who inhabit our lives.

What Christ taught, what we are supposed to believe and the relevance of Christian ministry to the sick are found among all these examples. The ministry to the sick and the medical miracles of our time are the signs of in-breaking of the *eschaton*—to live so long and to survive such killing and, in theological terms, evil things as the plague show the fulfillment of the age which is to be found in the fullness of life that Jesus shared with us. It is the life that each of us is given as a gift from the Father. Still, this same life passes from our sight as we age, grow sick and die. While the end times are seen in the wonders that make our lives so much better than in times past, life itself is still not an end in itself. Old age is not something to be hated; rather it is to be seen as the completion, the fulfillment of that gift given at our conception. In the ministry of Jesus, we see with blinding clarity that death is not separate from life. The way in which we face our own mortality as well as the way we minister to those who are sick and dying will affect those around us. We either proclaim or deny our heavenly citizenship.

That is why every Christian and the church have a place at the side of the sick, why we minister to the sick and why it takes faith to be healed, to grow old and to die well.

Another return to Galilee is often problematic for people of faith—the return to Nazareth in Galilee—the return to his hometown where Scripture says, "He could work no miracle there, though he cured a few sick people by laying hands on them. He was amazed by their lack of faith" (Mark 6:5–6). Outside the context of faith, Jesus does not seem to want or be able to cure. This is troubling. How could the all-powerful God not be able or want to cure? If this was true when he was walking on earth, how much truer is it now that his presence is only recognized by faith? It probably comes as no surprise to the medical community, and it should come as no surprise to the faith community, that unless we believe we are going to be cured, unless we believe that something or someone is going to cure us, there is really very little that either community can do for a person.

There is no magic formula—no hocus-pocus, no potion—in any sense of those words by which a person can be healed or comforted. Pastoral care, like any other kind of care, must be tailored to and by the individual person, and that is why there is a desperate need for an increase in ministers who can care for the sick among us. This is as much a theological as a pastoral reality. The theology of sickness and the movement toward the end of life claim that this is the time of fulfillment, the time when Christ is most clearly revealed and visible. The clarity comes from the images of the cross, where the suffering of those who are weak or dying is seen as the image of the crucified one. The invisibility is seen in the garden, where Jesus seems so alone. It is a time when faith has much more to say and much more to answer for, to call into the darkness to the one who has the power to save us from our suffering, and to submit that we are heard. It is in times when the possibilities of this world and this life begin to shrink to the confines of neighborhood, house and sickroom that faith is tested, and thus needs support. As ministers, this attitude can open our eyes to blindness we did not even know we had—the plank in our own eyes, our pat answers which do not address the reality before us. As our eyes are opened we see the needs of the person, the revelation of the cross in the people to whom we minister, and we see the need to walk along that road to Emmaus with our hearts burning—to stand before the mystery and accept and minister to it as such.

If we really believe all this, who must we be, who must be involved, who is the real *alter Christus*, who is healed, who is sick, who is sinner? The "where" and "what" of healing ministry will flow naturally from this, but before we get there let us consider the "who" of ministry to the sick.

The who is the *alter Christus*, the real presence and struggle of Christ in the world, and it seems that a series of circles can be drawn around the who of this ministry, the who of this time of grace. The first circle, however, is a very small one indeed; it is around the person herself or himself. It is in sickness, recovery, more sickness, and finally death that the reality of the cross is seen. The cross is not a great topic for a plaster statue; it is blood, saliva, urine, sweat, pain, pain and more pain. Nevertheless, sickness, recovery, death and dying are forms of real presence. It is not very nice, nor can it be controlled or put in a tabernacle, but this view of suffering shows that the cross, the real presence, is glimpsed only briefly once the journey is over and the bread is being broken. Still it is the real true body, blood, soul and divinity, presence of Christ. The struggle of sickness and of dying is the struggle of Christ to lay down his life and love us to death. As Christians, we see the death of Jesus reflecting the life he led. The life of Jesus, which was one great act of passion for the world, a life of miraculous love and power, of strength to face any obstacle, of the ability to be a true sign of the presence of God in our world, all this life was poured out on us at that moment on the cross and he poured out this life willingly in such a way that the centurion could only say, "Surely this was the Son of God" (Mark 16:39). Thus life and death are not separate; the life of Christ and his passion and death were in fact one great moment of salvation, and the message which Christ sends us from the cross and through all ages, before and since, is that this time, whatever it holds, and this place, wherever it may be, are to be seized and shaken and lived out in their fullness regardless of the consequences. Although Christ knew that his passion for the world would require his death, the passion itself was worth the final price. The road to Jerusalem and the cross seemed, to the unwise, to be a way of tears and destruction, but Jesus believed with every fiber of his being that the unwise were wrong. If that is true of Christ, it is to be true of the followers of Christ. We too must live lives worthy of a Christian death. As Mark Searle wrote as his death approached, "I have lived the paschal mystery long enough not to forsake it or to doubt it just when it becomes most real."[1] As ministers, this reminds us that we will reap in our ministry to the sick what we have sown in our ministry to the healthy. If our people have lived the paschal mystery, they will be ready when their time comes. It means preaching on the meaning of life and the fulfillment of that life in death. If this sounds traditional, it is, but it is not outdated. We see it all around us as people search for meaning in their lives. We must live passionately so that when we or one to whom we minister pass to eternity, when those who surround the event look upon it, there must be no doubt that those who suffer and those who minister are sons and daughters of God. If this is how we are called to live our lives and face our deaths, so too are we to bring this message from Christ to those to whom we minister, the sick and the well, the old and the young alike.

Those who minister medically or spiritually and those who are part of the immediate family and circle of friends form a very important

---

[1] Gerard Lukken, Mark Searle, "Semiotics and Church Architecture. Applying the Semiotics of A.J., Greimas and the Pafis School to the Analysis of Church Buildings," *Liturgy Condenda*, vol. 1 (Kampen, The Netherlands: Kok Pharos, 1993), 2.

group of people. It is the struggle of us all to get well, to accept long-term illness, to accept the mortality we have spent a lifetime denying; this is the wild rage of battle that the sick live out in communion with Christ, it is the battle in which we all participate as health care professionals and ministers of the Gospel. The ministers and health care professionals are, therefore, not separate from the suffering. Moreover, neither is the church.

The struggle extends beyond the one who suffers and the "professionals" to the family, and especially the loneliness of those who are suddenly half of a couple or part of an incomplete family—here the cross is often lived out in deeper shadow than for the one who may already be in a coma. All those involved are in need of healing. Where is the church to be found? At the foot of the cross in Mary and John, at the foot of the bed, at the doorstep of those who are left alone. Where else would we be? This is a third return to Galilee—the return where the mother and brothers of Jesus come to his aid because they think he is sick. The reply of Jesus reminds us that all for whom we care are mothers and brothers. "Even as you did this to one of the least...you did it to me" (Matthew 25:40). Theologically this is because those who suffer and those who care are the ones who have taken up the cross.

So, what can the larger circle of the church offer? It can offer what is often needed most: space. The space that the church offers is the bare cross, the place where you and I are invited to participate in the sufferings of the Lord. In one sense, we do not have much to offer; but it is, in another sense, everything that is needed. Our presence takes the lonely struggle and makes of it a common experience. St. Augustine wrote about this space in terms of a battle for someone becoming a Christian person in the arena with crowds on both sides cheering on either the devil or the future Christian. We cheer the person on; we make the person and their family aware that we and the whole of the company of heaven are cheering for them. There was a wonderful hospice program in Baltimore, and the holy sisters who ran it would start giving instructions to the dying about what they needed to ask for when they got to heaven. "Tell St. Joseph we need a new freezer." While this might seem a bit wild to us, to the one who was dying it gave a purpose to the event, and made of death a positive action. The living church is the arena for this struggle, for this positive act. We belong there, catching the drops of blood, saliva, urine and sweat into the chalice of pain and seeing there the life of the church as

111

the body of Christ being poured out for the peace and salvation of all the world. We need to see here the hope of resurrection dawning, the hope fulfilled in the final return to Galilee, in which Jesus appears to his disciples and makes everything okay. He heals their brokenness and makes them his witnesses. We need to see here the hope of the *Exsultet* of Easter—here the hope of baptism, here the dawning of the end times.

But just where is "here"? It is the highways and the byways—the roadside where a man went up from Jerusalem to Jericho and fell in among thieves. The place of ministers is anywhere there are people in need. It is in the apartment complex where the old are left to die, it is in the streets where people lie dying from drive-by shootings, and it is also still in the wards of hospitals, where people seek out the meaning of their suffering, in some cases alone. This trend is a return to older ways—a return to a time and a place where it was the job of family, friends and parish to care for the old, the sick and the dying. It was and it is our job as family, friends and church to participate in the healing ministry of all our people, wherever they may be.

What does the church expect of our ministry to the sick? I would not be surprised if many of us do not know what the church expects of a parish community when someone falls ill. The first thing that is expected is that a parish must have some means of finding out who is sick, and not just by waiting for the phone to ring at the rectory. We all, as members of the community, have a responsibility to keep watch and pray for those who are older, and to notice when anyone is not present with the community or when someone is not looking too good. This is the job of the entire parish family.

When someone falls ill there is a whole series of things that needs doing, but the most important is our presence. Before we bring Communion to the sick, before we break out the oils, the rites say that it is our job simply to visit and to be present to those who need to be able to share their illness. This task comes from our place at the foot of the cross. The person who is sick, or becoming enfeebled, or dying, needs to know that their life and its trials are part of the mystery of the cross. They and we need to know that this is a holy place, where we ought to stand barefoot in awe of the wonders that God is working even in our sight. That is why we minister to the sick and should go to pray with them. They and we need to know and name what is happening as an act of God. Even if the person wants to be alone, the person still needs to know that we are there and are seeing this as a moment of revelation, and that we are ready when the time comes to talk. This is especially true of those who are not seriously ill, but just more alone than they should be.

In times of sickness or approaching death, or at any time in the lives of those who are older, the opportunity should be there to celebrate the Rite of Penance, to become more in tune with what in life is out of step with the will of God. This is not because the aged or the sick are greater sinners, but because sickness and the dangers of old age can make us more aware of ourselves, of who we are and who we are not.

Communion to the sick should be made in a special visit—and not in a perfunctory way. It is in fact preferable to celebrate this Communion in the context of the celebration of the Eucharist. In a hospital or other institution, the celebration of Communion should link the parish community and all the sick in the same place. The individual manner of Communion, like a private Mass, is always an aberration and should only be celebrated in special circumstances.

The celebration of anointing of the sick acts as a summary of these other three ministries to the sick and apart from them really makes little sense. Unless we have visited the sick, and seen in their sickness the sufferings of Christ, we have not really prayed with them. Unless we have helped them to return to the Lord more fully through the Rite of Penance, unless we have been faithful in bringing Communion to the sick, we have not helped them become aware of the real communion that they have with Christ and with all of us, or of the deep bond with the Holy Spirit that this communion signifies. Unless all these things are in place, anointing comes like a shot in the dark and can really seem like a magical event. I know of no sacrament for which there is so little preparation for celebration, and, to my mind, this is something of an embarrassment. Granted, when critical sickness takes us completely by surprise there is simply not enough time to celebrate all these other elements as preparation for the anointing of the sick; however, the time allows us the opportunity to do more than we are doing.

Of course, the needs of the individual who is sick must be taken into account. If the person is a daily communicant, is it enough to bring Communion once a week? If family and friends have abandoned a person, does a weekly visit of ten minutes or less constitute sufficient ministry?

I am not suggesting that the presbyters, chaplains and pastoral ministers need to start working an additional thirteen hours to the sixteen they already work each day. At the same time, it is only right to recognize what the church puts before us as the ideal of care, and then to seek out ways to come as close as we can to this ideal.

As death approaches, the church is called upon to recognize this fact. This is one of the great gifts the church has to offer. In a world that prefers to deny death, the church and its ministers are called to speak the truth. In beginning the celebrations that are preparatory for death, the church again creates the space where the words that need to be spoken can be said. It frees a person to speak of last wishes, to speak of true loves, and to give a new and final testament to the life that has been led. It is at the moment when we are able to accept death that we can speak words such as this, words of faith, hope and love. How sad when this cannot be communicated. I am not suggesting that the church needs to encourage hysterical scenes in our hospitals, but through the ministry of the church deep truths can be made clear. When we prepare to help someone pass to eternity, to the arms of Abraham, to the holy city, we know that they will be missed, remembered for their good points, and have their faults lovingly forgotten. Nevertheless, it is the rites of the church, we believe, that create the place where such realities can be seen and spoken to each in a unique way.

It comes as a surprise to many people that Roman Catholics do not have eulogies in the traditional sense of the word. To praise people after their death seems to us to be misplaced. If we truly loved them, they felt it all along, for Catholics are supposed to be people who love to celebrate the love we feel for one another. This is to be especially true in the ministry we have to the dying, in the celebration of last Communion, which is, in fact, very similar to our first Communion. The celebration of *viaticum* is part of the final initiation of the person into the heavenly kingdom. It is a new baptism, a new dying and rising, but at its deepest level it is the same baptism received so long ago. This food for the journey is not something that can be slipped into a dying person's mouth like the coin to cross the river Styx, despite the obvious parallels. The celebration of *viaticum* is an act of love in which the dying person ministers as much as he or she receives ministry.

Then, as the moment of death approaches, as the person prepares to lay down the life, to give that life over to God who gave it in the first place, there is a commendation for the dying, a *bon voyage* in the fullest sense of the phrase. In the medieval rites of the church, the deacon would sit at the feet of the dying person and read the passion, including the resurrection. As Christians, this is what we believe we are seeing as someone gives up their life for us. It is that important and in a real way salvific. The death of a member of the body of Christ is a passion, making of the person a co-redeemer, "making up," as St. Paul says, "all that is lacking from the sufferings of Christ" (Colossians 1:24).[2]

All of this time and presence that the church calls its ministers to offer a sick person should make it immediately obvious that everyone in the parish must be part of the healing ministry of the church. The needs of family and friends and those who work in the medical field which multiply that amount of time only serve to confirm this call to every member of the parish. The healing ministry of the church in the twenty-first century must be this kind of collaborative and multifaceted effort. Anything less would deprive those who suffer of what they need, and will deprive all of us of opportunities to meet the Lord.

---

[2] This is the literal reading given in footnote "m" of the *Jerusalem Bible*.

2

The Rite Parallels
the Journey of Life

In all of liturgy, we must be about what is authentic, what is real. The *Order of Christian Funerals* (OCF) reflects the church's long-held understanding that loss, sorrow and grief are real. Only in the acknowledgement of sorrow and loss can the mourner begin the process of healing. This acknowledgement is the first step toward the integration of another's death into the fabric of each life touched by that death.

The following article is the story of one parish's celebration of the *Order of Christian Funerals*. This parish model was developed by close attention to the authentic spirit of the OCF, reflection upon the resources that were available and the careful catechesis that must be part of parish life.

That same attention, reflection and catechesis will allow any parish to celebrate the funeral rites similarly. What is clear is that participation in each "station" (i.e., the wake and vigil, the funeral Mass and the committal) of the rite parallels the journey of life, death and resurrection that our faith calls forth from each of us.

Too often, pastoral staffs practice ministry separately, each one going about the "business" of the Gospel individually. The response to the OCF that is described can only be accomplished if pastoral ministers are willing to truly collaborate, to work together for the common good. This working together is challenging, but it is worth the struggle. For in the end we have also accomplished the full, conscious and active participation to which we are all called by the liturgical documents.

Since this article was first published, the author has moved to another state and had the opportunity for a year's sabbatical and study in yet another area of the country. That study, particularly, has led to some reflection on the issues of cultural diversity. Many fine resources are available to address the American experience of ethnic diversity, but one can observe other more subtle diversities, such as the cultures that are the result of the different geographies of North America, the various economic realities of our cities, the predominant age groups that are served by particular parishes and the changing populations of city parishes. Whatever the diversity might entail, it is important for the parish staff to help one another observe and comment upon that diversity so that the funeral rites reflect the true nature of the parish and address the needs of the divergent groups.

Continuous reflection and discussion of the rites of the church keep those rites living and vibrant so that they are always helping all of us to "sing a new song to the Lord."

—Mary Jo Quinn, SCL

Celebrating the Order
of Christian Funerals

Mary Jo Quinn, SCL

The celebration of the parish funeral is the culmination of one person's journey of faith and the beginning of a new journey for the survivors. It is at this most profound time of loss and grief that the parish must take very seriously its obligations as a center of faith and life. Having been a full-time member of the same parish staff for sixteen years, I have come to believe that if a parish can only attend to sickness, death and grief well, it has done its "job."

To do this job well, a parish must invest itself with time and resources and be convinced of its responsibility to provide, at some level, the personnel needed for this important task. Personnel should include ministers of pastoral care (a group of parishioners who are trained to visit the sick, sharing the Eucharist when called upon to do so); a group of parishioners who work at ministering during the funeral rites; music ministers who can oversee musical leadership at necessary liturgical moments; a core of parishioners who will provide follow-up attention in bereavement; and a priest who understands the rites of the church and is committed to presiding appropriately.

In larger parishes, it is perhaps simpler to accomplish these tasks because of the presence of professionally trained staff members. In smaller parishes, the needs remain and it is up to the parish leadership to develop resources and training to meet these needs.

It has been my privilege through these past sixteen years to enter many different parts of the journey from sickness to death with a number of people. Typically, I have entered the process soon after the death, as the family begins the immediate process of preparing the funeral rites: the vigil service, the funeral liturgy and the rite of commendation. This preparation will be the concern of the ensuing pages of this article.

In preparation for the publication of the *Order of Christian Funerals* (OCF), extensive catechesis and enrichment began at all levels—for the clergy and pastoral ministers, for pastoral musicians and for parishioners on November 2, 1989 (All Souls Day). The OCF presented all of us with some new challenges. The principal challenges were, and remain, the sincere participation of the parish in all aspects of the funeral experience and the catechesis that can facilitate that participation.

How is this catechesis accomplished? We began with a series of diocesan workshops presented by a team drawn together by the office of worship: Carol McEvoy, a therapist with hospice experience; S. Mary Agnes Hogan, the pastoral care minister in our parish; Fr. Ed Hislop, pastor of Saint Mary's, director of the office of worship, a professional liturgist; and myself, director of music at Saint Mary's and musical consultant for the office of worship. These presentations were day-long experiences for clergy, pastoral ministers, musicians and funeral industry personnel, based on the premise that the OCF embodies our best understanding of human death and survivor grief. The workshops anticipated the promulgation of the revised OCF and drew on our own parish experience.

At the local level, we had a citywide meeting with funeral home personnel to explore the differing practices of various parishes and cemeteries and to deal with the aspects of the OCF that applied particularly to the funeral home. It was then that our parish began a move to have the vigil service in the church rather than in the funeral home. Now, when there is a need to have the vigil in the funeral home—because of parish conflicts or family wishes—we always receive a phone call or two asking if the newspaper notice is in error. "Are we allowed to have the vigil service in the funeral home?" has often been the question.

At the time of the promulgation of the OCF, the Federation of Diocesan Liturgical Commissions (FDLC) commissioned a set of bulletin inserts* to be used at the parish level. These inserts remain one of the best resources we have found on the experience of death and its celebration in the parish. We still prepare sets of them each November, and make them available to any parishioners who want them. In addition, we have prepared our own document on cremation, explaining how the church's understanding has grown through the years and when cremation ought to occur following death (i.e., after the funeral rites).

Each November the church provides us with a wonderful "mini-season" in which to refresh our catechesis. Beginning with the Solemnity of All Saints and the following day's Commemoration of all the Faithful Departed (All Souls) and continuing through the month of Gospel reflection on "the last days," we have excellent opportunities to preach about the funeral rites, to use the music of the rites, to recruit, and to provide training for parishioners who visit the sick and help

---

*Editors note: The FDLC bulletin notes "Life Is Changed Not Ended" (#44800PQ) and *La Vida Se Transforma* (#44870PQ) are available from Oregon Catholic Press.

with various aspects of the funeral ministry. Every time a mourning family comes to the parish to celebrate the rites with a deceased loved one, a new catechetical moment begins.

The funeral liturgy itself both calls forth participation and moves one to participation (as does all liturgy well celebrated). The order of the rites must be honored by calling forth the ministry of many, as readers, eucharistic ministers, greeters, ushers, musicians. Before and after the services food is provided by the parish, often in the form of a luncheon in the parish social hall following the journey to the cemetery and internment. Many of our funeral ministers have come from those who have experienced the parish celebration themselves through the death of a relative or friend.

In addition to the challenges of participation, there remain the musical challenges, ministerial and ritual. As in the church's entire liturgy, parishes must develop pastoral musicians who understand their role as *leaders*, not *doers*, of the assembly's song. While we have come to understand this role fairly universally at the Sunday liturgy, in many places the music minister's role at the funeral is still in need of development. Music ministers who are truly pastoral ministers need the support of clergy and parish to grow in that role. Musicians who have not yet moved toward the "pastoral" part of music ministry need continuing formation.

Music challenges abound. What about the "favorite" song? What about the "traditional" song? What about the "Irish" song? Why do we have to have music at all? Most of us will agree that the time for rationality is usually far from the time after death, but it is helpful for staff professionals to have come to an agreement as to how to answer these questions. It is imperative that someone on the staff be able to address these questions fully, lovingly and liturgically.

In our parish, we have developed a fairly straightforward procedure for our ministry to mourning families. Except when someone from the parish has been present at the time of death, the first formal contact with the parish is usually at a meeting arranged by the pastoral care minister and/or the priest. If possible, the priest and the music minister are present at this meeting. After prayer together, sometimes using one of the more informal rituals provided in the OCF, the family is invited to talk about the death experience, if possible, and to begin the sharing of memories that will continue long after the formal rites. The family is also given a packet of materials containing the FDLC inserts, the booklet *Through Death to Life: Preparing to Celebrate the*

Funeral Mass (Ave Maria Press), and the booklet *Prayers for Those Who Mourn* (LTP). The family is led verbally through each rite so that they will be familiar with the liturgy. The readings for the liturgy are discussed and sometimes decided upon during this meeting. Otherwise, the family is asked to choose the readings together at a later time and notify the parish of their choices. Parish record-keeping papers are completed and the family is asked for suggestions of those within the parish who could serve as liturgical ministers. If the family is unable to suggest any names, ministers are drawn from the list of parishioners who have agreed to serve as funeral ministers. These people are contacted by the parish and given readings and other information. Musical choices are solicited and the music minister suggests where these might be used within the rites, either during the vigil service or at the funeral Mass. We always prepare a special leaflet for each service containing all the music needed. The name of the person and the date of the funeral services are also on this leaflet.

Several years ago, we adopted a model for the vigil service (suggested by James Hansen) that provides a way of remembering the deceased in song and story and has become an important piece of our parish tradition. Jim suggested that a short musical refrain, from Scripture, form a sort of "connector" for all those who share stories. Favorite (and sometimes Irish) songs can be part of that memory time. The refrain he suggested is "Maybe Now and Then" (Huijbers/Oosterhuis) but we have used various favorite psalm refrains also.

The presider's homily sets the stage for the remembering time. Our pastor usually introduces the telling of the story as the time we understand the deceased person in the context of the Gospel—what has his or her life told us about God's life? At the conclusion of the homily, the music minister plays, then sings, the chosen musical piece a few times, inviting the participation of the assembly. Then, if necessary, as the music continues softly, the presider invites, by name, the first person who will share a memory to a microphone that is not at the ambo. At the conclusion of that person's reflection, the refrain begins again, inviting the participation of the assembly. The next person then comes to the microphone. If a favorite (Irish) song is to be sung, someone must introduce it as a favorite of the deceased and the same scriptural refrain is sung both before and after. At the conclusion of the sharing time, the presider moves to the ambo and quotes again from the Gospel that has been proclaimed, and the music concludes.

The repetition of a musical refrain accomplishes several things. Most importantly, it situates each story and memory in the context of prayer and ties it to the Scripture. It also "covers" the empty space, the time when a person is approaching the microphone or deciding if indeed he or she will even speak. The song also gives the entire assembly, along with the speakers, "recovery time," and a space to leave one story and move to the next. Overall, we have found this form usable, and very helpful.

The "traditional" song, especially for Catholics, is often either the Gounod or Schubert setting of the *"Ave Maria"* or Franck's *"Panis Angelicus."* I am always concerned that the music minister is able to sing the requested piece well (most of us have heard poor renditions of these pieces) and that the piece can be appropriately used within the liturgy. I have often suggested that the piece be used as a prelude. As the OCF has become more intimately connected to our Sunday liturgy, such requests have become rarer.

In parishes that are clearly committed to music at the liturgy, the last question—Why music at all?—is easily answered. However, we cannot expect people to celebrate the funeral liturgy with song if song is not a consistent expectation on Sunday.

Usually the music minister(s) is one of the parish music ministry. While the option of a family member serving as music minister is offered, that person is always supported by the parish musicians and the family is invited to consider the difficulty that a family member may have in truly entering the role of minister. Sometimes it is best for the family musician to sing the "favorite song" at the vigil or to take part in the funeral Mass along with others, especially if the person is very closely related to the deceased and/or is not a professional singer.

On the day of the funeral Mass, the family is invited first to gather at the baptismal font, to wash the casket with handfuls of water, to clothe the body with the white garment of the pall and to place the cross on the casket. Although it is presumed that these rites occur at the arrival of the body in the church before the vigil service, local custom has suggested that they take place as part of the funeral Mass. The family then processes into the nave of the church with the casket and presider in song. The song used here is from the parish repertoire, one of gathering and proclamation of God's goodness.

All of the music used within the funeral Mass is drawn from the parish repertoire and in collaboration with the wishes of the family. The psalm used during the proclamation of the Scripture is most often Psalm 23, a familiar setting of the shepherd psalm. The family is invited to participate in the preparation of the table by carrying the gifts of bread and wine. This is an excellent place for younger children to participate. The Mass setting is a familiar one and the Communion processional is also sung. The Communion processional is never the time for one of the "favorite" songs.

As the liturgy concludes, the casket is incensed and a setting of *"In Paradisum"* ("May the angels lead you into paradise") is sung. While the rite does provide the option of incensing the casket during the preparation of the gifts, it seems more appropriate to do so at the end, as a farewell. A musical setting that has worked very well for us is "Songs of the Angels" (Bob Dufford). This song has become a presumed part of each funeral liturgy and most parishioners know it by heart. During the singing and the rising of the incense, one can almost feel mourners begin to "let go" of their loved one and truly enter the next stage of their journey of grief and healing.

The procession to the cemetery usually occurs immediately. At the Catholic cemetery, the proper equipment has been acquired so that the casket can be lowered into the grave at the prayer of committal. This has been another part of catechesis, both with mourners and with funeral directors and cemetery personnel, a catechesis that has emphasized the importance of doing what we have come to the cemetery to do. During the lowering of the casket, we often sing again "Songs of the Angels" or a series of alleluias, even in the cold and snow.

Regarding cremation, when I began working at Saint Mary's, perhaps fifty percent of our funerals included cremation that had already occurred before the celebration of the funeral rites. Since we have committed ourselves to the work of catechesis, the number of families who choose cremation before the rites is very small. The funeral directors understand well that it is not their job to engage in this conversation to the exclusion of the parish. When families do choose cremation, whether before or after the rites, their choice is respected, the cremated remains are present during the rites as is permitted by local custom, and burial occurs immediately after the liturgy. The appendix on cremation from the *Order of Christian Funerals* reminds us "the practice of scattering cremated remains on the sea, from the air, or on the ground or keeping cremated remains in the home of a relative or friend of the deceased is not the reverent disposition that the church requires."

As a pastoral minister/musician, I have come to believe that the *Order of Christian Funerals* is one of the most important fruits of the liturgical reform. It is incumbent upon us as church professionals to fully mine its riches.

3

Options for Celebrating
a Catholic Wedding

Rituals change slowly. Like a beach rock whose shape is only gradually reformed as waves wash over its surface over the course of months and years, rituals are gradually reshaped over extended periods of time.

It's helpful some things don't seem to have changed: as this book goes to print in 2003, there is still no U.S. edition of the revised marriage rite promulgated by the Vatican in 1990 and anticipated in this article. Other things show signs of gradual change: more couples are taking advantage of the encouragement given in the church's 1969 *Rite of Marriage* to include the bride, the groom and their parents in the wedding entrance procession rather than limiting family participation in this procession to the bride and her father.

While weddings in American parishes have not changed dramatically since this article first appeared, there have been developments that, over time, are reshaping the landscape of Catholic wedding celebrations. More parishes seem to be taking a positive approach to working with engaged couples, presenting them with a variety of good options for celebrating a Catholic wedding, rather than merely handing out written guidelines that dwell on prohibited practices, or asking couples what they want to do at their wedding and then rejecting all of their ideas.

The first part of the article offers five general principles to provide engaged couples with positive assistance in the preparation of the wedding liturgy. Parish-based wedding liturgy and music preparation sessions are increasingly common ways to implement these principles. In these sessions, clergy, liturgists, music ministers, wedding coordinators and/or family life ministers from the parish present musical suggestions and liturgical options from the *Rite of Marriage* to a group of engaged couples who will celebrate their marriages over the next several months. Common to these suggestions and options is their ability to invite the participation of the entire assembly rather than rendering them mere spectators. In some places, such as the Washington, D.C., parish mentioned in the article, this type of session is built into the parish's marriage preparation program. In other places, it is part of a day's worth of events that begins with introducing the engaged couples at a Sunday Mass, continues with a brunch for the engaged couples served by the community's family life ministers, and concludes with the session on liturgy and music.

The second part of the article reviews many of the options available in the celebration of the Catholic wedding liturgy. It is not at all unusual for engaged couples, as well as some pastoral ministers, to resist some of these specific suggestions if they have never seen them incorporated in a wedding. Seeing is believing, and couples who might have dismissed the notion of greeting their arriving guests at the church door or priests who might not have been able to envision standing at the front of the aisle to receive the couple's vows are often more open to such practices once they've seen them. Toward that end, the videotape *Our Catholic Wedding* (Liturgy Training Publications; available from Oregon Catholic Press) is a very helpful resource, illustrating how such practices can be both beautiful and more fully reflective of the church's faith concerning marriage. As such, it is a good complement to both this article and the workbook to which the article refers, *Celebrating Marriage* (Pastoral Press, 6095PQ).

—Paul Covino

Here Come the Bride and the Groom
Another Look at Weddings and the Rite of Marriage

Paul Covino

During the mid-1980s, I served as liturgy director for a large parish in Washington, D.C. Each year, between one hundred twenty and one hundred fifty couples celebrated their marriage in this church. Prior to the wedding, each couple participated in a parish-based marriage preparation program led by married couples, separated and divorced parishioners, and staff members. Meeting in groups over the course of six weeks, the couples prayed together, reflected on their faith and discussed issues such as communication, sexuality and the sacramental nature of Christian marriage.

Evaluating this program after its first year, all agreed that it was a success. Couples gave the program high marks and other parishes in the area began to ask how they might undertake a similar program. Only one consistently negative comment surfaced: the program offered no assistance to the couples in the preparation of the wedding liturgy. As one engaged woman wrote, "I came to this program expecting six weeks on how to plan my wedding. Instead, we dealt with major issues that my fiancé and I will face throughout our married life. Still, I would have liked some help with the wedding ceremony." The next year, the program grew to seven weeks with the addition of a session which covered the preparation of the wedding liturgy.

This episode was an eye-opener for our staff. In retrospect, we had failed to realize how intimidated most couples felt when confronted with decisions regarding the wedding liturgy. They didn't know where to begin. We had, of course, given each couple a book with all the prayers and readings for the wedding, but that did not address the host of other issues such as music, ministries and ritual options. For people who had never been involved in preparing any type of liturgy and who now faced the preparation of a wedding with all its unique features, that little book was simply not enough. They were looking to the parish for some guidance with the wedding, and we were not supplying it.

This experience prompted me to write the book *Celebrating Marriage* (Pastoral Press 6095PQ) with three good friends and colleagues: Larry Madden, Elaine Rendler and John Buscemi. That, in turn, led to workshops on weddings for dioceses and various organizations around the country. One of the things that I discovered was that, in general, parishes and dioceses were quite clear in telling couples what they could not or should not do in the wedding liturgy. There have certainly been some outrageous things done at weddings over the years, and guidelines have often been written to avoid such things in the future. At the same time, we haven't been as forthcoming with positive guidance to couples on what options *are* available to make the wedding a life-giving liturgical experience for all involved.

Working with couples: A positive approach

How, then, might we offer assistance to couples in the preparation of the wedding liturgy, and do so in as positive way as possible? The answer will vary from parish to parish of course, but a few general things seem to be true across the board:

Begin liturgical preparations with couples long before the wedding. Couples are usually more open to ideas and suggestions when the wedding date is still several months away. As the date gets closer, the couple is naturally anxious for closure on the myriad details of the wedding. The time to make suggestions to couples regarding the wedding liturgy, therefore, is well in advance of the wedding date. This is usually quite possible since couples frequently set the date for their wedding a year in advance. Invite couples to begin their preparations for the wedding liturgy as soon as they have finalized the date of the wedding with the parish. The priest or deacon, pastoral musician, liturgy director, pastoral associate or a marriage preparation minister could hold an initial meeting with each individual couple or with groups of couples to review the *Rite of Marriage* and to present musical and liturgical suggestions. One or two follow-up meetings could then be scheduled to finalize the details. The added time will let the couple think over the suggestions without the pressure of making a decision right away.

Present options that invite the active participation of the entire assembly. As pastoral musicians and clergy well know, many couples have certain assumptions of what must be included in the wedding liturgy. These assumptions are often reinforced by the weddings they've attended or seen on television. Other couples, as we noted previously, don't know where to begin. Pastorally, it is much more helpful to give couples a host of good options rather than to ask what they want and then systematically turn down each request.

Share with the couples the vision of marriage that is presented in the *Rite of Marriage* and suggest options that will invite the participation of those who will gather to celebrate their marriage. Warn couples to avoid practices that render the assembly mere spectators.

Pay attention to the non-verbal, as well as verbal, elements of the wedding liturgy. Preparing the wedding liturgy is not simply a matter of choosing prayers and readings. There are many non-verbal elements which play an important part, such as the music, the environment of the church building, the manner in which people are greeted, the way that processions move, and the placement of the couple and the other worshipers. When carefully prepared, these non-verbal elements complement the verbal ones. Ignored or poorly prepared and celebrated, they can negate even the most beautiful of texts.

Distinguish between what is essential and what is not. Many of the practices that couples assume are part of the wedding liturgy actually do not appear in the *Rite of Marriage* at all. It is important to let couples know that practices such as the lighting of the unity candle and the seating of guests carefully on the "bride's side" or the "groom's side" are not necessary and to distinguish such practices from what is essential to the Catholic wedding liturgy.

Remember, good parish liturgy is the best foundation for effective wedding preparation. Obviously, many engaged couples do not participate in Sunday worship on a regular basis. Nevertheless, a couple's attitude toward liturgy is formed through their experience of liturgy in the parish. As Austin Fleming points out, "The health and vitality of parish liturgy will have significant impact upon the weddings celebrated there. Weddings will, in some ways, reflect the liturgical life of the local assembly." (*Parish Weddings*, Liturgy Training Publications, Chicago) If, for example, music lacks life and does not invite participation at Sunday Mass, couples will certainly wonder why the assembly at their wedding should be bothered with singing. If hospitality is not evident week after week, couples cannot be expected to understand its importance in the wedding. Conversely, couples who grow up in parishes where participation and hospitality are evident in the Sunday liturgy will be more likely to expect these values to be present in the wedding liturgy.

Making the most of the rite

In 1990 the Vatican promulgated a revised marriage rite entitled *Order for Celebrating Marriage*. Over the course of the next several years, the International Commission on English in the Liturgy (ICEL) will prepare an English translation of the revised tie and the U.S. bishops will have a chance to incorporate adaptations for our country. The Vatican will then be asked to approve this version of the rite for use in the United States. Until that time, our guidebook for weddings is the *Rite of Marriage* which was promulgated in 1969. Although twenty-five years old, this rite still contains some surprises and holds out a vision of weddings that is largely unfulfilled. Read in conjunction with the basic liturgical principles presented in other liturgical documents, the *Rite of Marriage* offers sound advice and numerous options for celebrating marriage.

Opening rites. What happens before the procession even comes down the aisle sets a tone for the entire wedding. Participation by the assembly, which is usually weak to non-existent at weddings, can be significantly enhanced by paying attention to basic liturgical principles of gathering an assembly for worship. There is, for example, no reason why the bride and groom cannot be at the door with their parents greeting their guests as they arrive. This simple act of hospitality lets the guests know that the couple is glad they are present. The unnecessary custom of hiding the bride from the groom before the wedding just needs to give way to the more important concern for hospitality.

Ask the members of the wedding party to distribute the worship aid for the wedding and to seat the arriving guests. Male *and* female members of the wedding party can do this. Seat people as far forward in the church as possible, and fill one row before seating people in the next row. Avoid the artificial distinction in seating between "bride's side" and "groom's side." If guests do not know one another, ask the members of the wedding party to introduce people to those they will be sitting next to. Have light, upbeat music playing as people gather. Take a few moments to rehearse any music that may be unfamiliar to the assembly. All of these things encourage a sense of community among the various people gathered for the wedding.

The entrance procession, according to the *Rite of Marriage* (20), proceeds as follows: "The ministers go first, followed by the priest, and then the bride *and* bridegroom. According to local custom, they may be escorted by at least their parents and the two witnesses." You read it correctly: bride and groom in the procession. This form of procession reflects the church's faith regarding marriage. Christian marriage does not consist in "giving a woman away," but in a covenant relationship undertaken by two equal partners. It is becoming more common to include both sets of parents in the procession as well. This acknowledges the transition for the bride and groom from their families of origin to the new family they are creating through marriage. Seen in this way, the procession is much more than the bride's grand entrance and, accordingly, "Here Comes the Bride" does not make sense as the accompaniment to this procession.

The seating of the couple during the wedding liturgy should reflect their role as minister of the sacrament of marriage. If they are in the sanctuary, by all means have them facing the rest of the assembly. It just does not make sense to have the couple turn their backs to their guests! There is also no reason to have kneelers in front of the couple's seats. The *Rite of Marriage* does not mention kneeling.

Liturgy of the Word. Couples often spend a good deal of time choosing the readings. It is disappointing, then, when the readings are poorly proclaimed in the wedding liturgy. Many people in the assembly at weddings rarely hear God's word in the Scriptures, so it's all the more important to have the readings proclaimed well. Encourage couples to identify good readers from among their guests. Someone who serves as a lector on a regular basis would be the ideal choice. Otherwise, think of who will proclaim God's word most effectively. If there are relatives or friends whom the couple wants to involve in some way during the wedding liturgy but who are not capable public speakers, consider asking them to bring up the gifts.

Marriage Rite. Everyone in the assembly wants and deserves to hear the exchange of vows. After all, the assembly is present to witness this marriage and offer support and congratulations to the couple. Have the couple face the assembly for the marriage rite. The priest or deacon can stand at the front of the assembly or slightly off to the side so that all can see and hear. Since this is the most important promise the bride and groom will ever make, encourage them to say the vows to one another directly. Repeating the vows line by line after the priest or deacon and simply saying "I do" really weakens this central action of the wedding.

Occasionally, couples request a song after the exchange of rings. This usually ends up being a solo that adds time, but little else, to the wedding. A more effective way to bring music into the marriage rite might be to invite the assembly to sing a joyful refrain (such as the "Celtic Alleluia") after the exchange of vows and again after the exchange of rings. This is more in the style of "ritual music" that serves the liturgical action that is taking place and invites participation by the entire assembly.

The General Intercessions, which conclude the marriage rite, offer a way of raising up the prayers of the couple and their families while also remembering the more universal needs of the world and the church. For example, petitions could be included for sick and deceased family members; for parents, godparents and others who helped to form the couple in their faith; and for the parishes of which the bride and groom have been part. Broader concerns to remember include the poor and needy of the town where the wedding is celebrated married, separated and divorced people and the unity of Christian churches.

Liturgy of the Eucharist. Not all weddings are celebrated within Mass, but for a nuptial Mass the liturgy of the Eucharist is much the same as for Sunday Mass. The major difference is the addition of the nuptial blessing before Communion. Encourage participation by suggesting well-known musical settings of the acclamations for the eucharistic prayer. As the prayer that binds all Christians regardless of denomination, the Lord's Prayer should be eminently accessible to all at a wedding. This implies reciting it rather than singing it. What was said above about lectors applies also to eucharistic ministers. The ideal choice is people who serve in this ministry on a regular basis. Otherwise, ask people who are gracious and reverent and who can attend the rehearsal for instructions. A good rule of thumb is one eucharistic minister (the presiding celebrant) for the sacred bread and two for the sacred wine per one hundred guests. Don't remove the individual person's option to receive the sacred wine by not offering it during a wedding.

Concluding rites. The final blessing is one of the most beautiful prayers in the wedding liturgy. There are four forms of this prayer, the last of which was composed for the United States version of the *Rite of Marriage*. In some parishes, the assembly is invited to join in this blessing by extending their arms toward the couple as the priest or deacon proclaims the prayer.

Engaged couples get plenty of ideas—and, sometimes, a good deal of pressure—from family, friends and the glossy wedding publications sold in bookstores. The church needs to offer couples its wisdom and guidance concerning marriage and the wedding liturgy early in the engagement period. The wedding liturgy is a rich and wonderful treasure. Don't miss the opportunity to unlock its full potential with the couples who will celebrate their marriage in the church where you minister!

4

A Visible Presence
of Christ at Prayer

Nearly ten years after Patrick Malloy's article "The Rich Liturgical Pallet of the Church: The Liturgy of the Hours," the church is still waiting to embrace this "forgotten stepchild" of the liturgical movement. Forty years after the council it is the Liturgy of the Hours together with the Eucharist and the sacraments that must again go together in every cathedral and parish community. The Liturgy of the Hours in any parish community is but an exercise of baptismal ministry, the church standing together with arms outstretched. The spiritual potential of the celebration of the hours is great. The element of praise alone has the ability to sweep us up into the mystery of Christ so that we can be his very presence in the world. The hours give voice to the praise of God in creation and unite us with the prayer of Christ. This praise, as Robert Taft, SJ, suggests, is a "school of prayer" for the church and as such it is a prayer that is self-transcending, doxological and prophetic. The Liturgy of the Hours is a celebration of the Trinity and its psalmody that is both praise and lament and can move the community to acts of justice. To encounter and be encountered by the God of creation, taking on our lips Mary's prayer, "may it be done to me according to your word" (Luke 1:38), moves us from the individualistic attitude in the church and society today, "I did it my way."

The Liturgy of the Hours is the communal prayer that will fill people's hunger for devotional and scriptural experiences, it is the prayer that can sustain the life of many within the faith community, and it is the way the church has traditionally marked the hours of the day and the seasons of the year with prayer. No one (catechumens, other Christians, alienated Catholics or people of good will) is excluded from participation in the Liturgy of the Hours, and the leadership for the Liturgy of the Hours is not limited to ordained ministers. Therefore bishops, priests, deacons, pastoral ministers and laity must form themselves with an appreciation for the Liturgy of the Hours so that the whole church can be a visible presence of Christ at prayer.

When celebrating the hours, the parish community enters into the rhythm of the liturgical year and experiences more fully the paschal mystery. This is why the mandate of the General Instruction of the Liturgy of the Hours is so important: pastors of souls should see to it that the faithful are invited and helped by liturgical catechesis "to celebrate the principal hours in common, especially on Sundays and holydays." (GILOH 23)

The celebration of the hours can provide a healing rhythm for people caught in the frenzied pace of twenty-first century living. The music and liturgical symbols of light and incense can carry us beyond the present into the paschal mystery of Christ. As Dr. Malloy indicates in his article, the restoration of the ancient cathedral office would help satisfy this need in the church today. When the body of Christ gathers to celebrate the hours we hear and see and smell the presence of Christ, "the light in the darkness, the sun that never sets."

—Michael R. Prendergast

The Rich Liturgical Pallet of the Church: The Liturgy of the Hours

Patrick L. Malloy

On Ash Wednesday evening, there was hardly a seat left at St. Peter's Church in Danbury, Connecticut. The size of the assembly was not surprising. After Christmas and Easter, Ash Wednesday is the most popular feast of the liturgical year. Two Masses had already been celebrated in the church that day. But the service itself was surprising. Not the usual Eucharist, this was Evening Prayer. The parish was learning a new way to pray.

In fact, Evening Prayer is an old way to pray. It stands along with Morning Prayer and services at other times of the day in a tradition called the Liturgy of the Hours. The history of the hours stretches back to the earliest days of the church. The Liturgy of the Hours is a counterpart of the Eucharist, not an alternative to it. Hours and Eucharist join together as integral parts of the liturgy of the church. Paul VI wrote that the Liturgy of the Hours is "a kind of necessary complement to the fullness of divine worship that is contained in the eucharistic sacrifice." (*Apostolic Constitution*, November 1970)

Some Catholics have discovered the Liturgy of the Hours and pray it regularly. Some pray it privately. Others gather with friends or members of the parish. Some, like the people of St. Peter's in Danbury, assemble for full, public, parish-wide celebrations of the Liturgy of the Hours. Yet such celebrations are rare. The Second Vatican Council's *Sacranctum concilium* (SC 100) expressed a hope that the hours would become popular, just as they were in the early church. Thirty years later, few Catholics even know that the hours exist.

Even among Catholics who have never heard of the Liturgy of the Hours, however, some have experienced it. They have seen their parish priest pacing in the church yard reading from a small book. He was probably reciting the texts of the Liturgy of the Hours. Perhaps they have been on retreat or have participated in small Christian communities where they celebrated Morning or Evening Prayer. These two prayers form "a double hinge of the daily office and are therefore to be considered the principal hours." (*General Instruction of the Liturgy of the Hours*, GILOH 37) Or they have visited monasteries or religious houses where the sisters or brothers pray the hours. For many communities these liturgies are at their very heart. Or they have taken part in the daily celebration of Evensong in the great cathedrals of England. This is yet another form of the hours, celebrated according to the liturgical tradition of the Anglican Communion. For most people and parishes, however, the hours are a buried pastoral treasure that awaits rediscovery by the modern church.

What follows is a short course in the Liturgy of the Hours, with a brief history and theology of this form of public prayer and concrete suggestions for implementing the Liturgy of the Hours in a parish today.

History and theology

The apostle Paul offers the church an ideal: pray always. Christians of his time tried to cultivate a spirit of constant prayer by regularly pausing to pray. Generally, they gathered as a community to pray at sunrise and sunset. They prayed alone or in small groups during the workday and at bedtime. Some even learned to wake in the middle of the night to pray to the God who never sleeps. These daily prayers were the seeds of the Liturgy of the Hours. From place to place and year to year, the details varied, but the community's dedication to daily prayer did not.

What drove the early Christians to pray with such fervor? It was their profound experience of Jesus. The rising sun reminded them of him, risen from darkness and death. It moved them to pray. The working hours, too, brought him to their minds. They remembered his trial at mid-morning, his crucifixion at noon and his death at mid-afternoon. At each of these three times, they paused to pray. When the sun was setting and the lamps were being lighted for the night, again they thought of Jesus, the sun that never sets, the light shining in darkness, and they assembled to pray. For the early Christians, everything was a reminder of Jesus.

In their experience, he was a person of the present, not the past. They knew that Jesus moved among them and that they were living and suffering, dying and rising with him every day. The reign of God had begun, and they were a part of it. In the Eucharist they used the common elements of bread and wine to remember him, and in baptism they used ordinary water. In the Liturgy of the Hours, they used another natural symbol—time—to celebrate the presence of Jesus.

By the fourth century, the daily prayer of the church had evolved in many ways because the church had evolved in many ways. For centuries, Christianity had been an illegal religion. In the early fourth century, it not only became legal but was even favored by the Roman emperor.

136

Because of his support, Christianity became popular and it grew. Some of its members desired to devote all of their time and energy to Scripture study, prayer and hospitality. To free themselves for this vocation, they chose not to have spouses or families, tried to live simply and "apprenticed" themselves to wise men or women who would train them in the Christian life. Those men and women who followed this way of life were called "monks," and the places where they lived together were called "monasteries."

The monks, of course, prayed the Liturgy of the Hours every day, but so did the Christians living in parish communities. Only their styles of celebrating the hours differed. Liturgists call the monks' form "Monastic Hours." They celebrated these liturgies in their monasteries, usually apart from the parish community. Liturgists call the form prayed in the parishes "Cathedral Hours" because at the time the cathedral, the bishop's parish, was the only parish in any city or town.

The cathedral hours included all the qualities that make a liturgy interesting for most people: predictability, symbols, music, gestures and processions, the possibility of praying about the ups and downs of life. If a parish liturgy committee were trying to craft a theologically sound, scripturally rich and pastorally inviting prayer service, they could choose no better model than the cathedral hours of the early church.

Although the cathedral hours held wide popularity in the fourth century, as the years passed and as Christianity became more common, fewer and fewer people attended daily prayer. At the same time, daily Eucharist became ever more customary. Gradually Morning and Evening Prayer, as well as non-eucharistic public prayer at other times of the day, moved into the background. It continued to be celebrated in some cathedrals, in monasteries, in other religious houses and occasionally in parishes. In most places, however, the priests were the only ones who prayed these prayers, and they usually did so privately.

Members of the early churches would not have believed what had become of their daily liturgies. Today, however, the Liturgy of the Hours in its full, public form is emerging from history. In 1970 the Second Vatican Council revised the books containing the texts of the hours, retaining many aspects of the monastic hours but recapturing more facets of the cathedral hours. The hours of the dead, taken from these books, is included as one of the wake services in the *Order of Christian Funerals*. The celebration of the hours is also suggested by the document *Sunday Celebration in the Absence of a Priest* as a suitable Lord's Day liturgy. These books are a wonderful resource for personal prayer and the starting point for preparing a public celebration.

SIMILARITIES BETWEEN MONASTIC HOURS AND CATHEDRAL HOURS

In both monasteries and cathedrals…

The hours were celebrated at specific key times or "hours" each day.
Morning and evening were the two most important hours.
All monks or parishioners were expected to join the community for the hours daily.
The core of each hour was a selection from the psalms.

DIFFERENCES

MONASTIC

- Only monks attended.

- Services were often quite lengthy.

- Monks sat quietly as one person read texts to them or said prayers in their name.

- Texts changed greatly from day to day.

- Texts were chosen because they came next in the Bible. For example, if Morning Prayer ended with Psalm 20, midmorning prayer began with Psalm 21. The images in the texts did not matter.

- Each hour moved along at a steady pace: a monk read a psalm while the rest listened prayerfully, the leader said a prayer, the reader moved on to the next psalm, and the pattern continued. A certain number of psalms was read at each hour.

- Nearly everything was recited.

- Monks conducted the services, without any representatives of the wider church.

- Quiet and introspection filled the liturgy.

- Monks quietly meditated on the texts.

CATHEDRAL

- Ordinary Christians attended.

- Services were relatively brief.

- Members of the assembly sang various pieces of music and made liturgical gestures.

- Texts were almost identical from day to day.

- Texts were chosen because they were appropriate, e.g., psalms in the morning spoke of sunrise or a new day, psalms at bedtime spoke of God watching over the sleeping world, and so forth.

- Public hours—Morning and Evening Prayer—contained great variety: movement and stillness, petition and praise, light and darkness, singing by cantors and responses by the assembly, prayers by leaders and "amens" by all.

- Nearly everything was sung.

- Many parishioners celebrated, along with their presbyters and deacons, while the bishop presided.

- Ceremony and symbol filled the liturgy.

- Assembly members expressed praise, thanks and petition.

The exact form of the hours given in the official books may need some modification for parish use. For use in parishes, families or small Christian communities, which are becoming more numerous, even further adaptation may be necessary. For example, the official version of the hours appoints three psalms for Morning Prayer and three for Evening Prayer; perhaps two, or even one, would be better at first, as people are just becoming familiar with this liturgy. The texts in the official Liturgy of the Hours also change frequently, as they did in the Monastic Offices. As a Christian community learns to celebrate the hours, and perhaps even after it has made them its own, it may be better to repeat texts each time, keeping at least a number of them the same. When the *General Instruction on the Liturgy of the Hours* says, "There are…circumstances occasionally arising when it is permissible to choose suitable psalms or other texts," (GILOH 252) it gives pastoral liturgists the freedom to make prudent choices. These, however, must be based upon the history and theology of the hours, as well as their basic structure and the style of their prayer texts.

Structure of the hours

Morning and Evening Prayer share a common structure: introductory rites, psalmody, reading, gospel canticle, petitions and concluding rites. Families or groups gathered for a meeting can use this format to pray a brief five- to ten-minute liturgy. By consistently using this structure for small group prayer as well as large public celebrations, the parish will come to share a dependable tradition of praying together.

The following outlines are guides for parish committees preparing celebrations of the Liturgy of the Hours. They include not only texts but also ritual suggestions, all of which may be simplified for use in small groups and family settings.

Signs and symbols are central to the hours. Use them generously. Liturgy is an event, not a collection of texts. It is something that the assembly does, not something it merely reads or sings, and certainly not something it thinks. In the liturgy Christians worship with all their senses and their entire bodies. Liturgies that do not take this into account leave the assembly feeling uninvolved and uninterested. When celebrated well, the Liturgy of the Hours is inviting and involving, highly symbolic and ceremonial. Even in a home, symbols can be richly used. For example, a simple evening candle lighting rite and prayer may precede dinner.

1. Outline of Morning Prayer

In the parish, Morning Prayer holds special promise for the days of the Triduum, when morning Eucharist is not celebrated but many members of the parish nonetheless desire to gather for liturgical prayer. During the Triduum, texts reflecting the images of the paschal mystery are most appropriate. The official Liturgy of the Hours is a good place to start.

A. Introductory Rites

 1. Entrance. As the ministers enter the room, the assembly stands. As the leader sings or says, "Lord, open my lips," all make the sign of the cross on their lips and respond, "And my mouth will proclaim your praise."
 Leader: "Glory to the Father, and to the Son, and to the Holy Spirit."
 All: "As it was in the beginning..."
 2. Morning hymn, containing images suitable for morning or images of the feast, sung by the assembly.

B. Psalmody

All except the cantor are seated.

 1. Psalm, followed by doxology (Psalm 63 and Psalms 146–150 are standard morning psalms).
 2. Period of silence for prayer (at least 30 seconds).
 The assembly stands as the leader says, "Let us pray."
 3. Prayer by the leader based on the psalm (see below for suggestions for composing these prayers).

If more than one psalm is sung, the same pattern is followed for each. The people bow their heads as they sing or listen to the doxology, "Glory to the Father..."

C. Reading

 1. Brief reading (usually only a few verses, echoing images of morning or of the feast).
 2. Period of silence (at least 30 seconds).

D. Gospel Canticle: The Canticle of Zechariah, commonly called the *Benedictus* (Luke 1:68–79). The assembly stands, as it always does during a proclamation of the gospel, and makes the sign of the cross. Incense may be burned to honor Christ present in the proclaimed gospel. The leader may incense the people as they sing, as a sign of their dignity.

E. Petitions

    1. Intercessions (for the grace to live the day ahead, like the General Intercessions at Mass).

    2. Lord's Prayer.

    3. Closing prayer (see suggestions below for composing such prayers; on special feasts, the prayer can be taken from the official Liturgy of the Hours or from the *Sacramentary*).

F. Concluding Rites

    1. Blessing.

    2. Sign of peace (the leader or assistant may invite the people to share this).

2. Outline of Evening Prayer

Cathedral Evening Prayer began as the community lit lamps for the night, with special hymns, prayers and ceremonies. The official Liturgy of the Hours does not contain these ceremonies, but their rich symbolism and strong emotion give them great pastoral value.

A. *Lucernarium* (Rite of lighting candles)

    1. Procession with the evening light. (The people gather in near darkness. Small candles are distributed to them as they arrive. Ministers enter in procession, carrying incense and a large burning candle. The procession stops in the midst of the people; all turn toward the light.)

    2. Greeting.

Leader: "Light of Christ."

All: "Thanks be to God."

    3. Candle lighting. (After the greeting, the people light their candles from the large candle, passing the light from person to person.)

    4. Evening hymn (celebrating Christ, light of the world).

    5. Prayer of thanks for the light.

    6. Lights. (The electric lights are turned on and the people extinguish their candles. Ministers move to their chairs as the candle and incense are put in prominent places.)

If the *Lucernarium* is omitted for simplicity, Evening Prayer begins with a greeting:

    "God, come to my assistance."

    "Glory to the Father..."

B. Psalmody

    1. Psalm, followed by the doxology. (Psalms 121 and 141 are standard evening psalms. If Psalm 141 ["Our prayers rise like incense..."] is sung, a server places incense on the burning coals during this psalm.)

    2. Period of silence for prayer (at least 30 seconds).

    3. Prayer by the leader based on the psalm. (See suggestions below; if more than one psalm is sung the same pattern is followed for each.)

C. Reading

    1. Brief reading (usually only a few verses echoing images of evening or of the feast).

    2. Period of silence (at least 30 seconds).

D. Gospel Canticle: the Canticle of Mary, commonly called the *Magnificat* (Luke 1:46–55). The assembly stands, as it always does during a proclamation of the gospel, and makes the sign of the cross. Incense may be burned to honor Christ present in the proclaimed gospel. The leader may incense the people as they sing, as a sign of their dignity.

E. Petitions

    1. Intercessions (for the needs of the church and the world).

    2. Lord's Prayer.

    3. Closing Prayer.

F. Concluding Rites

    1 Blessing.

    2. Sign of peace (optional).

PRAYERS IN THE HOURS

1. Short liturgical prayers and how to compose them

Short prayers or "collects" occur in two parts of the hours: after each psalm and at the end. The prayers after the psalms are generally called "psalm prayers." The leader voices all these prayers in the name of the assembly. An easy way to remember the four-part format of these prayers is the rhyme: you, who, do, through.

A. YOU. Begin by naming God in a way that is related to what you are going to ask in the prayer. For example, if you intend to ask God to send rain for the crops, you might begin "O Bountiful God" or "O Creator of the world."

B. WHO. Call to mind a wonder God has done in the past which shows why you believe that God will do what you ask. For example, the prayer for rain might continue, "...after you made the earth, you brought forth plants and fruit trees to provide food for all living things."

C. DO. Ask God clearly for what the community needs. The prayer might continue, "We ask you to send rain upon our dry and parched earth, so that your people today might have a share in the good things of your creation."

D. THROUGH. Close the prayer by offering it in the name of Jesus. Be sure to use the standard form, "We ask this through Christ, Our Lord." That is the cue for the people to voice their "Amen."

2. Psalm prayers and how to compose them

Psalm prayers particularize the psalms. They express what the text means to the particular community on the particular occasion. Always, the prayers aim to relate the psalm to the mystery of Jesus, present in the community.

A. Read the psalm carefully, asking yourself, "How does this psalm relate to what we are celebrating in this hour? How is the mystery of Jesus' life, death, resurrection and action in the church reflected in this psalm?"

B. Follow the four-part pattern for composing a liturgical prayer, but include the key images of the psalm. The following two prayers are based upon Psalm 23. One is intended for the wake service of a very old man. The other is for Evening Prayer before the parish potluck dinner. They illustrate not only the four-part pattern but also how the situation colors the specific meaning of the psalm:

Parish celebration

After the liturgy preparation committee thoroughly understands the history, theology and structure of the hours and the style of its parts, it is ready to plan an actual celebration. By following these basic guidelines, the committee will help the parish to embrace the hours as an uplifting and significant part of its liturgical life. Just doing the hours does not suffice. The aim of the committee must be to make the hours truly popular.

WAKE	POTLUCK
O Gentle and loving Shepherd,	O faithful Shepherd,
in the waters of baptism you claimed our brother, John, as your own. All the days of his life, you kindly watched over him.	our lives overflow with your goodness: with food and drink, with our brothers and sisters in this parish community.
Lead him now to a place of refreshment and peace, and one day reunite us with him.	Move among us tonight as we celebrate your kindness, and make us worthy stewards of all you have given us.
We ask this through Christ, our Lord.	We ask this through Christ, our Lord.

1. Pair the hours with an event already significant to the community

Every parish has days that are special in its life. Members of the community need not be coaxed to assemble on those days. In fact, they may actively seek ways to celebrate. For example, Ash Wednesday, the memorial of Saint Blaise, with its traditional blessing, and All Souls Day appeal to basic human needs and mysteries: our sinfulness, our struggle against illness, our helplessness as loved ones die. The strong seasons of the liturgical year, especially Advent and Lent, also appeal to many people's spiritual yearnings and bring them to church at times other than Sunday Mass.

Those who prepare the liturgy know that the most important festival of the year is Easter and the fifty days that prolong it. Everything must be done to highlight the paschal season and the mystery which it explicitly celebrates. But liturgists must also be both wise enough and respectful enough of the community to honor its spontaneous religious impulses, as far as tradition and good theology will allow. The question a liturgy committee should ask before introducing the hours is: on what occasion will a significant portion of the parish genuinely desire to assemble for prayer? This is not the same as asking when they *should* want to assemble. If the Liturgy of the Hours is to become popular, it must be paired with an occasion that is truly popular.

2. Advertise

Even on popular feasts, people may avoid unfamiliar services. A brief explanation in the bulletin can help. Even better, the pastor or another representative of the liturgy preparation committee can announce the liturgy and encourage the people to attend it. Perhaps the committee could ask the leaders of the various parish groups to invite their members to join in this new celebration. Personal invitations put people at ease. For example, for Evening Prayer on All Souls Day or during the month of November, the pastor could send a letter to the families of those who have died during the last year, personally inviting them to the service. During the intercessions, the names of the dead could be mentioned. After the hour, a reception could be a way for the parish to continue its care to the bereaved.

3. Draw from music the community already knows

What church musician has not wondered aloud, "How can I get the people to sing?" Part of the answer to this complex question is to allow the community to sing the music it knows best. As with any other skill, confidence in singing comes with familiarity. Most parishes already have music in their repertoire which is suitable for the hours.

Each hour is made up of these possibly "musical" building blocks:

Psalms
Hymns
Greetings/Responses
Canticles
Petitions
Periods of Silence

In each category most parishes have significant repertoire. For example, many responsorial psalm antiphons from the hymnal or seasonal liturgical booklet can be used in the hours. The parish probably also knows hymns suitable for the hours. The most ancient of all the evening hymns, the *Phos hilaron*, has been translated in a variety of ways into English. The community may know a hymn tune of the same meter as one of the versions. (For instance, see "O Radiant Light" [Long Meter] found in *Music Issue/Breaking Bread* and *JourneysongS* second edition) The well-known tune could be paired with the new text, with due regard for copyright.* The community could then make the sentiments of the text its own with ease and confidence.

---

*Editor's note: Several examples of long meter texts can be found in the following Oregon Catholic Press hymnal anthologies: *Take With You Words* by Genevieve Glen, OSB (11725 PQ) and *Awake My Soul* by Harry Hagen, OSB (11641PQ).

Some parishes may already use versions of the gospel canticles, which are the high point of Morning, Evening and Night Prayer. Several examples of metrical settings of the *Magnificat*, the gospel canticle at Evening Prayer, and the *Benedictus*, gospel canticle for Morning Prayer, are found in most hymnals. Bernadette Farrell's setting of these canticles employs the metric tune for both texts. The assembly's confidence as it stands to sing this metrical canticle would make it the real high point of the service.

The importance of using tried and true music during the parish's initial celebrations of the hours does not mean that new music can never be introduced. In time, after the parish is familiar with the format of the hours and has grown comfortable in celebrating them, new elements can be introduced. Innovation must be gradual. Several contemporary composers have produced settings of the hours. The tradition also offers material from other centuries. Chant, often neglected today, can have a part in the hours. A cantor can sing the verses of a psalm using classical chant melodies, while the assembly responds with a refrain. Whatever musical choices are made, the assembly's ability to participate must be the first consideration. That means beginning with what the parish knows best.*

4. Provide Orders of Worship

Before setting out on an unfamiliar journey, most people consult a map. An *Order of Worship* is a kind of map. It tells the assembly where it is going and what twists and turns it will make along the way. An order of worship for Evening Prayer might look like this, with the music, titles and Scripture citations inserted where appropriate.

This order of worship, through use of type faces and indentations, shows the assembly what the pieces of the service are and how they fit together. It also indicates the postures the assembly will take throughout the service. This will allow the community to pray the liturgy without the self-consciousness that comes from not knowing what to do next. When the parish celebrates the Liturgy of the Hours the first time, or even the first few times, a brief account of the history and theology of these services might be included on the order of worship.

---

*Editor's note: Oregon Catholic Press has the following collections of music for the Liturgy of the Hours: *Lord, Open My Lips* by Cyprian Consiglio, OSB Cam. (11629PQ) and *O Joyful Light/As Morning Breaks* by Michael Joncas (9477PQ).

EVENING PRAYER
(*name of occasion, e.g., The Dedication of the New Organ*)
(*name of parish*)

SERVICE OF LIGHT
Please stand as the musicians enter

Greeting
Evening Hymn
Thanksgiving for the Light

PSALMODY
Please be seated

Psalm #
Psalm prayer
Psalm #
Psalm Prayer

READING

GOSPEL CANTICLE

Please stand

PETITIONS

General Intercessions
Lord's Prayer
Concluding Prayer

CONCLUDING RITES

Blessing
Dismissal
Sign of Peace

Many contemporary resources, such as OCP's *Journeysongs*, *Breaking Bread* and *Music Issue,* include their own orders of worship for the hours.* These can be very useful. They can also be less than ideal, however, for two reasons. First, they often include music that a parish may not know. Second, they necessarily lack material that will be important for a particular celebration of the hours. For example, at

---

*Editor's note: Oregon Catholic Press hymnals *"Glory and Praise"* Second Edition (#11454PQ) and *Journeysongs* Second Edition (#510PQ) both contain on order of worship for celebrations of the Liturgy of the Hours.

Evening Prayer for Ash Wednesday, a short homily and the blessing and imposition of ashes would come after the reading. A "generic" order of worship would not include this information, nor would it include music that the community would sing during the procession to receive the ashes. For times when special activities are included in the celebration of the hours, a special order of worship will help the assembly to move easily through the liturgy.

5. Treat the Liturgy of the Hours as "formally" as you would Mass

When a parish gathers to celebrate Mass, it is an official event. Those in charge of the liturgical environment prepare the space. The pastor or another priest on the staff presides. Ministers of hospitality greet worshipers at the door and offer them whatever will be needed for the liturgy. Other ministers are assigned to exercise their proper roles. Thanks to planning and preparation, to discussion and rehearsal, the Eucharist proceeds smoothly. The Liturgy of the Hours deserves this same attention. The liturgy preparation committee will have to:

• "Choreograph" the rite. The committee planning the liturgy should picture it concretely. This will mean carefully outlining what will happen, taking note of where people will stand, how they will move from place to place, what objects will be needed, where they will be placed in the worship space and so forth. In outlining the choreography, the committee should keep in mind that the Liturgy of the Hours, like all liturgy, is celebrated by everyone who gathers. It is not done by the ministers for the assembly. How can the church be used so that it all becomes liturgical space and the people experience themselves as actors and not audience?

• Make a list of all the ministers needed to facilitate the liturgy. Although the list will vary depending upon the circumstances, greeters, a leader and an assistant, a cantor, instrumentalists, a thurifer, a reader, a leader of the intercessions, sacristans and environmental designers are likely. Someone will even have to be assigned to turn on the electric lights after the *Lucernarium* of Evening Prayer!

• Prepare books or booklets for the ministers. Just as the presider for the Eucharist uses a special book containing all the texts and direction for his task, so, too, the presider at the Liturgy of the Hours needs a ritual book. The designer of the book should:

1. Choose a cover, e.g., a service binder or presentation folder in the color of the liturgical season covered with art worthy of the liturgy. *
2. Include directions so the presider will not have to remember every detail. For example, after each psalm, include a directive such as: *After the psalm, pray quietly for approximately 30 seconds. Then look up and say, "Let us pray." Stand, and when the assembly is settled, open your arms and pray.* Then give the text of the prayer.
3. Take care that pages do not have to be turned in the middle of a prayer. If the presider has his or her arms outstretched, a page turn would be clumsy.
4. If the cantor will not have a suitable stand to hold music, assemble a cantor's book also. The other ministers can use the same order of worship as the assembly, but they should make notes in them. For example, after each psalm, the assistant might write: *Put down order of worship and prepare to hold the presider's book so the presider can pray with extended arms.*

• Schedule a rehearsal. Since the ministers will model for the assembly how to participate in this new liturgy, their certainty will make the assembly more certain. Halting movements and obvious confusion among the ministers will distract people and lessen their ability to focus upon the texts, music and ceremonies of the liturgy. At the rehearsal, a member of the committee who understands the history and theology of the Liturgy of the Hours should briefly explain it to the gathered ministers. This will give them a deep understanding of what they are doing and will help to transform their service from "going through the motions" to embodied prayer. A rehearsal is more than an opportunity to talk about the liturgy, however. At a good rehearsal, the ministers actually walk through it, using the actual objects they will use during the celebration. Only in this way will they discover the most efficient and graceful way to perform each action and how to perform the various actions in concert. The rehearsal is a logical time for the ministers to make notes in their orders of worship or books.

---

*Editor's note: Oregon Catholic Press has service binders and presentation folders suitable for such occasions.

Why bother?

To understand, to plan and to celebrate the Liturgy of the Hours in a parish is not a simple matter. Nonetheless, the benefits far exceed the bother.

The hours:

• provide a "non-eucharistic" way for the church to pray, and they fill the gap left by the death of so many kinds of devotional prayer.

• celebrate the presence of Christ often overlooked, namely in the proclaimed word and in the gathered church.

• offer groups of Christians a liturgical way to pray when no presbyter can preside for worship.

• provide a consistent but flexible format for prayer, adaptable for innumerable situations: parish-wide celebrations, prayer before or after meetings, family prayer and wake services.

• serve as a forum for learning new ways of doing things without hurting anyone or causing resentment.

• give families a way to take the liturgy home; what is done in the hours can be done in a simpler way in the home.

• invite the community to pray in a way that is truly earthy and incarnational, using natural symbols—sunrise, nightfall, fire, smoke—and involving all the senses.

• tie people today into a tradition as old as the church itself.

During the first week of Lent, a woman in a supermarket in Danbury, Connecticut, was overheard asking another, "Were you at that evening service at St. Peter's on Wednesday? I hear it was beautiful." Indeed it was. For in the midst of the community's remembrance of its sinfulness and mortality, people heard and saw and smelled the presence of Christ, the light in the darkness, the sun that never sets. And they knew that Easter was on the way.

5

Beauty and Hope

At some point early in my life, I fell in love with that "prayer of the church" known as the Liturgy of the Hours. The private and sometimes silent and hurried duty of praying the office from the breviary was not attractive to me. It was the gathering together of a diverse group of people for the communal celebration of the hours that impressed me—men and women, young and old, expressing, through the poetic words of the psalms, some of their deepest emotions. For the words of the psalms tap into our joy, our fear, our expectation, our disappointment, our love and, yes, even our anger. It is all there for us, helping us to express with one another, in a place of prayer and peace, our humanness. There is beauty and there is hope!

And so, when I eventually found myself in the choir stalls at St. John's Abbey in Collegeville, Minnesota, praying the Liturgy of the Hours, I was like a thirsty man drinking from the deepest of wells—I was at home!

One cold, early winter night in Minnesota I walked with a Lutheran friend who, with excitement in her eyes, said to me, "Michael, the O antiphons begin tonight." Rhoda was eager to get to the Abbey Church.

In the cool bleak countryside, in a warm monastic church, we entered into the mystery filled with beauty and promising hope. Together as pilgrims we joined the memory and the memory and the story: Wisdom. Lord. Root of Jesse. Rising Sun. King. God with Us!

The O antiphons help us to get in touch with our yearning for hope and for love. Their poetic beauty inspires us to trust that the Lord Jesus is keeping the promise of abiding presence in our world.

Ero Cras: Tomorrow I will be here! Tomorrow has come. It is today; it is always and for ages unending. And so, may those of us who lead the church in musical prayer be inspired by the O antiphons so that we will bring them to life for so many who need to hear that comforting promise of Christ's loving presence.

—Michael P. Mernagh

Ero Cras: Tomorrow I Will Be Here

Michael P. Mernagh

Snow dusts the ground. The branches of the barren trees reach out long, bony fingers toward the sky as if searching for warmth. In a little town, in a small church, people make their way to Mass. A worship space decorated with fabric, branches, a wreath, a tree and cedar and spruce swags greets them. Their nostrils fill with the scent of burning candles and incense. The warmth of the church contrasts with the cold clinging to their coats. It is that time of year again.

The priest wears a royal purple vestment to follow the procession up the aisle as the assembly sings the signal that the journey has begun:

> O come, O come Emmanuel,
> And ransom captive Israel,
> That mourns in lonely exile here,
> Until the Son of God appear.
> Rejoice! Rejoice! Emmanuel
> Shall come to thee, O Israel!

It is Advent!

There is no mistaking it once we hear those wonderfully familiar words, "O Come, O Come, Emmanuel." The season of hopeful expectation for the birth of the Savior is upon us.

Many of us have sung this hymn for years without knowing its origin, its history and its meaning. As a pastoral musician I played it many times, but not until graduate school did I hear of the so-called "O" antiphons from which "O Come, O Come, Emmanuel" is based. The antiphons are a gem embedded in the church's rich and long tradition and preserved, in a particular way, by our monastic brothers and sisters.

The following history, background and suggestions for use are intended to inspire pastoral musicians and liturgists to use these antiphons.

Some History

The O antiphons derive their name from the fact that each of the seven begins with "O": *O Sapientia* (Oh Wisdom), *O Adonai* (Oh Leader of the House of David), *O Radix Jesse* (Oh Root of Jesse), *O Clavis David* (Oh Key of David), *O Oriens* (Oh Rising Sun), *O Rex genitum* (Oh King of the Nations) and *O Emmanuel* (Oh God with Us).

In monastic churches and other settings, the antiphons are sung at the beginning and at the end of the "Canticle of Mary" during Evening Prayer on the seven days preceding the vigil of Christmas. Fr. Columba Kelly, OSB, a monk of Saint Meinrad Archabbey, musicologist and expert in chant, said, "The texts and probably the music date from around the time of Pope Gregory the Great, between the sixth and seventh centuries." Kelly stated that the earliest notated examples of these antiphons are found at the abbey of St. Gall in Hartker's Antiphonal, which dates from around the end of the tenth century.

The O antiphons were considered so important in medieval monasteries that they were assigned to the leaders of the monastery: the first to the abbot, the next to the prior, and so on. Sometimes they were even sung three times before the *Magnificat*, three times before the doxology, and three times after the doxology. Similar in structure to orations or other ecclesiastical writings, each antiphon begins with an invocation to the Messiah that is rooted in the images of the Hebrew Scriptures. The image in each invocation is developed and expanded so that it says a little more about the Messiah, and finally there is an invitation—a calling out to God—to come and to act according to the title used in the antiphon. The O antiphons intensely address God and cry out for his presence. They are prayers of entreaty that increase in anticipation of the celebration of the nativity.

The "greater antiphons," as they are sometimes called, are powerful prayers that give voice to our need for God's presence; they help us to articulate our total dependence upon God and our faithful trust in God.

The theology of the O antiphons

O Sapientia (December 17)
O Wisdom,
Who came forth from the
mouth of the most high,
Reaching from end to end mightily, and
gently governing all things:
Come,
To teach us the way of prudence.

Sirach 24

In this first antiphon, we call upon the word of wisdom spoken by the mouth of the most high God, whose power knows no bounds in time and space. Jesus the Messiah is the word and wisdom of God made flesh, a powerful and tender guide. We seek and ask the God of wisdom to direct our lives by inspiring us to make choices that are life-giving and growth-promoting.

> *O Adonai* (December 18)
> O my Lord of Lords,
> And leader of the house of Israel, who
> Appeared to Moses in the fire of the
> burning bush,
> And on Sinai gave him the law:
> Come,
> To redeem us with outstretched arm.
>
> Exodus 3, 15, 24
> Deuteronomy 5

The second antiphon calls upon the Lord of lords who led the chosen people out of bondage in Egypt. It is the same Lord who called Moses to the task of being God's instrument of liberation, appeared to him in the burning bush, and gave him the law. This antiphon reflects our trust in the God whose powerful outstretched arm created, redeems and continues to embrace the cosmos in love. We are challenged to seek freedom and justice for all people.

> *O Radix Jesse* (December 19)
> O Root of Jesse,
> Who stand as a sign for
> the peoples,
> Whom kings will meet
> with silence,
> Whom nations will entreat
> in prayer:
> Come,
> To set us free, delay no longer.
>
> Isaiah 11

From humble peasant roots, King David emerged as a mighty and powerful tree for the people of Israel. It is from this same humble beginning that a new king comes, one who, without the trappings of an earthly king, holds power over all, comes. Aware of the need for humble, honest and loving leadership, we become persistent in our call to the one who can deliver us from our own trappings of materialism and power.

> *O Clavis David* (December 20)
> O Key of David,
> And scepter of the house

of Israel,
Who open, and no one closes,
Who close and no one opens:
Come,
And lead forth from the house
of bondage,
The captive sitting in darkness and the
shadow of death.

Isaiah 22, Revelation 3:7

David's key and scepter were nothing in comparison to the key and the scepter of the Messiah. Jesus is the key of David, who can open the hearts and minds of those whose lives are locked up in fear, disease and sin. We need this key so that our own hearts may be opened, emptied of all that keeps us from being who we are called to be, and filled with the grace of God that transforms our lives and leads us to full personhood.

O Oriens (December 21)
O Rising Sun,
Splendor of eternal light,
And sun of righteousness:
Come,
And enlighten those sitting
in darkness
And the shadow of death.

Zechariah 3:8, 6:2; Isaiah 9:2, 60:1–3;
Wisdom 7:26; Luke 1:78; Hebrews 1: 3

This antiphon is about light, brightness and warmth. At least in the north, the days of Advent can be gloomy at times and we often find ourselves waiting for the sun to shine. Light has power to give life. We cry out to the rising sun, whom we trust will arise even in the grayest of times when it seems like we will never see the light again. It appears—huge, fiery, powerful and capable of dispelling darkness and giving and supporting life. Christ, the sun of justice, becomes more visible, more accessible, as we are enlightened by his presence.

O Rex Gentium (December 22)
O King of the Nations
Whom they have long awaited,
The cornerstone,
Who makes both sides one,
Come,

Save us
Who you fashioned out of clay.

> Jeremiah 10:7; Haggai 2:8;
> Isaiah 28:16; Genesis 2:7;
> Ephesians 2:14

Here is a cry to Israel's promised one, and it is our cry to the Christ whom we desire. Just as Israel waited for a king who would bring them together again and make them a great nation, so we wait for Christ who is the cornerstone of our lives. Christ shapes our lives like clay vessels on the potter's wheel. He is the king of our lives.

O Emmanuel (December 23)
O Emmanuel,
Our king and law-giver,
The expectation of all nations
And their Savior:
Come,
To save us,
O Lord our God.

> Isaiah 7:14, 33:22; Genesis 49:10;
> Zechariah 9:9; John 20:28

The seventh of the great O antiphons is where we finally hear that great and wonderful name Emmanuel, God with us. What greater gift and what more profound reality is there than to say that God is with us as one who knows our experience and who shares in our life with its suffering and joy? The last of the O antiphons expresses the goal toward which Christian pilgrims walk as we make our way to the stable of our hearts. There we will find our God reborn in us once again.

Finally, whether by clever design or by chance, the first letter of these titles backwards spells the Latin words *ero cras,* which mean "tomorrow I shall be here." Brilliant!

The O antiphons outside monastic walls

Well, what is the point of reflecting upon these antiphons? Most of us are not monks who will go to the abbey church for vespers from December 17 to December 23. For the most part, we have four weeks, a relatively short time, to prepare for the nativity of Jesus. So in addition to singing "O Come, O Come Emmanuel" occasionally during Advent, how can we use the antiphons? How can we introduce them to our communities in a way that will have an impact upon them? How can we use pastoral creativity to adapt the O antiphons to the church's liturgical life? The following are some thoughts and ideas.

157

Devotions

For a number of years following the "liturgical housecleaning" after the Second Vatican Council, it seemed that celebrating the Eucharist was our only liturgical expression. Much of the devotional life of Roman Catholics in North America was abandoned as the church explored the liturgy of the word and the Eucharist. Mass was now more accessible to Roman Catholics due largely to the language change from Latin to the vernacular. The eucharistic celebration was restored to its central place while devotional practices such as novenas, forty hour and adoration and Benediction of the Blessed Sacrament either moved into the background or disappeared.

Things are now changing. While the celebration of the Eucharist is central to Catholic Christian life, devotions are making a comeback in the Roman Catholic Church. An opportunity is presented.

Given the deep well of our Catholic tradition, we need not limit ourselves by shallowly dipping into the devotional practices of the immediately pre-conciliar church. The well is deeper. Why not finally take up the challenge of making the Liturgy of the Hours regular practice in our houses of worship? Why not mine our liturgical tradition, explore, adapt and use some of what we discover to nourish the lives of our communities? The great O antiphons are but one example of how we can do this.

A few ideas

Even if your place of worship does not regularly sing vespers (Evening Prayer), you can still incorporate the antiphons into your Advent season. Perhaps the parish community could study the texts, the history and development of the antiphons during the Advent season. Each study session could begin with an adapted Liturgy of the Hours or Liturgy of the Word wherein the O antiphons would be either recited or sung.

For example, one could use Rev. Eugene Lindusky's "The Great O Antiphons" as a musical source for theological reflection (found in *Choral Praise* Choral Edition 9093PQ and *Choral Praise* Vol. 1 8723PQ). As part of the study sessions, have a couple of cantors sing the antiphons while the group simply listens and reflects.

Or, one could plan an evening of prayer and music similar to "Lessons and Carols" (for an example see *The Advent of Our God* 9217PQ) by using various musical settings of the antiphons as well as readings that would highlight the images in the various antiphons.

Perhaps one of the antiphons could be focal (in music, prayer, word and preaching) in each liturgy during the season of Advent: one for each Sunday, one for communal reconciliation, one for an evening of reflection and one for Evening Prayer or Night Prayer.

In addition, I strongly recommend using the antiphons before and after the *Magnificat*, according to ancient tradition, as you sing Evening Prayer from December 17 to December 23.

Some of you may already be saying, "Be realistic! People do not want to come to church seven nights in a row." No, the entire parish community may not, but let us not underestimate the faithful. It is our ministerial responsibility to be creative so that people, rather than not wanting to attend, would rather not miss. Many of our people are tired and stressed and would welcome a half hour to an hour of quiet, well-planned and well-executed prayer. They will not, however, be excited about coming to church to face the death-like hues of mercury vapor lamps, poor music or none at all, and a service during which they are bombarded with nothing but words.

Let's be counter-cultural! Rather than caving in to or even supporting the frantic and often zombie-like activity preceding Christmas, we can offer those to whom we minister a refuge of peace and prayer each evening on their way home from work. People will come!

A few years ago, I visited the Jerusalem Community (a modern-day urban monastic community) at their place in Paris, France. Each evening at 5 p.m. people from around the city of Paris gathered with these monastics to fill the church and to celebrate a hybrid Byzantine Rite/Latin Rite eucharistic liturgy that lasted almost an hour and a half.

Another suggestion is that a liturgy in the Taizé style could be planned around a setting of the antiphons. The Taizé community has shown us that simple repetition is a very effective way of settling people down, breaking down barriers and centering prayer.

Finally, I encourage all pastoral ministers in music and liturgy to consider using some chant in your places of worship. Fr. Kelly has written thousands of chants in the vernacular and has created some wonderful settings for the O antiphons. The antiphons are recorded on the CD "Gregorian Chant for Advent and Christmas" (08925). This CD is available by calling Abbey Press (1-800-325-2511).

Conclusion

Our church has a rich tradition that overflows with expressions of faith by our forbears who sculpted, painted and penned their belief in the greatest of God's gift to us, his son Jesus. The great O antiphons should be brought to life in our places of worship. We can draw inspiration from the people who crafted these antiphons and be as creative by incorporating them into our faith lives and our worship. Celebrate using the O antiphons in the Liturgy of the Hours, in your Advent reconciliation liturgy, an evening of lessons and carols, or even in a special evening of instruction and song with our sisters and brothers of other Christian churches. In our prayer and worship, we will surely hear the Lord Jesus respond, *"Ero cras*! Tomorrow I shall be here!"

6

Good Friday Is Not a Funeral—
Or Is It?

Fifteen years have passed since I pondered the first part of this assertion, and I still believe it. Today I would add the second clause and its question mark precisely to emphasize what a valuable "school of the faith" we have in the solemn liturgy of Good Friday. Year in and year out Good Friday continues to remember the true Christian meaning of the cross and in so doing teaches us how central the cross is to our lived faith. Nowhere, I would still wager, do we come more closely in touch with the suffering and death of Jesus, the Christ, than when we stand before our own crosses of suffering and death. At no time in recent history have we as a nation shared in the sufferings of others as deeply as in this year of terror. And yet, nowhere does our faith in the resurrection of Jesus, the Christ, mean more to us or give us more hope than when we can look beyond our crosses and even our mortal resting places to the empty tomb and its pledge that death does not have the last word.

The solemn liturgy of Good Friday teaches that our suffering in union with that of Jesus is salvific. That is, Good Friday not only remembers the death of the Lord but the modality of that death, the cross. Pope John Paul II expressed this clearly in his 1984 Apostolic Letter *Salvifici doloris* ("On the Christian Meaning of Human Suffering"):

> Those who share in Christ's sufferings
> have before their eyes the Paschal Mystery of
> the Cross and Resurrection, in which Christ

descends, in a first phase, to the ultimate limits of human weakness and impotence:
indeed, he dies nailed to the Cross. But if at
the same time in this *weakness* there is accomplished his *lifting up,* confirmed by the power
of the Resurrection, then this means that the
weaknesses of all human sufferings are capable of being infused with the same power of
God manifested in Christ's Cross. In such a
concept, *to suffer* means to become particularly
susceptible, particularly *open to the working of the
salvific powers of God,* offered to humanity in
Christ. (23)

When Christian funeral liturgy fails to take seriously the reality of
the death it embraces, it also fails to take seriously the suffering and
death of Jesus and its power to transform even death. Although
Calvary already professes belief in the victory of Easter, the *trophy of the
cross* remains *cross,* the awful instrument of human suffering. With both
its triumphal elevation of the cross and its proclamation, "This is the
wood of the cross on which hung the Savior of the World!" the Good
Friday liturgy successfully reflects an integrity we can all expect of
good funeral liturgy as well. No, Good Friday is not a funeral in any
conventional sense, but our funerals can and should mirror its liturgical
fidelity to the paschal mystery.

—H. Richard Rutherford, CSC

Good Friday Is Not a Funeral

H. Richard Rutherford, CSC

The solemn liturgy of Good Friday, the Passion of our Lord, is not a funeral. This liturgical truism never hit home more vividly than in a situation I experienced in the early years of post-Vatican II renewal when the nationally televised funeral of President John F. Kennedy was still very vivid in our memory. I was assisting with the long-range planning of the Easter Triduum (Holy Thursday through Easter) in a liturgically active Catholic community.

When the discussion turned to Good Friday, a prominent member of the planning group suggested that it would appropriate to set the mood for the liturgy commemorating the death of Jesus by introducing the solemn beat of a great kettle drum during the entrance procession. Everyone would recognize its significance and what could be better than to show Jesus the same honor that we accord national figures at their funerals. My insistent plea that liturgy of Good Friday is not a funeral failed to convince the committee that the kettle drum might indeed be so effective as to set the wrong mood!

From the earliest pilgrimages to the sacred shrines of the Holy Land, popular piety has done much to dramatize the realism and pathos of Good Friday. Extraliturgical wakes with a statue of the crucified Jesus and procession to a replica of the garden tomb are part of my own ethnic memory; passion plays in drama (Oberammergau), literature (*The Greek Passion*) and artistic masterpieces (Michelangelo's *Pietà*) continue to impress us with the utterly human suffering and reality of the Lord's death.

But because of our need to hear and to celebrate again and again the good news that death does not have the final word, the liturgy of Good Friday never absorbed the trappings of a funeral. This is easily understood when we see that most solemn of days in its rightful place as part of the Easter Triduum. It is expressed most succinctly in the *General Norms for the Liturgical Year and Calendar*:

> Christ redeemed us and gave perfect glory to God principally through his paschal mystery: by dying he destroyed our death and by rising he restored our life. The Easter Triduum of the passion and resurrection of Christ is thus the culmination of the entire liturgical year. (18)

This extended celebration of the solemnity of Easter as the context for our commemoration of the Lord's passion and death provides our best guide to observing Good Friday. In turn, the liturgy of Good Friday thus celebrated spells out for us in words and actions the fundamental meaning of Jesus' death, casts some dramatic light on our Christian way of thinking about death, and models for us the pastoral sensitivity with which we dare to "celebrate" the death of our own loved ones in the Christian funeral.

What do these three have in common? The following reflections are the beginning of an answer, treating the funeral, the cross and one nearly forgotten facet of the Christian attitude toward death.

The Christian funeral

Although our celebration of Good Friday, caught up in the paschal mystery of the death and resurrection of Jesus Christ, is not itself a funeral, it reveals most vividly what it is that makes a funeral Christian. All the various rites of the new Roman *Order of Christian Funerals* express the faith that the Christian mystery of Christ's death and resurrection is involved in the mystery of human death.

The Gospel simplicity of Jesus' own burial on Good Friday awaiting the dawn of Easter well expresses the manner with which the *Order of Christian Funerals* invites Catholics to accept courageously the death of their loved ones and to surround it with the church's liturgy. In these grief rituals, the paschal death and resurrection of Jesus give human death Christian meaning.

The image of the cross

Just as the paschal event of Good Friday and Easter shaped the Christian funeral historically, so too can the liturgy of Good Friday shape our attitude toward death. One example is the cross itself.

Historically, some five centuries passed before the early Christian symbol of the cross came to carry a painted representation of the crucified Jesus on it. It would be another four hundred years before we find examples of the crucified figure, life size and sculptured in the round, the origin of the familiar crucifixes of medieval and recent times. For the first five hundred years of Christian spirituality, therefore, the sign of the cross and the cross itself expressed the paschal meaning of Good Friday.

The *chi rho* symbol of Christ encircled by a laurel wreath of victory and affixed atop a cross was called the "trophy of the cross" and proclaimed unequivocally the paschal significance of Jesus' death. Long before vivid scenes of the crucified Jesus in agony came to characterize the cross as a passage (passover) which Jesus had to endure in order to reach the glory of resurrection, the "trophy of the cross" proclaimed with the Gospel of John and early Christian writers that the hour of Jesus' death is at once the hour of his glorification.

Pascha/Passion

St. Augustine summarized the twofold meaning of *"pascha,"* in which we recognize our English words Pasch and paschal, by explaining the traditional usage of that time. From the semitic tradition, *"pascha"* carried the meaning of passover, with all its biblical history and symbolism.

Paul's exhortation to the Corinthians, "Christ, our passover, has been sacrificed; let us celebrate the feast..." (I Corinthians 5:7–8) still echoes in the Easter readings, and the Easter Proclamation (*Exsultet*) still sings, "This is our passover feast, when Christ, the true Lamb, is slain, whose blood consecrates the homes of all believers."

Have you ever wondered why this seemingly Good Friday theme is so prevalent in the liturgy of Easter? Why not, when all of the Easter Triduum makes up one great extended celebration of the Easter event?

This becomes unforgettably clear when one takes part in the full celebration of Christian Initiation (baptism, confirmation and first Eucharist), in which the new Christians are baptized by immersion. Few symbols strike our religious imagination as vividly as this visual proclamation of the one paschal mystery in Jesus' death and resurrection:

> You have been taught that when we were baptized in Christ Jesus we were baptized in his death; in other words, when we were baptized we went into the tomb with him and joined him in death, so that as Christ was raised from the dead by the Father's glory, we too might have a new life (Romans 6:3–4).

The other meaning that *"pascha"* had in early Christianity, according to St. Augustine, came from its proximity to the Greek word for suffering (*pathos* and *paschein*) in which we see the root of our words "pathos" and "passion." Among the Christians, "passion" in reference to the cross brought together Jesus' suffering and his death in one technical term.

Christine Mohrmann, the renowned scholar of early Christianity, explains that "passion" embraced the death, both of Christ and the early martyrs. It strongly suggested to the early Christians the idea of victory and heavenly glory that would follow death, again both for Jesus and the martyrs. This combination of ideas—passion, death, victory and glory—is very understandable in those times of persecution.

What all this has to do with the cross, Good Friday and the *Order of Christian Funerals* is well stated by Richard Martin in a graduate essay at the University of Portland:

> Our tradition understands that Jesus' life was lived out in orientation to his coming passion and death, that intimately woven into Jesus' way of being was a dying to self, a giving of oneself completely to that imaginative mysterious part at the basis of all our experience...
>
> In the end, death not only speaks of life in the funeral (rites), but life must also speak of passion.

As the week we call "holy" again comes to its climax in the Easter Triduum, Christians everywhere lay aside their mourning dress and with St. Augustine exalt in the "trophy of the cross" and in the meaning of the sign we bear: "What is the sign of the cross that we all know, other than the cross of Christ? If this cross be not traced upon the foreheads of the faithful, or over the water from which we are born anew, or over the oil with which we are anointed, or over the sacrifice which we are fed, then none of these acts is accomplished according to the rite."

PART 4

Eucharist

1

Still Safeguarding the Balance

Coming back to this article ten years after its publication shows an example of how the thinkers of the liturgical movement and the leaders of the church are thinking along the same lines. In 1994 Patrick Malloy surely could not have known that in 1995 the Pastoral Message of the Kansas Bishops on Sunday Communion without Mass would be issued, followed in 1998 by the monumental work of Pope John Paul II, his apostolic letter *Dies Domini: On Keeping the Lord's Day Holy*. And yet these three documents speak as with one voice on the nature of Sunday and the meaning of Communion.

The two documents of the church repeat in a forceful way the insistence that Dr. Malloy made: Sunday is meant for Eucharist. The Kansas bishops were very concerned that the link between Sunday, the Eucharist and Communion would be destroyed by a multiplication of Sunday Celebrations in the Absence of a Priest. The issue they brought forward is still before us today: what is a diocese to do when there are not enough ordained ministers in order to have Sunday Eucharist celebrated in every parish? This link is made even clearer in the apostolic letter of the Holy Father. There can be no doubt but that the church insists that it is not just receiving Communion, it is the celebration of the Eucharist tied to a life of prayer and service to those in need that gives Sunday its special character. A Sunday observance without Eucharist is an anomaly, just as Communion without reference to Eucharist and to service is an anomaly.

The need for a life of prayer and service brings the other aspect of the article to the fore. In order to support the life of faith, Sunday needs more than Eucharist, more than Communion. In these days when so many who work in the church feel burdened by a list of a million things to do, there is good cause for limiting the number and types of celebrations and activities that a given parish does. Still, this article, together with the two subsequent documents of the church, make it clear that it is insufficient to offer communion services or even Eucharist as the sole diet of the Sunday assembly. Our parishes need to be places where prayer of all sorts and service are seen as part of a normal Sunday observance.

So it is that Sunday is to be the center of the week of prayer and service, just as receiving Communion is to be the center around which our lives are led. God has given us the Lord's day in order to show the value of this time apart from our usual concerns; it is our job to make the most of that time. God has given us Communion in the body and blood of Jesus; it is our job to let that Communion nourish our whole life of faith. To obscure either is to put an obstacle in the way of that which God is offering us in Christ.

—Glenn CJ Byer

The Rich Liturgical Pallet of the Church: Safeguarding the Balance

Patrick L. Malloy

Most Catholics know the hymn "On This Day, the First of Days." It celebrates the importance of Sunday, the first day of the week, in the story of salvation.

> On this day, the first of days,
> God the Father's name we praise,
> Who, creation's Font and Spring,
> Did the world from darkness bring.

> On this day th' eternal Son
> Over death his triumph won.
> On this day the Spirit came
> With his gifts of living flame.
>
> Text: 77 77; *Die parente temporum; Caracassion*
> *Brievary*, 1745; tr. by Henry W. Baker, 1821–1877, alt.

Sunday is the day when God created the world from darkness, recreated it through Jesus' triumph over death and assured its ongoing renewal through the gift of the spirit on Pentecost. In the history of salvation, Sunday claims a special place.

Early Christians held the day in such high esteem that, during the first few centuries of Christianity, Sunday was the only day of the week when they celebrated the Eucharist. On the other days of the week, those who were able assembled for other kinds of prayer, which we today would call "offices" or the Liturgy of the Hours. These services generally included psalms, sometimes hymns, occasionally a brief reading and almost always prayers of petition and thanks. Other sacraments and rites, such as baptism, penance and ordination, were celebrated when the occasion called for them. Weekly Eucharist and the daily Liturgy of the Hours, however, were the "bread and butter" of the church's public prayer.

Eucharist and other rites and prayers

The link between Sunday and the Eucharist did not last, however. Christians gradually began to celebrate the Mass on other days, and eventually on every day, and often more than once a day. They seemed to believe that if the Eucharist was a good thing—in fact, the highest form of prayer—then the more the church celebrated it, the better. The church could have slipped into an unhealthy fixation or a magical attitude toward the Mass—attending (or in the case of a priest, presiding for) as many as possible each day. Still, customs and legislation arose to guard against that pitfall. Although some of these had negative effects, they did encourage Christians to surround the Eucharist, the center of worship, with other rites and forms of prayer. The result was balance.

1. Number of Masses restricted. The tendency of priests to multiply Masses was kept in check by regulations allowing them to celebrate only two Masses each day. Christmas and All Souls' Day were the only two exceptions, when a priest was permitted to celebrate Mass three times. This regulation, which is still in effect, does not downplay the Eucharist but highlights its importance. Just as a family does not have a Thanksgiving-style dinner every day, lest the meal become too common and lose its special character, so the church realized that the frequency of Mass had to be regulated; otherwise, the Eucharist would come to seem too "ordinary" and unimportant. It could even be used for inappropriate purposes, for example, as a means for priests to earn greater income.

2. Time of Masses restricted and fast imposed. Other practices gradually developed which also helped to keep the liturgical and prayer life of the church in balance and to heighten respect for the eucharistic liturgy. Mass was never to be celebrated after noon, for example. This greatly restricted the frequency of the celebration. Equally significant was the long eucharistic fast. It extended from midnight to the time of Communion. Such a potentially long period without food was difficult for many people, especially children, and so they received Communion infrequently.

3. Feelings of guilt inhibit frequent Communion. In the Christian Scriptures, the apostle Paul spoke of believers as "a royal priesthood, a holy nation, a people set apart." Gradually, however, Christian people came to be very concerned with their own sinfulness and saw themselves as unworthy to approach the altar except on the rarest of occasions. Worshipers received the sacrament so infrequently that a regulation was passed: Christians were required to receive Communion at least once each year, during the Easter season. This rule is still in force today and is commonly called the "Easter Duty."

All of these forces together—the restriction in the number of Masses a priest could celebrate, the regulation forbidding Masses after noon, the demanding eucharistic fast and deep feelings of inadequacy—kept people from treating the Mass like a magic act or from making it their only form of worship. Instead, the Mass took central place in the church's worship and other forms of prayer grew up around it, like spokes emerging from the hub of a wheel.

In addition to the Liturgy of the Hours, which became less and less popular, new forms evolved. These other types of prayer are commonly called "devotions." Such devotional customs as the rosary, the *Angelus*, Order of Exposition of the Holy Eucharist, novenas and other prayers were less "official" than the Mass but were very dear to the people who prayed them. In these devotions, the people built up for the church of future generations a tradition of rich and varied styles and forms of prayer. The Eucharist was clearly regarded as the central and highest form of Christian prayer, but Christians experienced it within the broader context of all sorts of prayer and devotion.

The pendulum swings

By the early twentieth century, however, many members of the church came to the conclusion that the negative results of the various restrictions on the Eucharist outweighed the positive. Fewer and fewer people were receiving Communion, even on Sunday. Many wondered, "Should Christians who believe in the forgiveness of God through Jesus be so fearful of approaching the Lord's Supper? Or should restrictions concerning fasting and the hour of the day keep them away?" In response to these concerns, the following official decisions were made:

1. Receive Communion as often as possible. In 1905 Pope Pius X inaugurated a movement to encourage Catholics to receive Communion as often as they could. He said that "at each Mass the faithful who are present should communicate, not only in spiritual desire, but sacramentally, by the actual reception of the Eucharist." He even went on to say that Jesus wished Catholics to receive Communion every day. This was quite a shift from the previous attitude of most members of the church.

2. Children too may receive Communion. In 1910 Pius X went a step further. For many centuries, children had not been allowed to receive first Communion until they could fully understand the church's teaching concerning the Eucharist. Pope Pius made the requirement much simpler: they only had to be able to distinguish the eucharistic bread and wine from ordinary bread and wine. By inviting children to the Lord's Table, Pius made the Eucharist seem less intimidating and more accessible. He also encouraged children to receive the Eucharist frequently, even daily if possible. Once again, the church was being encouraged to change its approach to the Mass.

3. Evening Masses are possible. The conflict between modern work schedules and the prohibition against afternoon and evening Masses was finally addressed in 1953. On Epiphany, Pius XII gave permission for Sunday evening Masses. The bishop of each diocese was to make evening Mass available to workers who could not come to the Eucharist in the morning. They and others who truly could not attend morning Mass were the only ones who could satisfy their Sunday obligations in the evening, however. Pope Paul VI removed this restriction and made evening Mass a regular part of Catholic life. Surprisingly, history shows that never before had Mass been celebrated in the afternoon or evening, except in cases of genuine necessity. Pope Paul had set the church on a new eucharistic course.

4. The Communion fast gets easier. At the same time that Pius XII gave permission for evening Masses, he also lightened the eucharistic fast. How could someone who was working all day Sunday fast from the previous midnight until the time of the newly allowed evening Mass? Therefore, Pius eased the fast for those who attended evening Mass. Food could be taken up to three hours and beverages up to one hour beforehand. Compared to previous regulations, this was a generous compromise, and it made Communion at evening Mass possible.

Three years later, the midnight fast was abolished altogether, even for those going to Mass in the morning, and the three-hour fast was made the rule for all Masses. Finally, in 1964, Paul VI reduced even this rather light fast to one hour for food as well as drink. Since the fast is calculated, not from the time Mass begins, but from the time of Communion, this new regulation virtually destroyed the ancient custom of fasting before Communion.

Thus, in four steps, the customs that had kept a balance between the Eucharist and other forms of prayer had been destroyed. The push toward daily Communion, the permission for small children to approach the Lord's table, the institution of evening Masses and the near abolition of the Communion fast opened the way for an explosion of Masses and the gradual decay of other kinds of prayer.

Advantages and disadvantages

Is this shift good or bad? Like most developments, it is both. Surely, Jesus did not institute the Eucharist expecting people to be afraid to receive Communion. The comfort Catholics now feel as they approach the Lord's Supper is a wonderful gain. The ability of those who work on Sunday to assemble with other Christians for Eucharist, thanks to afternoon and evening Masses, is a great blessing for them individually and for the entire church. The relaxation of the Communion fast, even though it can lead to a casual approach to the sacrament, can also encourage a more mature approach by making believers decide for themselves how best to prepare for sharing in the Lord's Supper.

At the same time, these changes have made it easy for Catholics to overlook important parts of the church's tradition. Both the eucharistic event and the eucharistic food have been held in great reverence throughout history. Now there is a danger that they may be seen as common and, therefore, ordinary. Just as it is not good to approach the sacrament in terror, it is equally dangerous to approach it casually.

Through the ages, the church's prayer developed into an inviting and interesting sharing in the life of God—a table laden with many rich dishes. The current emphasis on the Eucharist, and especially on receiving Communion, threatens to reduce our liturgical fare to the entrée.

For the sake of having a balanced prayer life and for giving the Eucharist the central place it deserves, the church should once again explore its rich storehouse of public prayer. The need for forms of prayer other than Mass becomes obvious as the church faces a shortage of priests. We cannot maintain a liturgical life that demands the Eucharist at every turn. Some people, recognizing all the gains that frequent Communion has brought to the church, are suggesting that, when a priest is not available, Communion services should substitute for Mass. The church would be wise to consider other options, however, not in place of Communion services, but along with them. In the tradition, many such solutions already exist. None has as much to offer as the Liturgy of the Hours, the highly popular daily prayer that flourished in the church prior to what liturgist John Baldovin, S.J., had called our "monoeucharistitis."

2

Eucharist Only? Ten Years On

When Patrick Malloy wrote on how the Catholic community came to focus on the Eucharist as its exclusive form of worship, he held up a mirror to us and gently prodded us to think. Why did we have such a limited pallet of worship services? Were we, as liturgists and musicians, falling back on Mass because it could be done with little or no extra work, or perhaps because we knew that it would at least draw a decent crowd? What could we do to make the worship experience of the church a little richer?

In my own teaching, I would describe this phenomenon as the atoll theory of liturgy: let people alone and then expect them to climb the almost vertical slope to the summit of liturgical life once a week, only to be left to drop off the worship radar for the other one hundred and sixty-seven hours in the week once Mass was over. The problem is not just one of a need for variety in worship, but also of the more basic ability of people to participate in the liturgical life of the church at all. Without a life with many different opportunities for common prayer, the eucharistic liturgy is like visiting a distant cousin–we know that we have a connection, but we just don't have very much to talk about.

Two consequences flow from this reality: first, we need to encourage all opportunities for common prayer. Unless the group is attached to some schismatic or heretical sect, we need to support any group in the parish that wants to pray in common. They may pray in an especially pious or archaic way, but that is all right as a starting point. The second consequence is this: parish liturgists and musicians need to do the extra work to create this broad pallet of liturgical experience, even if large numbers of people do not attend. If we start from these two realities, then we can work toward bringing these groups into the liturgical life of the church, praying the hours and celebrating all the wonders that the liturgical year has to offer.

Today we are further down the road of the priest shortage and even more in need of growth in our liturgical life. Where there are signs of an increased desire for common prayer, it has often been in the area of devotions to the Blessed Sacrament. The politicization of this type of prayer (rampant in some places) has not helped in the overall development of a varied life of prayer. Everyone needs to take a deep breath and acknowledge that, on the one hand, this extension of the Eucharist is not the only form of good prayer, nor is it the new answer to every question of how to pray. At the same time it is a prayer that most easily flows from the Eucharist and allows participants the opportunity to let the power of the Mass fill the rest of the hours of their lives.

What the article said about Eucharist now applies to Eucharist and eucharistic devotions together. We have them, but let's work to take the next steps in this journey to a full and vibrant life of worship that offers us all the means to experience Christ in community and the motivation to action for the good of the whole world.

—Glenn CJ Byer

The Rich Liturgical Pallet of the Church: Eucharist Only?

Patrick L. Malloy

The church is suffering from a bad case of monoeucharistitis. For years people have noticed the symptoms; only last year, however, was the disease finally named. Liturgical historian John Baldovin, S.J., coined the term "monoeucharistitis." Like any good word, this one's meaning is rather obvious: inflammation or irritation (-itis) caused by limiting the worship of the church to one (mono-) rite only: the Eucharist.

Mass for all Seasons

In most Catholic churches, the Mass is the only ceremony meant for the entire parish. There are, of course, other rites: the sacrament of reconciliation is celebrated regularly but in a rather private way. Baptisms and marriages also take place but in the presence of only a select group. The sick are anointed but usually in their own homes or in hospital rooms. Baptism, reconciliation, marriage and anointing of the sick are truly acts of the entire church, celebrated in its name, determining its membership, internal relationships and order. Practically, however, these rites are not parish-wide celebrations. Only one is: the Mass. It is the one liturgical occasion at which every member's presence is not only welcomed but encouraged and, on Sunday, expected.

To make matters even more eucharistic, Catholics often celebrate Mass when small groups gather for special events. Meetings sometimes begin with Mass. Retreatants may expect a retreat house to provide daily Mass. Diocesan or state conferences seldom occur without one—likely more than one—Mass.

Ask Catholics over forty. They say it was not always this way. Monoeucharistitis, although it infected the church centuries ago, has, until recently, remained almost dormant. Mass was but one event in the average parish's diverse worship schedule. During the liturgical year, the more memorable events were May crowning, forty hours, processions, patronal feasts, parish missions and first Friday observances. Lenten stations of the cross drew large crowds. Weekly novenas, rosaries and holy hours were popular. Sunday vespers became a tradition in some places, with the pastor delivering a sermon as part of the service. Such ceremonies throughout the year and the week often combined with Exposition of the Blessed Sacrament and Benediction. Thus, church worship had variety. Mass was the centerpiece of liturgical fare, but it was not the only thing on the table.

Some of these occasions and rites were of doubtful value; others, although good in themselves, gained far too much prominence and made the Mass seem relatively insignificant. Two liturgical events, Exposition of the Blessed Sacrament and Benediction, may have reinforced in some people's minds the notion that the Eucharist was something to be looked at, not something to be done and consumed. Still, despite their pitfalls, all these modes of worship created a diverse and interesting repertoire of Catholic public prayer. Times have changed. Today parishes celebrate Mass and not much else.

Perhaps monoeucharistitis is less a disease than a deprivation. The church is so fixated on the Mass that all else falls by the wayside. If Mass is good, more Masses are better, and other forms of public worship can be allowed to die. This seems to be what Catholic parishes decided. But a crisis is just around the corner. In order to maintain its high volume of Masses, the church will need what it no longer has: a large number of priests. As the pool of clergy shrinks it will become impossible to celebrate Mass at every occasion; it even will be impossible to celebrate Mass every day. What is the church to do?

Was it always this way?

A look at the days before monoeucharistitis may help. For the earliest Christians, the Eucharist was a weekly event. It occurred on Sunday. On that one day, all believers gathered to celebrate the Lord's life, death, resurrection and glorification, and to rejoice that through baptism and Christian living believers could share in this paschal mystery of Christ. On other days of the week, members of the community who were able gathered for prayer. However, the entire church assembled for Eucharist only on Sunday.

In some places each household received eucharistic bread to take home for the week. It was kept in a special place in the house and was reverently eaten each morning before anything else. In this way believers would daily break their fast with Communion. Here is the root of our word "breakfast." This daily partaking of the eucharistic food celebrated a twofold unity: the unity of the communicant both with Jesus and with his body, the church. Daily communion from the reserves in the tabernacle thus stretched the Sunday celebration through the week.

Although the entire Christian community assembled for Mass only on Sunday, small groups gathered for it on other days. Indirectly this custom came from "pagan" Romans. Long before the dawn of Christianity Romans gathered at the tombs of their loved ones on the birthday of the deceased. There, family and close friends shared a meal. It was believed that this meal brought about a communion not only among the living but also with the spirits of the dead. Romans who later converted to Christianity continued this custom at the graves of martyrs, holding the memorial meal on the anniversary of death rather than on the anniversary of birth—a "heavenly" rather than "earthly" birthday. Furthermore, they eventually substituted the Mass for the meal. They saw the Mass as a way of achieving a special unity with the martyr (now in glory) and with the Lord (present here in a particular way for the martyr's heroic death). Important though these gatherings were, they appealed only to small sub-groups of the church. The entire church was not expected to attend and did not. Sunday remained the one day of the week for Christians to gather as a body to celebrate Mass.

Gradually these celebrations at the tombs became more popular than the regular liturgies of the community. People began to go to cemeteries for memorial Masses rather than to churches for the daily community prayer. Eventually many stopped attending even Sunday Mass so that they could be present instead at the saints' tombs. The life of the church suffered, since the entire community rarely assembled to hear the scriptures, share the Eucharist and celebrate the presence of Christ in his body.

Bring the tombs to the churches

A decision was made: if people want to be at the tombs rather than at the church, then why not bring the tombs into the church? This was a radical and, to most people, disturbing proposal. It went against an ancient taboo that forbade burial of the dead within city limits. Nonetheless, leaders of the church saw no alternative. The change in custom became even more urgent as barbarian invasions threatened the Roman Empire. Civil authorities in many cases were able to defend major cities, but territories beyond city walls were more difficult to protect. This left the cemeteries unguarded. The bishops thus saw additional reason to safeguard the saints' bodies within city churches.

At first the civil government resisted the proposal, but eventually authorities agreed. Saints' bodies were moved into parish churches, usually under the altar. Finally people had reason to return to celebrations in the church. This is the origin of the relic stone. Until the reforms of the Second Vatican Council, which convened in 1963, Mass could be celebrated only on an altar that contained the relic of a saint. Gradually, as churches acquired more and more saints' bodies, or even small parts of saints' bodies, memorial Masses became increasingly common. Parishes started to celebrate memorial Masses even of saints whose relics they did not have. Thus began the custom of the daily parish Mass.

Monasteries and the "private Mass"

The transition from the one-per-week Mass to the one-per-day Mass and eventually to the many-per-day Mass was also encouraged by monasticism. Christian monasticism began as a lay movement. Many early monasteries actually forbade priests to be members. Some communities were less severe in this regard, but all carefully regulated the behavior of the clergy, not only of the ones who joined, but also of those who came as visitors. Even the most important of all Western monastic rules and the guiding document of all modern Benedictine and Cistercian communities, the "Rule of Saint Benedict" (480 C.E.), reflected caution about the clergy. As priests became more numerous in the monasteries, however, they quickly gained power and changed the face of Christian monasticism. Lay members of the monasteries, who today are called "brothers," became second-class citizens. It is one of the great ironies of the vowed life that the ordained eventually dominated. Such domination was exactly what early monastic founders feared.

Monasteries were full of priests who had no parish pastoral work. These men were ordained as ministers of the sacraments but had no communities in which to serve. This strange situation gave birth to the practice of "private Mass." Priests in the monasteries prayed the eucharistic liturgy alone, usually for the intention of someone who had made a donation to the monastic community. Thus, in each monastery, Mass would be celebrated as many times each day as there were priests in the community. In some larger houses, this meant hundreds of Masses each day. While the practice had little direct effect on parishes, there was an indirect impact: it showed, as the weekday memorial Masses of the martyrs and saints had done, that the Mass was not directly linked either to Sunday or to the assembly of the community. It was a rite that could be used for any occasion. The church had been infected with monoeucharistitis.

Where from here?

For centuries, however, the affliction was kept in check. Mass had the central place but not the only place. Various liturgical regulations and powerful strains of spirituality maintained balance in the church's public prayer. Only recently, due to a confluence of many forces, has monoeucharitsitis emerged full force.

3

Rites of Preparation,
Somewhat Restrained

Since 1994, when the following article was first published, little has changed in either the understanding or the practice regarding the rites for the preparation of the altar and the gifts for the celebration of the Eucharist. The pertinent numbers of the fifth edition of the *General Instruction of the Roman Missal* (GIRM), nos. 73–77 and 139–146, are essentially unchanged from the previous edition of the GIRM. Nevertheless, there are several points that bear repeating.

First of all, these are rites of preparation for the eucharistic prayer and for Communion. As preparatory rites, they must stand in proper proportion to the central rites of the Liturgy of the Eucharist. In practice, they must be somewhat restrained, although on occasion they may take on a more solemn character.

These rites are more of action and gesture than of word and text. One still sees priests who always insist on saying the two prayers for the placing of the bread and chalice on the altar. The GIRM (142) clearly indicates that when there is singing or instrumental music, which should be the norm for Sundays and solemnities, they should be said in a quiet voice. Let the visual action of placing the gifts on the altar speak for itself. Even when there is no singing, there is no requirement that these prayers be said aloud—they may be, but never need be, said aloud. (GIRM 142)

The primary gesture in these rites is not of offering or raising up, but of setting down or solemnly placing the gifts on the altar. The offering gesture of the Eucharist is found at the end of the eucharistic prayer when the chalice and paten are elevated during the final doxology. (GIRM 152)

Incense may appropriately be used on more solemn and formal occasions. The gifts, the altar, the priest and the people may all be incensed. (GIRM 75) The manner of incensation has been greatly simplified from that required in the Tridentine Mass. Now the gifts are incensed with three swings of the censer (center, left, right) or by making a cross over the gifts with the censer. The altar is incensed with single swings of the censer as the priest circles it. The priest and people are incensed with three swings of the censer. (GIRM 277)

The cup may be prepared at the side table (credence) by the deacon rather than at the altar. This allows the action of the priest placing the chalice on the altar to come to the forefront.

The chalice may be covered with a white or colored veil when the cup is placed on the side table before Mass begins. (GIRM 118) The new edition of the GIRM indicates that the use of the veil is no longer an obligation.

When Communion is distributed under both kinds, it is preferable that only one cup is on the altar and that additional wine be placed in a flagon or pitcher. This allows the symbolism of one cup to be evident to the assembly. Communion under both kinds should be normative for the Sunday celebration of the Eucharist.

The use of one paten, plate or dish also helps to communicate in a non-verbal manner the one bread of the Eucharist; the priest does not need to have a separate paten. The people are to be communicated with bread consecrated at the Mass being celebrated. Accordingly, care should be taken to consecrate a sufficient amount of eucharistic bread at each Mass.

Proper attention to the actions and gestures of these rites of preparation and presentation and care for the details of these rites will make them flow smoothly and allow them to be seen for what they are: the preparation of the bread and wine which will become the body and blood of Christ and of the eucharistic assembly which will receive them.

—Alan F. Detscher

The Preparation of the Gifts and the Altar

Alan F. Detscher

Of all the parts of the Order of Mass that Pope Paul VI revised in 1969 and ultimately published in the *Roman Missal* of 1970, the rites for the preparation of the gifts and the altar are probably the most changed from the Tridentine *Roman Missal* of Pope Pius V. Although the rites changed, many clergy and lay people still understand them in terms of the Tridentine Missal. Symptomatic of this is the continued use of the term "offertory," elevations of the plate and cup, use of music that stresses offering and minimal washing of hands by the priest as he declaims his sinfulness. Other practices arose: saying all the prayers aloud and presenting symbolic gifts.

A look at history

Second Century. The earliest description we have of the eucharistic celebration is by Justin Martyr (c. 150 C.E.). Justin, a layman and scholar, tried to explain the Christian faith and liturgies to non-believers in his *Apology*. In the course of his defense he described the Sunday eucharistic celebration when it was combined with baptism and when it was not. In both descriptions he explained that the table is prepared by deacons, who place on it as much bread and wine mixed with water as they needed for those present and those absent. He noted that the bread and wine for the Eucharist were brought by the faithful, who also brought other gifts for the poor. The collection did not take place at the time of preparation but at the end of the celebration. (How interesting that the collection is one of the most ancient features of the liturgy!) Once the table was prepared, the *president* (bishop) went to it for the eucharistic prayer. Justin made no mention of songs or prayers to accompany the preparation. The preparation was purely functional. Deacons prepared things quickly and simply.

Third Century. Around 250 C.E., Hippolytus of Rome wrote what has become our second eucharistic prayer. In his writings he too described how deacons prepared the table for Eucharist by taking the necessary bread and wine from the gifts people brought. Again we find no prayers or songs accompanying the practical action of preparing the table. When all was ready, the bishop and presbyters came to the table and laid their hands on the gifts. Then the bishop proceeded with the eucharistic prayer in his own words. The description of the bishop and presbyters laying their hands on the gifts was new. This ancient gesture continues today in the eucharistic prayer when the priest extends his hands over the gifts and invokes the Holy Spirit to transform them into the body and blood of Christ. This invocation in the eucharistic prayer is known as the *epiclesis*.

Seventh Century. In the seventh-century *First Roman Order* we find an elaborate description of a solemn Mass celebrated by the pope. When the liturgy of the word was over, the choir began to sing what was later called the offertory song. Essentially it was a psalm sung responsorially: verse and refrain. Eventually the verses disappeared and only the refrain remained.

Deacons first covered the altar with a large corporal. The pope, archdeacon, deacons, subdeacons and other officials then collected loaves of bread from various groups and placed them on a linen cloth. The archdeacon and deacons received flasks of wine and poured the wine into a large cup. The archdeacon arranged the loaves on the altar and prepared a large cup of wine to which water was added by a subdeacon. Acolytes held the remaining wine. The pope went to his chair to wash his hands. Then he came forward to place loaves for the clergy and himself on the altar with the cup next to them. When all was ready, the choir stopped singing and the pope said a brief prayer. Eventually this prayer was said inaudibly and became known as the Secret Prayer, but its more ancient name was the Prayer over the Gifts, the title the church has restored. This variable prayer was the *only* prayer during the preparation. Despite the increasing complexity of the preparations due to the large number of ministers, the essential elements are the offering of the bread and wine by the people and the placing of these gifts on the altar. At this stage in history three new elements were added: the offertory song, the washing of hands and the prayer over the gifts.

Tenth Century. By the tenth century a new layer of complexity developed. This new complexity became firmly set in the sixteenth-century *Roman Missal* of Pius V. Earlier preparation rites were practical: bread and wine were placed on the altar in quantities sufficient for communion. With the Middle Ages, practical things received symbolic interpretations. Prayers and actions multiplied and greatly confused the nature of the preparation of the altar and the gifts. These added prayers and actions actually anticipated the language and, to some extent, the structure of the eucharistic prayer. Some new prayers focused on the unworthiness of the priest. Others used words referring to the bread and wine as if they were already the body and blood of Christ. Many expressions of offering were used throughout the preparation, and it was commonly referred to as the "offertory."

Sixteenth Century. The *Tridentine Missal* had an offertory song. The cup and plate were unveiled—the corporal had been spread at the beginning of Mass—and the priest took the plate and raised it in a gesture of offering as he said a prayer of offering. He then placed the host on the corporal and slid the plate under the corporal. Then he poured wine and a small amount of water into the cup as he said a prayer based on the ancient opening prayer of Christmas. He elevated the cup and said another prayer of offering. The cup was placed on the altar and covered. The priest bowed and said a prayer asking God to accept the offerings and a prayer asking the Holy Spirit to bless the sacrifice. If incense was used, the offerings were incensed at this time with elaborate series of crosses and circles. The altar, priest and members of the assembly were also incensed. During the incensation the priest recited Psalm 141:2–4. Then he washed his hands as he recited Psalm 25:6–12. He then bowed and asked the Holy Trinity to accept the offerings. Finally, he invited the people to pray that the sacrifice be accepted by God and after their response he said the prayer over the gifts inaudibly.

Missal of Paul VI

The reformed Order of Mass of Pope Paul VI after the Second Vatican Council radically simplified the preparation of the gifts and the altar. The rite is described in the *General Instruction of the Roman Missal* (GIRM), #49–53 and 100–107:

> 49. At the beginning of the liturgy of the Eucharist the gifts, which will become Christ's body and blood, are brought to the altar.
>
> First the altar, the Lord's table, which is the center of the whole eucharistic liturgy, is prepared: the corporal, purificator, missal, and chalice are placed on it (unless the chalice is prepared at the side table).
>
> The gifts are then brought forward. It is desirable for the faithful to present the bread and wine, which are accepted by the priest or

deacon at a convenient place. The gifts are placed on the altar to the accompaniment of the prescribed texts. Even though the faithful no longer, as in the past, bring the bread and wine for the liturgy from their homes, the rite of carrying up the gifts retains the same spiritual value and meaning.

This is also the time to receive money or other gifts for the church or the poor brought by the faithful or collected at the Mass. These are to be put in a suitable place but not on the altar.

50. The procession bringing the gifts is accompanied by the presentation song, which continues at least until the gifts have been placed on the altar. The rules for this song are the same as those for the entrance song (26). If it is not sung, the presentation antiphon is omitted.

51. The gifts on the altar and the altar itself may be incensed. This is a symbol of the Church's offering and prayer going up to God. Afterward the deacon or other minister may incense the priest and the people.

52. The priest then washes his hands as an expression of his desire to be cleansed within.

53. Once the gifts have been placed on the altar and the accompanying rites completed the preparation of the gifts comes to an end through the invitation to pray with the priest and the prayer over the gifts, which are a preparation for the eucharistic prayer.

According to the *General Instruction*, clearly the rites are no longer seen as an offertory but rather as preparation for the eucharistic prayer and Communion.

Preparation of the altar

First, the altar is prepared by bringing the corporal to the altar and unfolding it. There is no justification for leaving the corporal on the altar all the time or for having it pressed flat. Its purpose is to catch particles of the Eucharist, and it serves as a sign of reverence for the Eucharist, which is placed on it. After the distribution of Communion, the corporal is refolded and returned to the side table. Other things necessary for the Eucharist also are placed on the altar: purificator, *Sacramentary*, cup. Nothing unrelated to the actual celebration of the Eucharist should be placed on the altar. Before Mass begins, the altar is covered with a single altar cloth—nothing more. Out of respect for the altar, other objects such as papers, hymnals or eyeglasses are not placed on the altar. Although flowers are not placed on the altar, they may be arranged suitably near it. At least two lighted candles are placed either on or near the altar. A cross is on or near the altar and clearly visible to the assembly. (GIRM, 268–70)

Preparation of the gifts

Presentation. The revised rites stress the procession of the gifts by the faithful, their presentation to the priest, the placing of the gifts on the altar and the prayer over the gifts. These are the central rites of this portion of the liturgy. The prayers of the priest, the incensation and the washing of hands are all clearly secondary elements.

The procession of the faithful with the gifts is a restoration of the ancient practice of the church. It is a constant reminder that the bread and wine are the gifts of the church, gifts that are transformed and returned to the faithful as their spiritual food and drink: the body and blood of Christ. The collection is also a part of the gifts of the faithful and should be included in the procession. Although it may at times be appropriate to include symbolic gifts in the procession, this normally should be avoided. During the collection, procession and placing of the bread and wine on the altar, a presentation antiphon with or without psalm verses or a suitable song may be sung. If there is to be no singing, the antiphon is not recited and is simply omitted. The text of the song should not focus on offering but on praise. Instrumental music or an additional song may be appropriate if the collection takes a long time. Since the gesture of placing the gifts on the altar is more important than the prayers of the priest as he does this, the song should not conclude until the priest is ready to invite the people to pray and say the prayer over the gifts. Instrumental music may be used in place of a song throughout the rite until the priest is ready to begin the prayer over the gifts and its invitation. Other options are indicated in the statement of the Bishops' Committee on the Liturgy: *Music in Catholic Worship* (1983), 71.

Placing the gifts on the altar. After the ministers receive the gifts, the cup may be prepared at the side table by the deacon or the priest himself. When the priest reaches the altar, the deacon hands him the plate with the bread. It is preferable that all the bread for the Eucharist be in one container that does not look like a cup but rather like a dish or plate. Only materials that are suitable for this function and not common dishes should be used. In spite of the admonitions of all the popes of this past century, it is still common to find most of the hosts for a particular Mass taken from the tabernacle.

The *General Instruction* states:

> 56. (h) It is most desirable that the faith-
> ful receive the Lord's body from hosts conse-
> crated at the same Mass and that, in the
> instances when it is permitted, they share the
> chalice. Then even through the signs com-
> munion will stand out more clearly as a shar-
> ing in the sacrifice actually being celebrated.

If Communion is to be given under both kinds, the wine to be consecrated in addition to that in the cup should be in a suitable pitcher or flagon designed for this purpose.

Inaudible prayers. In contrast to the Tridentine offertory rite, the present rite is one of solemnly placing gifts on the altar. The gesture used by the priest to do this has completely changed. He is to hold the plate slightly raised above the altar (about a hand-breadth) as he says the prayer. The plate is not held up high as in an offering gesture; this is done only at the final doxology of the eucharistic prayer. The prayer that accompanies the gesture should be normally said inaudibly, especially when the people are singing. The priest should not wait for the music to stop before he says the prayer. Even when there is no singing, there is no obligation to say the prayer aloud; it always may be said inaudibly.

When the cup is brought to the altar, it is placed to the side and not on the corporal so that the act of placing the cup on the altar may be clearly seen. The cup may be prepared at the side table or at the side of the altar by the deacon or priest. The prayer for mixing the wine and water is always said inaudibly. The priest takes the cup or receives it from the deacon and, holding it slightly raised, says the prayer inaudibly.

The two prayers for placing the gifts on the altar are new compositions based on ancient Jewish blessings at table. On occasions when the priest does say them aloud the people may respond "Blessed be God forever" but the response is not required. The prayer that follows the two blessing prayers is always said inaudibly. It is based on a prayer found in the Tridentine rite.

Incensing and washing. The gifts, altar, priest and all members of the assembly may be incensed simply, without the elaborations of the former "offertory." Incense depicts prayer rising to God. It honors the gifts, the altar and the people.

The priest washes his hands, reciting the accompanying psalm verse inaudibly. Hand washing used to have a practical function after all the gifts were received. Now it serves more as a sign of spiritual cleansing. Since it is a washing, the previous practice of wetting the tips of the fingers rather than the whole hands should be discontinued. Larger vessels and more water are needed now. There is no provision for omitting the washing of hands. All actions up to and including the washing of hands may be accompanied by song or instrumental music. Once the priest has washed his hands, the music should stop. This requires attention by music ministers.

Prayer over the gifts. The priest invites the people to pray, and they respond. This invitation and response has taken various forms over the years. It serves to conclude the preparation and call for the prayer of the people.

In this second function it is like the "Let us pray" of the opening prayer and the prayer after Communion. After the people's response, the priest may pause for a moment of silent prayer and then sing or say the prayer over the gifts.

Conclusion

Often misunderstood, the preparation of the gifts and the altar is to be brief. It prepares for the eucharistic prayer and Communion. From gifts God has given us we present bread, wine and money. Money assists in the continuing work of the church. By the word of Christ and the invocation of the Holy Spirit, bread and wine will become the bread of life and the cup of eternal salvation, which we receive in holy Communion.

The preparation should always be simple so that the notion of offering can stand out clearly in the eucharistic prayer. The preparation is not a liturgical high point. The eucharistic prayer and Communion form the climax. The right perspective will surface when all ministers of the assembly understand the function of the ritual elements of the Mass. It confuses matters to reintroduce things that reflect a previous theology and practice. Blessed be God forever!

4

Gifts Are Prepared for Distribution

This article, first written in 1996, is still valid and does reflect the rubrics and other indications in the GIRM 2002 and the *Ordo Missae* 2002. For the moment these are only found in the Latin texts as printed in the *Missale Romanum–Editio Typica Tertia* (Third Edition) published by the Vatican Press in 2002.

The first three gestures referred to in the article remain exactly the same, and so the suggestions for their understanding and use remain worthwhile. The numbers in the new GIRM and the *Ordo Missae* are different, but their texts and so their interpretation remain the same.

The only point where there has been some development is in the fourth gesture, *Just before the Distribution of Communion*. With that in mind I will look at the "new texts" for this gesture using the "new numbers" for reference. For my quotations from the GIRM 2002, I will use the "English Language Study Translation" Secretariat for the Liturgy of the National Conference of Catholic Bishops, 2000, changed to conform to the Latin as appears in the 2002 *Missale Romanum*. For the quotations for the *Ordo Missae* 2002 I will offer my own translation from the Latin text of the 2002 *Missale Romanum*.

We read as follows in the GIRM 2002:

> The priest prepares himself by the prayer, said inaudibly, that he may receive Christ's body and blood to good effect. The faithful do the same in silent prayer.

The priest then shows the eucharistic bread above the paten or above the chalice to the faithful and invites them to the banquet of Christ. Along with the faithful, he recites the prayer of humility in the words prescribed by the Gospels. (GIRM 2002 84)

At the conclusion of the prayer, the priest genuflects, takes the eucharistic bread, and, holding it slightly above the paten or above the chalice, while facing the people, says: *Behold the Lamb of God.* With the people he adds: *Lord, I am not worthy.* (GIRM 2002 157)

For a concelebration:

Then the principal celebrant takes a host consecrated at the same Mass, and, holding it slightly raised above the paten or above the chalice, facing the people says...(GIRM 2002 243)

For a priest and a server:

...if the minister is to receive communion, the priest turns to the minister, holds it slightly raised above the paten or above the chalice... says...(GIRM 2002 268)

Then in the *Ordo Missae* 2002 it says:

The priest genuflects, takes a host, holds it slightly elevated over the paten or over the chalice, facing the people, he says aloud...(*Ordo Missae* 2002 137)

And for a Mass with a priest and a server:

The priest genuflects, takes a host, holds it slightly elevated over the paten or over the chalice, facing the minister, he says aloud...(*Ordo Missae cuius unus tantum minister participat* 2002 26)

These citations of the GIRM 2002 and the *Ordo Missae* 2002 continue and strengthen the previous emphasis on the norm of using eucharistic bread consecrated at the same Mass. The eucharistic bread shown to the faithful must come from the present Mass and not from the tabernacle.

The other change is that the host from the same Mass may be held slightly raised above/over the paten (as previously) or above/over the chalice.

Looking at the *why* here allows us to see the required continuity of the gifts being prepared for distribution and the present celebration of Mass. The reason, therefore, for the added possibility of showing the chalice in this gesture would seem to suggest that the chalice here is being offered for the Communion of the faithful. It would therefore make best sense logically and liturgically to show the chalice to the people at this point only if the intent is to give Communion under both kinds. Otherwise, it is a misleading gesture, offering something (the chalice) not then given.

—Philip J. Sandstrom

Four Gestures
Similar but Not Identical

Philip J. Sandstrom

When a presider for Mass (presbyter or bishop) goes on vacation he gets a chance to do something he usually cannot do the rest of the year. He can go on a "busman's holiday" and sit with the assembly—not in his own church, of course, but somewhere else. A vacation can give him a chance to look, to think and to pray with others celebrating liturgy. Sometimes this experience breeds self-satisfaction—"we do better at home"—but more often it is a learning experience.

These vacations can be a source of ideas for new possibilities: for the ministers (reading, music leading, serving, ushering, processional movement); for the better placement of the furniture (altar, chairs, ambo, font); for audiovisuals (to draw the senses and the whole person toward the act of glorifying the Trinity and delighting in God's bride, the church); and for the presider if he has the humble courage to watch his brother presbyter and evaluate his own habits of presiding. The questions a presider must ask are, "How do I do what I do? Why? How is this work perceived by assembly members? What meaning do they take from what they hear and see?"

Ritual inertia

In the churches there are many well-known examples of unthinking "arrangements" that arose because of some half-forgotten event: cluttering the altar with extra books and papers; leaving the corporal open between celebrations and when not needed during the celebration; using book stands, candles, flowers and microphones, which hide rather than disclose the mysteries. Anyone sitting in the assembly can add to this list a favorite "mystification" or two. These are obvious to onlookers and they obscure the process and purpose of worship. They exist because of unthinking, unquestioning "ritual inertia" and they stick like barnacles.

It must be recalled that one of the main purposes of the liturgical reforms after the Second Vatican Council was to sweep the "liturgical mantelpiece" clean of the souvenirs of such inertial neglect that had collected for centuries.

Ritual momentum

In this article, however, I want to bring your serious attention to the inertial neglect not of some objects but rather of some gestures. Four times during the eucharistic liturgy the presider is directed by the *General Instruction of the Roman Missal* (GIRM) and the *Ordo Missae* to make *similar but not identical gestures*: 1. at the preparation of the gifts, 2. during the eucharistic institution narrative (consecration), 3. during the doxology at the end of the *anaphora* (eucharistic prayer) and 4. just before the distribution of communion.

It is necessary to consider why these similar but not identical gestures are called for and how they look to the assembly for whose worship, after all, they are being done. It is also necessary to keep in mind the purpose of the reform after the Council and not rely only on inertia or folk memories in performing them. We examine these gestures in order from the instructions given in the *Sacramentary*:

At the preparation of the gifts

At the altar the priest receives the paten with the bread from a minister. With both hands he holds it slightly raised above the altar and says the accompanying prayer. Then he places the paten with the bread on the corporal. (GIRM 102)

The priest stands at the side of the altar and pours wine and a little water into the chalice, saying the accompanying prayer softly. The minister presents the cruets. He returns to the middle of the altar, takes the chalice, raises it a little with both hands, and says the appointed prayer. Then he places the chalice on the corporal and may cover it with a pall. (GIRM 103)

The *Ordo Missae* gives the same instructions (19, 20, 21), giving also the texts of the prayers to be said "inaudibly" (*secreto*). Only if there is no music may the presider say these words audibly—he need not do so—that "the people may respond."

Looked at calmly here, what is taking place is not any grand gesture of offering but rather a formal table setting. It is an indication to the assembled people that these are the gifts to be used and received at this celebration. We are going to ask the Lord to change them for us and to change us to be effectively nourished on divine life. In secular terms this is the same gesture we see in good restaurants, on television or in the movies when the chef brings out the specialty of the day and places it on the table before the guests. The foods are shown with love and pride and then put cleanly and with dignity on the table. The chef and the presider perform the same action straightforwardly as a ritual service before the guests and assembly members. The action is an important part of their respective ministries. It is important for the event, but *it is not the event itself.* (Family customs of meals for Thanksgiving and Christmas come to mind here; just think of the "solemn entrance" with the ham or turkey that precedes the joy of the banquet.) The "slight raising above the altar" prescribed here is only to call the attention of the assembly to today's gifts of bread and wine—no more and certainly no less.

During the eucharistic institution narrative

During the eucharistic institution narrative (consecration) there are no specific instructions for gestures prescribed in the *General Instruction of the Roman Missal.* The instructions are exactly the same, however, in the *Ordo Missae* for all the *anaphoras,* with only one slight variant in Eucharistic Prayer I (Roman Canon): "He looks upward" during the consecration of the bread. No further variants occur in the other eucharistic prayers: the three others in the center of the *Sacramentary,* the three for children, the two for reconciliation and the one newly approved for English speakers, *Eucharistic Prayer for Masses for Various Needs and Occasions.* The common texts for relevant instructions in all these *anaphoras* follow:

- The words of the Lord in the following formulas should be spoken clearly and distinctly, as their meaning demands...
- He takes the bread and, raising it a little above the altar, continues...
- He bows slightly...
- He shows the consecrated host to the people, places it on the paten, and genuflects in adoration...
- Then he continues...
- He takes the chalice, and, raising it a little above the altar, continues...
- He bows slightly...
- He shows the chalice to the people, places it on the corporal, and genuflects in adoration...

Here we read "raising it a little above the altar." "He shows the consecrated host/chalice to the people." The *action* of showing is not too different from "holding it slightly above the altar," but the *why* is very different. One must look carefully at the *why.*

200

The purpose of "raising it a little" is to focus attention on the gifts during the repetition of the words of the Lord: to focus the attention of both the presider and everyone else present. By means of these iconic gifts we all can share in the saving covenant of Jesus: the paschal mystery. Therefore, they are to be held up "a little" for our concentrated attention when the Lord's instructions and words are ritually repeated. In each case the consecrated gifts are to be shown to the people for veneration. There is here no indication for further lifting up the gifts. Rather, it seems there is to be a pause for veneration.

There is no indication or reason for the presider to hold the gifts over his head—unless some part of the assembly is behind his back. (This was the reason given for the presider to hold the gifts over his head before the Second Vatican Council in the Missal of Pope Pius V. The presider used to have his back to the people, but this is rarely true nowadays.) When the presider holds the gifts over his head, he likely is giving a glaring example of "inertial drift" or folk memory, doing something called for neither by the instructions themselves nor by the needs of people gathered behind him.

During the doxology at the end of the *anaphora*

The third instance of the gesture is during the doxology at the end of the eucharistic prayer. The instructions here are exactly the same in all the *anaphoras*:

He takes the chalice and paten with the host and, lifting them up, sings or says:..

Notice that it is no longer "slightly" or "a little" but wholeheartedly "lifting them up, sings or says..." This is the real elevation of the Mass. Historically and functionally this elevation shows the assembled people that, through the grace of the successfully completed eucharistic prayer, the Holy Spirit has made these gifts the body and blood of Jesus and the divine nourishment of the faithful.

We read further:

> At the final doxology of the eucharistic prayer, the deacon stands next to the priest, holding up the chalice as the priest raises the paten with the eucharistic bread, until the people have said the acclamation: Amen. (GIRM 135)

The doxology of the eucharistic prayer
may be sung or said by the celebrant alone or
by all the concelebrants with him. (GIRM 191)

Here the deacon performs his task with the chalice, all the concelebrants join in the triumphant doxology and the people add their ratifying "Amen." In the middle of the second century, Saint Justin (layman, philosopher, theologian and martyr) described this event in his *First Apology* (65:1): "When [the presider] has finished the prayers and thanksgiving, all the people give their assent by saying 'Amen.'" "Amen" is Hebrew for "So be it." God's gifts are to be held up in triumph for the people's approval, not slightly or a little but really lifted up. This is the joyful *culmination* of the celebration. It leads directly to the fourth instance of the gesture.

Just before the distribution of Communion

We read as follows:

The priest then shows the eucharistic
bread to the faithful. He invites them to participate in the meal and leads them in an act
of humility, using words from the Gospel.
(GIRM 56g)

These instructions are added:

The priest genuflects. Taking the host, he
raises it slightly over the paten and, facing the
people, says aloud...*(Ordo Missae* 133)

"Raises it slightly" recalls the gesture at the preparation of the gifts, and "shows the eucharistic bread" reminds us of the eucharistic institution narrative or consecration. Looking at the *why* here allows us to see both the continuity of the gifts being prepared now for distribution and the focus of attention on the iconic gifts needed for salvation. This is not the *culmination* but its *continuation* in our sharing it as nourishment.

Obviously it does make more logical—and liturgical—sense if the people are being served, as the *Ordo Missae* strongly suggests in the section (17) on the preparation of the altar and the gifts:

It is most desirable that the faithful
receive the Lord's body from hosts consecrated
at the same Mass and that, in the instances
when it is permitted, they share in the chalice.
Then even through the signs Communion

will stand out more clearly as a sharing in the sacrifice actually being celebrated. (GIRM 56h; also *Eucharisticum mysterium* 31)

Conclusion

I hope I have given my brother presbyters—and all interested in worship that is good, intelligent and correctly done—something to think about and perhaps to act upon. Why we do what we do is at least as important as how we do it, especially if it helps us overcome inertial neglect.

5

Center and Summit
of the Entire Celebration

When I was invited to write "The Assembly's Ownership of the Eucharistic Prayer: Why and How" for *Today's Liturgy* back in 1994, the primary official document guiding Roman Rite celebration was the fourth edition of the *General Instruction of the Roman Missal* (GIRM). A new edition of the GIRM appeared in 2000 as a published extract from the third edition of *Roman Missal*. When that third edition of the *Roman Missal* in Latin finally saw the light of day in printed form in 2002, this new edition of the GIRM likewise appeared in a further edited and corrected form. Although at the time I am writing this introduction, neither the *Roman Missal* 2002 nor the GIRM 2002 has been officially translated into English, I have been able to consult the Latin texts and find some interesting correlations with my 1994 article.

The fundamental theological understanding of the eucharistic prayer has not changed between the fourth and the fifth editions of the GIRM; indeed, many of the passages about the eucharistic prayers remain word for word the same. However, my 1994 article noted that only nine eucharistic prayers were officially approved for use in the United States. With the approval of the *Eucharistic Prayer for Masses for Various Needs and Occasions* (the so-called "Swiss Synod" prayer) in an official English translation, ten eucharistic prayers are now available in the euchology of the Roman Rite. GIRM 2002 emphasizes that the laity are not to recite or sing portions of the prayer reserved to the presiding celebrant (such as the "Through him, with him, in him..."); rather they are to recite or sing the interventions (responses to the

Opening Dialogue; Holy, Holy, Holy; Memorial Acclamation; Great Amen), explicitly mentioning for the first time other acclamations during the prayer as approved by the competent territorial authority (i.e., bishops' conference).

My 1994 article distinguished between a Roman "proclamatory" model for the postures assumed during the eucharistic prayer (standing except for the "consecration") with an American "devotional" model (kneeling from the post-*Sanctus* through the doxology). Interestingly, GIRM 2002 adds a reason for remaining standing (because of health concerns) to the reasons previously given for remaining standing even through the consecration in the Roman "proclamatory" model. However, the American bishops have requested and received permission from the Congregation for Divine Worship to continue the American "devotional" model for posture during the eucharistic prayer. In response I would simply repeat the argument I made in 1994 that "manifesting the unity of the praying assembly and the unity of the eucharistic prayer" remain good reasons for having all assume a standing posture throughout the prayer's proclamation.

In 1994 I suggested a variety of gestures that might enhance the laity's participation in the prayer: standing in *orant* position for the proclamation of the preface and/or doxology; extending hands toward the bread and wine (like concelebrating presbyters) during the first *epiclesis*; praying with hands open-palmed during the intercession. I was delighted to read in the new GIRM that, if the laity remains standing throughout the consecration, they are to bow toward the altar (along with the ordained concelebrants) when the presiding celebrant genuflects after the consecration of each element. Clearly the gesture of bowing toward the elements is not seen by those who constructed GIRM 2002 as a properly clerical gesture: it belongs to all the baptized.

In 1994 I noted that on May 15, 1975, *Passim quaeritur* directed that elements of the eucharistic prayer that should be sung should be printed in place and not relegated to an appendix since this practice "has the...advantage of reminding the priest celebrant that these parts of the Mass are *as a rule* to the sung." It was therefore an anomaly to find that the second edition of the *Roman Missal* in its Latin printing (1975) did not follow this instruction. Happily, the *Roman Missal* 2002 does print *Eucharistic Prayers I-IV* with musical notation in place. Musical notation also appears for the two *Eucharistic Prayers for Reconciliation* and the *Eucharistic Prayer for Masses for Various Needs and Occasions*, but the prayers themselves are placed in an appendix. (No musical notation appears for the three *Eucharistic Prayers for Masses with Children*, but that is to be expected since the rubrical note states that these prayers are only to be proclaimed in the vernacular.)

GIRM 2002 does not address in any detailed way environmental issues associated with the eucharistic prayer. However, a request from the American bishops that multi-colored cloths be placed on the altar (as long as the uppermost cloth remains white) was approved by the Congregation for Divine Worship.

I concluded my 1994 article by suggesting that catechesis on the eucharistic prayer could be attempted by means of a short address before the prayer begins, reflecting on the eucharistic prayer during a homily, or using the usual means of informing the praying community (bulletin announcements, classes, and so on.). I believe with the promulgation of the *Roman Missal* 2002 and the GIRM 2002 we have a perfect opportunity to catechize a new generation on this central element of the eucharistic prayer. The Bishops' Committee on the Liturgy has created significant catechetical materials for the United States implementation of the new GIRM. Diocesan offices of worship are likewise providing fine catechetical aids for local worshiping communities. (I hope readers will permit me the indulgence of the office of worship under the direction of Vicki Klima). Members of the North American Academy of Liturgy are producing "Homily Suggestions" in which various aspects of liturgical catechesis are correlated with the Sunday lectionary readings. I hope in 2003, as I hoped in 1994, that we take this opportunity to deepen our own knowledge of and love for the eucharistic prayer, "center and summit of the entire [eucharistic] celebration."

—Jan Michael Joncas

The Assembly's Ownership of the Eucharistic Prayer: Why and How

Jan Michael Joncas

> Now the center and summit of the entire celebration begins: the eucharistic prayer, a prayer of thanksgiving and sanctification. The priest invites the people to lift up their hearts to the Lord in prayer and thanks; he unites them with himself in the prayer he addresses in their name to the Father through Jesus Christ. The meaning of the prayer is that the entire congregation joins itself to Christ in acknowledging the great things God has done and in offering the sacrifice.

These words from article 54 of the *General Instruction of the Roman Missal* (GIRM) provide a wealth of reflection for Roman Catholics on the central importance of the eucharistic prayer in their common worship. The article defines the eucharistic prayer as "a prayer of thanksgiving and sanctification," although reading the approved reformed texts will quickly indicate how much of the prayer remains supplicatory and intercessory. It indicates the ritual participants in the prayer: a "priest" (presumably a validly ordained presbyter or bishop) who vocally enunciates the prayer in the name of the "people" (presumably the baptized, although some of the texts extend their compass to include all humanity). It sketches the theological content of the prayer as acknowledgment of God's great deeds (what liturgical theologians term *anamnesis)* and sacrificial offering, as the community's self-oblation is conjoined to the "re-presentation" of Christ's own sacrificial self-offering at Calvary. It also declares the importance of this element of the Mass: the eucharistic prayer is the "center and summit of the entire celebration."

Contemporary commentators have noted that the ritual experience of the eucharistic prayer in parish celebration rarely matches the description given in the GIRM 54. Most liturgy planners tend to spend more time on "creative" additions to the preparation of the gifts and/or the Communion rite than on this center and summit of the celebration, since the eucharistic prayer is perceived as the exclusive preserve of the presiding cleric(s). Some communities have sought to increase the vocal participation of the laity in the eucharistic prayer beyond the pre-scribed norms by a variety of strategies, from having the assembly recite or sing portions (e.g., "Through him, with him, in him...") or the entire text of the prayer along with the priest-celebrant, to using texts other than the nine that are officially approved. Division in posture during the proclamation of the prayer (clerics standing, laity kneeling) reinforces the notion that the prayer "belongs" to the ordained. In pas-toral practice gestures during the prayer—praying with hands held aloft (the so-called *orant* position), praying with hands outstretched over the gifts and/or assembly during the *epiclesis* ("invocation"), lift-ing/presenting the bread and cup, bowing or genuflecting—are almost completely reserved to clerics in pastoral practice.

While a few complete musical settings of the approved eucharistic prayers have appeared and are employed in some places, in many wor-shiping communities only the "Holy, Holy, Holy," "Memorial Acclamation" and concluding "Amen" are sung while the rest of the text is recited; frequently the musical settings of these acclamations employ diverse keys, thematic material and styles that fracture the sense of the unity of the prayer. As Kevin Seasoltz OSB asserts:

> [A]ttention to the celebration of the eucharistic prayer remains undeveloped in comparison with the attention that has been given to other aspects of the liturgy...As a result most worshiping assemblies presume that the eucharistic prayer is a lengthy discur-sive monologue, uttered by the liturgical presider and interrupted occasionally by brief acclamations sung or recited by either a choir or the whole assembly. They often feel that they are being subjected to a barrage of irrel-evant or incomprehensible words...The problem can be solved only be attending to the non-verbal as well as the verbal aspects of the celebration and by grounding construc-tive efforts in a clear grasp of the eucharistic prayer as collective symbolic behavior.[1]

---

[1] R. K. Seasoltz, "Non-Verbal Symbols and the Eucharistic Prayer," in *New Eucharistic Prayers: An Ecumenical Study of Their Development and Structure*, ed. F. C. Senn (Mahwah: Paulist, 1987) 217.

This article will suggest some areas that may help the liturgical assembly to take "ownership" of the eucharistic prayer: posture, gesture, music, environment and catechesis. We will limit our discussion to the nine Roman Rite eucharistic prayers officially approved for Roman Catholic liturgical use in the United States.

Posture

GIRM 62 powerfully states the case for common posture among the members of the liturgical assembly:

> In the celebration of Mass the faithful are a holy people, a people God has made his own, a royal priesthood: they give thanks to the Father and offer the victim not only through the hands of the priest but also together with him and learn to offer themselves...They therefore are to shun any appearance of individualism or division, keeping before their mind that they have the one Father in heaven and therefore are all brothers and sisters to each other. They should become one body...above all by offering the sacrifice together and sharing in the Lord's table. There is a beautiful expression of this unity when the faithful maintain uniformity in their actions and in standing, sitting, or kneeling.

But an attentive reading of the GIRM and its "Appendix for Use in the Dioceses of the United States" reveals different models for the postures to be employed during the eucharistic prayer. GIRM 21 declares:

> [A]t every Mass the people should stand...from the prayer over the gifts until the end of Mass, except...[t]hey should kneel at the consecration unless prevented by the lack of space, the number of people present, or some other good reason.

However, in 1969 the National Conference of Catholic Bishops voted that GIRM 21 "should be adapted so that the people kneel beginning after the singing or recitation of the *Sanctus* until after the 'Amen' of the eucharistic prayer, that is, before the Lord's Prayer."

The Roman "proclamatory" model clearly prefers that the entire assembly, clerics and laity, should assume the same standing posture for most of the prayer. The assembly is directed to kneel for the "consecration" (presumably during the recitation of the institution narrative); this change in posture seems to indicate the centrality of the consecratory texts much as the prescribed bow at the words "by the power of the Holy Spirit/he was born of the Virgin Mary, and became man" indicates the centrality of the incarnation in the proclamation of the creed. Yet the same article notes that the assembly may stand throughout the prayer for a variety of reasons, both practical and theoretical. I would argue that manifesting the unity of the praying assembly and the unity of the eucharistic prayer could be one of the "good reasons" for having all assume a standing posture throughout the prayer's proclamation.

The American "devotional" model seems less coherent, since the same posture is prescribed for the assembly during the proclamation of a variety of diverse elements in the prayer: post-*Sanctus*, *epicleses*, *anamnesis*, offering, intercessions and doxology, in addition to the institution narrative. While kneeling as evidence of devotion during the institution narrative or as an expression of supplication during the intercessions might be appropriate, it is less easy to connect the kneeling posture with the proclamatory and invocative dynamics of the post-*Sanctus*, *epicleses* and doxology, not to speak of the difficulty of singing acclamations from a kneeling posture. As was already noted above, dividing the eucharistic assembly by posture into clerical and lay participants does not reflect the theology enunciated in GIRM 54 in which the "entire congregation" joins itself to Christ in the eucharistic prayer.

Gesture

The gestures prescribed in the rubrics for the eucharistic prayer involve only the priest-celebrant and clerical concelebrants. Both the GIRM and the *Ordo Missae* provide directions. Although the priest-celebrant prays most of the prayer in *orant* position, he is instructed to extend his hands when he proclaims "The Lord be with you," lift them up during "Lift up your hearts," and extend them again at "Let us give thanks to the Lord our God." He joins his hands together for the recitation of the "Holy, Holy, Holy." He blesses the bread and wine with a sign of the cross and holds his hands outstretched over them at the first *epiclesis*. A variety of manual acts and genuflections marks the institution narrative;[2] and he (with the deacon's assistance) lifts the chalice and paten with the host during the doxology. Eucharistic Prayer I prescribes even more gestures for the priest-celebrant, including bowing, signing himself with the sign of the cross and striking his breast.[3]

The GIRM and the *Ordo Missae* direct presbyteral and episcopal concelebrants to pray with hands outstretched toward the bread and wine during the first *epiclesis*, to gesture toward the bread and wine with their right hands "if it seems appropriate" during the institution narrative, to bow during the genuflections by the priest-celebrant in the institution narrative, and to pray in *orant* position during the *anamnesis*-offering and second *epiclesis*.[4]

Since no gestures are prescribed for the laity during the prayer, liturgical planners might want to exercise some creativity in this area. Perhaps all could be invited to stand in *orant* position during the proclamation of the preface and/or doxology; those accustomed to charismatic prayer would already be familiar with this ancient gesture of praise and thanksgiving. Similarly the assembly might extend their hands toward the bread and wine while the priest-celebrant extends his hands over them at the first *epiclesis*. Bowing and/or genuflecting after the institution narrative could be a profound communal gesture of devotion cued by the priest-celebrant's motion. Praying with hands open-palmed could be used during the intercessions. These patterns should not be changed from week to week or even from season to season; the community would learn to pray these gestures as second nature. (Such gestural participation further presupposes that the assembly's hands are unencumbered by seasonal missals, hymnals or worship aids during the eucharistic prayer.)

---

[2] H. A. J. Wegman provides a fascinating analysis of the presidential rubrics during the institution narrative in "The Rubrics of the Institution-Narrative in the Roman Missal 1970," in *Liturgia: Opera divina et humana. Studi sulla riforma liturgica offerti a S. E. Mons. Annibale Bugnini in occasione del suo 70 compleanno,* ed. P. Jounel, R. Kaczynski and G. Pasqualetti, *Bibliotheca* «Ephemerides Liturgicae» «Subsidia», 26 (Rome: CLV *Edizioni Liturgiche,* 1982) 319–28.

[3] For further insights see T. Fitzgerald, "Body Language in the Institution Narrative," *Liturgy 80* 20/3 (April 1989) 7–10; 20/4 (May–June 1989) 5–7.

[4] European scholars have written extensively on the meaning of these various gestures; see A. G. Martimort, "*Le geste des concélébrants, lors des paroles de la consécration: indicatif ou épiclétique?*" *Notitiae* 18 (1982) 408–12; E. Moeller, "*L'imposition des mains des concélébrants à la consécration: Geste démonstratif ou consécratoire?*" *Questions Liturgiques* 63 (1982) 50–52; C. Vagaggini, "*Ancora sulla estensione della mano dei concelebranti al momento della consacrazione: gesto indicativo o epicletico?*" *Ephemerides Liturgicae* 97 (1983) 224–40; idem, "*L'estensione della mano alla consacrazione: gesto indicativo o epicletico?*" *Rivista Liturgica* 56 (1969) 224–32 (French translation, *Paroisse et liturgie* 1 [1969] 46–53).

Music

Carefully choosing music for the eucharistic prayer may be the most immediately rewarding method for promoting the assembly's ownership of the prayer. At the simplest level singing the "Preface Dialogue," "Holy, Holy, Holy," "Memorial Acclamation" and concluding "Amen" could become the normal mode of vocally executing these texts at every Mass, weekend or weekday. Such a practice would combat the perception that music is an "optional extra" to be added to the liturgical texts on the basis of solemnity and taste rather than the lyrical means by which the texts are ritually performed. The chants printed in the *Sacramentary* might provide a fundamental repertoire for these four elements since they require no instrumental accompaniment, are thematically unified and employ a restricted vocal range. Priest-celebrants could be encouraged to chant at least the preface and doxology, although other elements of the eucharistic prayer (*epicleses*, institution narrative, *anamnesis*-offering) could likewise be chanted[5]

If the presidential texts of the eucharistic prayer are recited rather than sung or chanted by the priest-celebrant, perhaps carefully improvised instrumental accompaniments underlying the recitation may both unify the prayer and cue the assembly's acclamations without the need for a verbal announcement that breaks the prayer's focus (e.g., "Using Memorial Acclamation Three in musical setting B on page 26 of your missal, let us proclaim...").

Three recent works have suggested even more extensive musical adaptations of the eucharistic prayer. Lucien Deiss recommends inserting sung acclamatory texts (e.g., "We give you thanks, we worship you, we sing your praise and glory, Lord our God") during the post-*Sanctus* and/or institution narrative; he also suggests a sung supplicatory text (e.g., "Remember us, O Lord") during the intercessions.[6] After

---

[5] *Passim quaeritur*, a note on May 15, 1975 from the Sacred Congregation for Divine Worship concerning vernacular editions of the *Roman Missal*, directs that the preface dialogue, the prefaces themselves, the call for the memorial acclamation, the acclamations themselves and the other elements of the eucharistic prayer that might be sung should be printed with musical notation in the body of the edition and not relegated to an appendix since this practice "has the . . . advantage of reminding the priest celebrant that these parts of the Mass are as a *rule* to be sung; this is all to the good for the solemnity and effectiveness of the celebration." *Notitiae* 11 (1975) 132 (emphasis added).

[6] L. Deiss, *Spirit and Song of the New Liturgy*, rev. ed. (Cincinnati: World Library Publications, Inc., 1976) 95–99, 179.

listing seven contemporary practices in the French-speaking world, Joseph Gelineau calls for the "creation of an overall assembly action in which text, music, gestures and division of roles are integrated for 'making Eucharist together.'"[7] Considering the eucharistic prayer as a potential example of ritual "music united to a text," Edward Foley and Mary McGann offer six theses to guide musical adaptations of the prayer: the eucharistic prayer is 1. an action of the church, 2. presidential, 3. dialogical, 4. unified, 5. creedal and 6. related to the rest of the Eucharist. They further offer a classification of musical settings of the eucharistic prayer based on the amount of text actually set to music and a series of questions to be posed in analyzing these musical settings.[8]

Environment

The impact of the visual environment upon the quality of liturgical experience cannot be overestimated. Here only three areas for reflection will be posed. First, since the eucharistic prayer is a text prayed over bread and wine, how are the elements visually encountered by the assembly? GIRM 283 and 284 declare:

> The nature of the sign demands that the material for the eucharistic celebration truly have the appearance of food. Accordingly, even though unleavened and baked in the traditional shape, the eucharistic bread

---

[7] Gelineau's examples of practices include: "1. The reading by the presider of a eucharistic prayer of private origin...2. Improvisation of the entire eucharistic prayer by the presider...3. The use of a eucharistic prayer...which the presider takes as an 'operating model,' adopting its structure, flow and essential sections, but paraphrasing, enriching and making it contemporary. 4. The introduction into the received texts of acclamations by the assembly, for example, in the preface, the post-*Sanctus*, the intercessions [i.e., Deiss' model considered above]. 5. The framing of the presider's discourse by the verses of a hymn sung by the assembly. Some of these verses are sung at the beginning, at the *Sanctus*, at the *anamnesis*-offering, at the communion *epiclesis*, at the doxology. 6. The development of a more dialogued prayer in which the participation of the assembly (other voices, choir, the people) does not interrupt the presider's message..." While Gelineau considers the third practice "the most traditional and pastoral," he judges the others as "merely palliative": the first and second for using texts and forms unknown to the participants, the fourth and fifth for making the prayer more or less disparate, and the sixth for concentrating too much on the text alone. See J. Gelineau, *The Eucharistic Prayer: Prayer of the Whole Assembly. A Search for a Celebratory "Model" for "Making Eucharist Together,"* trans. M. A. Grover (Portland, OR: The Pastoral Press, 1985) 12–13.

[8] E. Foley and M. McGann, *Music and the Eucharistic Prayer, American Essays in Liturgy* (Collegeville, MN: The Liturgical Press, 1988).

should be made in such a way that in a Mass
with a congregation the priest is able actually
to break the host into parts and distribute
them to at least some of the faithful...The
wine for the Eucharist must be from the fruit
of the vine...natural, and pure, that is not
mixed with any foreign substance.

One of the difficulties in manifesting the assembly's ownership of
the eucharistic prayer is that there is usually such little connection
between the bread and wine offered and the actual foodstuffs consumed by the assembly in daily life. Although no one recommends
that we return to the style of "offertory" described in the *Ordo
Romanus I,* perhaps that document's stress on the gifts for the
Eucharist being chosen from among the food offerings brought by the
participants could inspire both the source and preparation of our own
eucharistic gifts.

Second, since the elements over which the eucharistic prayer is
prayed are placed on the Lord's table, how does the assembly visually
encounter the altar? In its material and shape does the community perceive it as a table? Or a mausoleum? Does its scale conform to its
usage? Is it a fairly modest surface for the community's ritual meal? Or
does it dominate the area? Is it reverently adorned with altar cloths and
candles, the best of the assembly's handiwork? Or does it become a
bulletin board for homemade posters and banners? Is it a temporary
repository for wilted flowers and dog-eared seasonal missals? Is it
accessible to everyone in the community? Or is it situated in a fenced-
off enclosure for the clergy?

Third, how does the area around the altar relate to the rest of the
assembly space? Frequently the so-called sanctuary is elevated above
the level of the assembly and occupies a position at the end of a long
nave. While some elevation may be necessary for visual access by the
assembly, excessive prominence of the sanctuary may reinforce the
idea of the eucharistic prayer as a clerical recitation-*cum*-gestures to be
listened to and watched by the assembly rather than as a common act
of gathered worship.

Catechesis

Finally, we might consider catechizing our communities on the
importance and meaning of the eucharistic prayer. Three opportunities
suggest themselves. GIRM 11 directs the following:

> It is…up to the priest in the exercise of his office of presiding over the assembly to pronounce the instructions and words of introduction and conclusion that are provided in the rites themselves. By their very nature these introductions do not need to be expressed verbatim in the form in which they are given in the Missal; at least in certain cases it will be advisable to adapt them somewhat to the concrete situation of the community. It also belongs to the priest presiding to…give the faithful a very brief introduction…to the eucharistic prayer (before the preface)…

Our present celebration of the Eucharist is frequently accused of being too wordy. However, it might be very appropriate to indicate to the assembly why the particular eucharistic prayer has been chosen for the particular celebration;[9] an individual text from a given prayer might be proposed for deeper meditation.

Although most homilies will be evocations of the word of God to a given community mediated through scriptural texts, GIRM 41 declares that the homily "should develop some point of the readings or *of another text from the Ordinary* or from the Proper of the Mass of the day, and take into account the mystery being celebrated and the needs proper to the listeners" (emphasis added). Clearly, then, it would be possible on occasion to preach from the eucharistic prayers themselves. An appropriate time for such preaching at the Sunday Eucharist might be when the "Bread of Life" discourses in John 6 are proclaimed on the Seventeenth through Twenty-First Sundays in Ordinary Time of Year B.

An exploration of the meaning of the eucharistic prayer might also be undertaken in the usual means of adult education—parish bulletins, lectures and discussion groups. Nevertheless, a fundamental principle should be recognized: the deepest and most long-lasting catechesis on the eucharistic prayers is their consistent and reverent celebration in the worshiping assembly.

---

[9] A guide for making such decisions and a source for more detailed catechesis on the eucharistic prayers can be found in *Normae pro adhibendis precibus eucharisticis* of 23 May 1968 (cf. *Notitiae* 4 [1968] 157-60; an English translation appears in International Commission on English in the Liturgy, *Documents on the Liturgy 1963–1979: Conciliar, Papal, and Curial Texts* [hereafter DOL] [Collegeville: The Liturgical Press, 1982] #'s 1931–1941, pages 609–12) and in the *Consilium* document to assist in catechesis on Eucharistic Prayers I–IV *"Au cours des derniers mois"* of June 2, 1968 (cf. *Notitiae* 4 [1968] 146-55; an English translation appears in DOL #s1942–1963, pages 612–19).

6

Pocket the Tabernacle Key

This article has its genesis in a formation program for extraordinary ministers of the Eucharist. A few years ago, a group of us on the Boston Archdiocesan Liturgical Commission decided to re-read the 1980 *General Instruction on the Roman Missal.* Most of us were surprised at some provisions, which, in our experience of parish liturgy, had been widely ignored. One of the most obvious was the stipulation that the faithful always receive the consecrated bread and wine from the Eucharist they celebrate, rather from the sacrament reserved for adoration and Communion of the sick. This led to further study and discussion. As we began to implement better practice in our own ministry, we learned that fairly subtle shifts opened up new reserves of meaning, deeply rooted in the tradition.

The next step was to devise a workshop to train Extraordinary Ministers of the Eucharist in the effective celebration of the Communion rite at Sunday Mass, and to write a study guide for them, including bulletin inserts. Several thousand persons enrolled in the three-session workshop, conducted in more than twenty regional sites. The centerpiece of the workshop was a liturgical catechesis on the Communion rite, including an opportunity to engage in ritual and symbol. Celebrating the Communion rite with ritual integrity was the goal, and the symbol of Communion from the same sacrifice was explored. Remarkably, perhaps because this symbol has not been attentively fostered, people were surprised that the provisions of liturgical law made such good common sense. They connected the dots with ease, and over time many parishes experienced a shift in ritual practice that was fairly easy to achieve.

217

Since the article was written the implementation of the new *General Instruction on the Roman Missal* has begun in many dioceses. This process is remarkably awkward: a definitive English translation of the Latin is not available, yet a long list of American adaptations in English is widely circulated. In some dioceses, efforts are being made to change patterns of parish celebration before the guiding document for this process is available. This has given rise to a range of emotions from confusion to dismay. The patterns worked out on the parish level over the last forty years have served us well and may prove difficult to change, especially with a widely held perception that the IGMR (*Institutio Generalis Missalis Romani* 2002) stresses the role of the clergy to the detriment of the lay faithful.

Some things spelled out in the 1980 GIRM are not clear in the IGMR, and will therefore have to be worked out in diocesan policy. For example, the 1980 GIRM mentions the importance of providing adequate bread for the members of the assembly, yet the newer document is silent. Perhaps it is silent on a matter which should be obvious, since the tabernacle is not seen as a source for the people's communion in the new document either. This may point to a certain clerical bias in the document. It must be recalled that a concelebrating priest is forbidden to receive from the reserved sacrament: for his celebration to be valid, he must eat and drink what has been consecrated in that liturgy.

What lies ahead? For the readers of this book, probably a good measure of reflection on the next generation of liturgical reforms. Bishops will choose various paths according to their best judgments as pastors, teachers and liturgists. Similarly, parishes will embrace some elements of the reform, adapt others, and as was the case with the 1980 GIRM, miss others entirely. However, the value of partaking in the Eucharist, rather than serving the people with the reserved sacrament from the tabernacle, is unchanged. The goal described in this article is very much within reach. More than one priest shared the most effective method of realizing the goal: at the beginning of Mass, they pocket the tabernacle key!

—James A. Field

Altar or Tabernacle?
The Source of Communion

James A. Field

As the busy sacristy slowly quieted and the ministers formed the entrance procession for Sunday Mass, the sacristan whispered a word to the priest. "The tabernacle is full, so I put your paten with a big host and half a handful of the little ones on the gifts table, along with enough wine for eight cups, since it looks like we have about six hundred people here." The presiding priest smiled in response: "Thanks a lot, Frank; you're a big help."

Would this scene play out similarly in your own parish's sacristy? If you can imagine this, in the words of NASA, "Houston, we've got a problem." The problem is that Frank is not helping at all. The problem is that our tradition, hundreds of years of papal teaching, eucharistic theology, liturgical law and common sense and hospitality all militate against the practice of Communion from the tabernacle at Mass. The problem is that this practice subtly undermines the capacity of the worshipers to see themselves in what is offered and to understand their role in the eucharistic prayer. For parish liturgical planners, the issue is creating a space where those who gather to celebrate the Eucharist can come to life in the body of Christ. Although we need to make some decisions in shaping the Communion rite in an individual parish, the basic plan is given to us in the liturgical books. While the accommodation of turning to the tabernacle for previously consecrated hosts makes sense on a utilitarian level, and of course depends on the theological grounds that Christ's presence is fully realized in the reserved sacrament, it is not permitted in liturgical law, and for good reason. Experience has shown that it is easy to correct this practice on the parish level. First, the eucharistic ministers, including priests and deacons, must grasp the issue and commit themselves to careful practice of the liturgical principle that the faithful have the right to receive Communion from the same sacrifice in which they have participated.

The *Sacramentary*, the ritual book containing the prayers and rubrics for the celebration of Mass, is clear on this issue. Turn to the "Preparation of the altar and the gifts" (in your *Sacramentary*) and the ritual direction is printed in red ink. This is a rubric, a direction for how the liturgical action is to be accomplished. "Sufficient hosts (and wine) for the Communion of the faithful are to be prepared. It is most important

that the faithful should receive the body of the Lord in hosts consecrated at the same Mass…Communion is thus a clearer sign of sharing
in the sacrifice which is actually taking place." (See also *General
Instruction of the Roman Missal* 56h.) Rubrics are more than stage directions. They are designed to protect the meaning of the symbol. When
a rubric is followed, the worshipers' capacity to enter into the liturgical
action is respected. In this case, the worshipers' ability to enter into the
themes and images of the eucharistic prayer is keyed to the ability to
see their lives in the gifts that are presented as the holy table is prepared. It is an action in tune with the images of the prayer: "Father, we
bring you these gifts. We ask you to make them holy by the power of
your Spirit, that they may become the body and blood of your Son"
(Eucharistic Prayer III). The rubric protects the meanings communicated
in the prayer.

The origins of eucharistic reservation, in which the consecrated
host is reserved in the tabernacle, are rooted in the ancient practice of
extending the fruits of the eucharistic banquet to those who were
absent through illness or imprisonment. Today, eucharistic reservation
has the dual purpose of providing a reserve source of hosts for the
Communion of the sick, especially the dying, and for adoration by the
faithful. Ideally, the sick are to receive Communion brought directly
from the parish Mass, and for this reason many parishes include a dismissal of ministers at Sunday Mass. Normally, therefore, the tabernacle is presumed to contain enough hosts to sustain the daily need of the
parish for *viaticum* (food for the journey) for the dying. In exposition of
the Blessed Sacrament, liturgical law presumes that the host for the
monstrance is brought directly from Mass, not from the tabernacle.
Liturgical law always protects the insight that the celebration of the
Eucharist is the source and summit of the Christian life. Interestingly,
in the only instance in which the faithful everywhere are communicated
from the reserved sacrament, in the celebration of the Lord's Passion
on Good Friday, Communion is not brought from the tabernacle, but
from the sacristy or other place, and the assembly is fed from the altar.
Similarly, in Communion services outside Mass, the focus is on the
altar, not on the place of reservation.

A few years ago, after completing a careful study of the guiding
documents of the Communion rite at Sunday Mass, parishioners in
one Boston parish assumed responsibility for baking all the bread for
Sunday Mass, preparing large unleavened loaves scored for breaking
into small pieces. For weeks prior to the shift from manufactured

hosts, teams of bakers practiced their craft, trying to produce a result that looked like bread and tasted like bread, yet contained no ingredients but wheat and water. At last, under the guiding hands of a woman who was a master of her Italian kitchen, the bakers were ready for Mass. A "Mass coordinator" made a quick last-minute count of the assembly, and set out enough 70-piece loaves for the assembly on a handsome plate, along with a carafe of wine. If any consecrated bread remained, the ministers would consume it reverently in the sacristy after Mass. At the preparation rite, the gifts were held high and carried solemnly through the assembly to the altar. Afterwards, the master baker's eyes were filled with tears. She had been going to Mass for more than sixty years, she said, and this morning she had understood something for the first time. Singing the hymn, she turned to the center aisle and saw the loaves from her kitchen, the work of her hands, being borne to the altar. As clouds of incense swirled around the loaves and the wine, tears of gratitude filled her eyes. "I never knew before that I was in the bread." Her life, what she loved and what she struggled with, her hopes and fears, were all kneaded into the dough and now set on the altar for the great prayer of thanksgiving. Alive in the offering, she came alive in the eucharistic prayer with a new intensity, understanding in an instant that her life was accepted by Christ, her prayer arose to the Father in him, and that in this holy exchange of gifts she was utterly transformed. "Say Amen to who you are," St. Augustine encouraged his people, "it is your own mystery you receive." (St. Augustine, Sermon 272, PL38: 1247) The Liturgy of the Eucharist in her parish, planned and prayed with such careful attention to the church's ritual plan, had the capacity to reveal to her the deep-down meaning of her life in Christ. She knew it all along, of course, but the clarity of the ritual made this meaning accessible. The transforming insight became available to her precisely because of the heightened attention in her parish to the church's ritual and pastoral plan.

The goal for a liturgical planner, therefore, is for communicants to receive Communion from the Mass in which they participate, not from the reserved sacrament consecrated at another moment. Pursuit of this goal often is assigned a low priority in pastoral planning, yet it is protected in law for priests. In order for a priest to validly concelebrate, it is essential that he receive holy Communion from the same sacrifice. In short, if a concelebrating priest receives the host from the reserved sacrament, rather than from the altar, he has not assumed the role of concelebrant lawfully. The value is the same for the lay faithful, although the law protects the value most forcefully concerning priests. The vigor of the law in this case should alert us that we are not dealing with picayune matters here, but are working to protect the core meaning of our worship.

The pattern for sharing holy Communion in the celebration of the Mass may be traced, of course, to the Last Supper, which has its roots in Jewish formal meals. The basic structure in that Jewish tradition is the taking of bread, blessing it, and sharing it with those present around the table, and the sharing of a cup of blessing with those who are united in the prayer experience. Jesus, in his gathering of his disciples, commanded them and us to "do this in remembrance of me." Readers who are skilled at the ancient parochial school art of sentence diagramming will parse this phrase "do this" in an interesting way. The verb, of course, is "do," and its subject is "you, understood." The diagram is exceedingly simple: *(you) do this.* "This," however, stands for something else: it is a pronoun with reference to an action. What is the "this" we are commanded to do? In the context of the meal, the command contains not only the blessing of bread and wine, but also the act of gathering itself, the telling of the story, the singing of hymns, the tender ministry expressed in the washing of the feet. It extends further to the willingness of Jesus to be broken like bread, and to have his life blood poured out in love. It is a command pointing to the basic structure of the Eucharist: taking, blessing, breaking and eating. The command of Jesus is about living a life of thanksgiving to God; it is about the doing of the whole life and witness of Jesus in our flesh, in our time. In its origins, therefore, the Mass is a meal in which participants experience a deep communion with each other and with God. Part of the "this" we are commanded to do in remembrance of the Lord is eating and drinking of the offering. It is a meal which draws its energy from the future; it is a meal that is not only a symbol of the future, but also the way of entering into God's future. How we share this meal, even in its smallest details, is therefore a matter of great consequence. In this light, Communion from the same sacrifice is hardly a small matter, but the norm.

Many religions have sacred meal traditions, stemming from the core human experience of story-telling and expressing the bonds of friendship in the sharing of food. Many religions likewise contain a sacrifice tradition, and primitive religion even extended to human sacrifice. Think of the gruesome practices of the ancient Canaanite people: consider how Abraham was freed from this burden when God freed

Isaac and promised that he would provide the sacrifice. Typically, in ancient Israel, the totality of the animal or grain offering was handed over to God by the giver, and consumed by fire. Some sacrifices, however, were communion sacrifices, in which part of what had been offered was returned to the givers to be eaten by them. Thus, those who had offered the sacrifice shared a sacred meal with God. It is precisely this insight that is at the core of the Mass: that those who give themselves to God in the sacrifice encounter him present in the meal. We dine with God, a sacred meal which is both a foretaste and a participation in the banquet of heaven.

This insight is protected in many places in our tradition. One of the most striking is in the Dedication of a Church and an Altar, a liturgy charged with luminous symbol and ritual. At the central moment of the ceremony, a field of fire is kindled on the altar table, which has already been anointed with chrism as a symbol of Christ. Clouds of incense swirl around the altar table as the bishop prays the great prayer of dedication. The altar, symbol of Christ, is hymned in this great prayer: "From here, may prayer, the church's banquet, arise…" In this same liturgy, the final movement is the inauguration of a Blessed Sacrament chapel. The prayers for this moment likewise express the church's faith. In no place does the prayer suggest that the tabernacle is ever to function as a source for the Communion of the faithful. It is a place set aside for adoration, a place suited to private prayer and devotion, which in turn leads the worshiper back to the altar to the public celebration of the Eucharist.

A knowledge of history is always helpful. From our vantage point, it is amazing that over the course of time, the communion of the people virtually disappeared from Mass. By the twelfth century, great saints and theologians began to urge the lay faithful back to Communion. In response, the church formed a plan for the Communion of the faithful, which could be inserted into the Mass as needed. The model for this plan was the existing plan for Communion of the sick. This included a *confiteor*, a showing of the host with the words "behold the Lamb of God," and a three-times repeated "Lord, I am not worthy," taken from the prayer of the centurion in Luke's gospel (Luke 7:6). Amazingly, Communion of the faithful became almost an intrusion into the celebration of Mass. Around this same time, the tabernacle was receiving more prominence in architecture. Increasingly, priests found it more convenient to communicate lay people after Mass had ended, from a supply of hosts in the tabernacle. It must be remembered that Communion remained a fairly rare experience in the life of the faithful.

In the sixteenth century, in the *Missal of Pius V*, used until the mid-twentieth century, there is a correction to this unfortunate trend. The plan for Mass expressed in this missal presumes that the people who approach the altar for Communion will receive hosts consecrated during the Mass in which they are participating: "at each Mass the faithful who are present should communicate, not only in spiritual desire, but sacramentally, by the actual reception of the Eucharist." (Council of Trent, session 22, cap. 2) The priest celebrant is directed in the rubric to place sufficient hosts in a vessel, or if only a few are receiving, on the paten. For six centuries, therefore, there has been a clear ritual direction for the faithful to receive from the same sacrifice in which they participate.

In practice, the requirements of the *Missal of Pius V* were often ignored. By the seventeenth century, most churches had one Sunday Mass, but no Communion of the faithful. Those who wished to receive would normally do so out of the public eye, so as not to boast of their spiritual life. In some places, people lingered after Mass to receive what had been set aside in the tabernacle. Elsewhere, people came almost in secret to an early Communion Mass before going to the public Mass. Biographies of the saints often point to these strange practices. In the mid-eighteenth century, St. Julie Billiart was so advanced in holiness as a child that her pastor permitted her to receive holy Communion at the age of seven, five years before the normal standard. Communion was so privatized and secretive that she was able to conceal this privilege from her family and neighbors.

Despite unfortunate practices at the parish level, papal teaching consistently defended the tradition of reception of Communion from the sacrifice. In 1742 Pope Benedict XIV, in an encyclical letter, urged priests to "satisfy the pious and just request (of the lay faithful) to be admitted to a share of that same sacrifice of which they also—in their own way—are the offerers. Indeed, she (the church) approves and encourages this practice and would blame any priest through whose fault or negligence such sharing of the Sacrifice should be denied to the faithful." (*Certiores Effecti*, 1742)

In the last one hundred and twenty years or so, Catholics have responded, slowly at first, to a call to more frequent reception of holy Communion. At the turn of the twentieth century, most Catholics, although they attended Mass at least every Sunday, normally received

Communion only a few times a year after their first Communion at twelve to fifteen years of age. As the practice of more frequent Communion grew, there was at first an amazing disengagement between the celebration of Mass and the reception of holy Communion. Papal teaching consistently resisted these unfortunate practices. Pope St. Pius X's 1905 encyclical on frequent Communion "*Sacra Tridentina*" not only recalls the teaching of Trent, but consistently refers to holy Communion as "approaching the holy table." There is never a rationale offered in papal teaching for Communion from the tabernacle for the Communion of the people at Mass.

Sadly, it was not uncommon up until the late 1950s for the distribution of holy Communion to be utterly isolated from the priest's Communion at Mass. Catholics of a certain age can recall Lenten Masses, long ago, when priests would communicate the faithful from the tabernacle before, during and after the celebration of the parish Mass, stopping only for a moment during the Gospel and the consecration. No one seemed to think much about it, even though there was a clear warning contained in the *Missal of Pius V* then in use. The goal was to receive Communion, and once this had been accomplished and a quick private thanksgiving completed, the commuter with briefcase and the schoolchild with lunchpail could hurry out to face the day. The Mass was conducted at the distant high altar with a priest quietly reciting the prayers and an altar boy or two to ring the bell. The first bell functioned to stop the distribution of holy Communion, and the bell after the elevation of the chalice started it up again. To borrow an apt phrase from Dave Barry: I am not making this up. If this were attempted today, most Catholics, and certainly the readers of this article, would be horrified; yet many do not blink at the vestiges of this improper practice when the tabernacle is made the source of holy Communion at Mass. In point of fact, there is no liturgical function for the tabernacle at Sunday Mass. There is never a direction in the liturgy to turn to the tabernacle, nor is it expected that what remains of the offering be returned there, but rather to the sacristy or a side table for the vessels to be cleansed and the sacred species to be consumed.

When forty years or so ago Communion was often disconnected from the celebration of Mass, the bad behavior highlighted above, while widely tolerated, was hardly endorsed. In fact, many modern popes, beginning with Leo XIII in the 1890s and continuing with St. Pius X and Pius XII, spoke to the issue of Communion from the same sacrifice. With the reforms of the Second Vatican Council, this practice is not merely endorsed, but protected in law.

The shape of our ritual is clearly given to us in our liturgical books and in guiding documents such as the *General Instruction of the Roman Missal*. One of the most striking features of the Order of Mass of Paul VI in the mid-1960s was the inclusion of a rite for the people bringing the gifts of bread and wine to the altar. The rubrics direct the priest to prepare sufficient bread and wine for the communicants. On the issue of obtaining hosts from the tabernacle, the rubrics are utterly silent. The 1967 Instruction *"Eucharisticum mysterium*, On Worship of the Eucharist"* describes the gradual unfolding of Christ's presence in the celebration of the Mass: in the faithful gathered in his name, in the word and in the Eucharist. For this reason, "it is more in keeping with the nature of the celebration that, through reservation of the sacrament in the tabernacle, Christ not be present from the beginning on the altar where Mass is celebrated." (EM 55) Liturgical law always protects the value of the people receiving from the sacrifice in which they partici-pate. Reverence for the Eucharist requires that those who prepare for worship commit themselves to fidelity to liturgical law, and therefore to protect the capacity of people to enter into the mystery of Christ.

Who celebrates the Mass? Christ, of course. Those who are bap-tized are alive in Christ, and in the liturgy are profoundly aware of his presence in their gathering. It may be said, therefore, that the baptized, the faith community, the church celebrates. In the liturgy, all of the baptized celebrate as Christ's body in this place, at this particular time. Those who celebrate are not passive receivers, they are called to "full, conscious, active participation" in the eucharistic liturgy, which is the "source and the summit of the Christian life." (*Sacrosanctum concilium* 14) As we have seen, the liturgy has been designed to serve this meaning and make it available. The liturgy constitution required that rites be drawn up so that "they express more clearly the holy things they sig-nify and that the Christian people, as far as possible, are to understand them with ease and to take part in the rites fully, actively, and as befits a community." (SC 21) More than forty years into this liturgical reform, it is high time to excise any bad practices which endure. Pastoral expe-rience has shown that the problem of communion from the reserved sacrament at Mass is relatively easy to correct.

The *Sacramentary* and our guiding documents set out the plan for celebration. Liturgical planners would do well to reread the *General Instruction of the Roman Missal*, the *Constitution on the Sacred Liturgy*, and *This Holy and Living Sacrifice* (found in *The Liturgy Documents*, Vol. 1), the guide to the Communion rite. In an era where Communion outside Mass is increasingly celebrated in some parishes, the value of protecting the celebration of the Eucharist as the distinctive form of Sunday worship is primary.

Planners who have studied these documents and who have changed practice in their own parishes offer the following advice:

1. Catechesis for the ministers of Communion, including priests and deacons

When the ministers grasp the importance of Communion from the same sacrifice, they will work diligently to preserve the integrity of the celebration. Some members of the assembly may not notice a shift in practice, but there will be a stronger basis for their ongoing catechesis and for liturgical preaching.

2. Counting

Someone—a Mass coordinator, eucharistic minister or sacristan— must be responsible for estimating the number of communicants at a Mass and for setting out enough bread and wine for the celebration. After a few weeks, it generally becomes easy to estimate what is needed and to set out additional bread and wine before the procession with the gifts, if needed. This is a basic exercise of hospitality to the gathered assembly: assuring that what is offered in the sacrifice is for their eating and drinking.

3. Bread to be broken

The antiseptically bagged, machine-produced hosts are convenient for counting, and can be weighed and counted out with a sensitive kitchen scale, but are not really the substantial bread the liturgical documents propose. Large hosts, scored for breaking into as many as 70 pieces, are available. Parishioners may also bake fresh bread. When these large hosts are used, there are clear advantages. First, everyone receives a fraction of something larger. Second, if the supply has been over-estimated, it is easy to give the last communicants larger pieces so that nothing is left over.

4. Single vessel for the bread

The sign value of "one bread" and "one cup," and the sharing of the assembly in the offering, are enhanced when the bread is arrayed on one large plate and divided among many smaller plates at the fraction rite. Similarly, a carafe or pitcher is sufficient for the wine. Many vessels on the altar obscure the meaning of the prayer. Additional vessels and cups are brought to the altar at the time of the fraction rite.

5. Liturgical preaching

Preaching at the Eucharist should move us from word to table: good liturgical preaching stirs up a hunger for the praise of God, leads us to active engagement in the eucharistic prayer and makes us aware of our hunger for communion with one another and with the Lord. Good liturgical practice provides a context for good preaching. Strong symbols and signs can be unpacked and explored in the homily and the participants formed to enter into them with understanding.

6. Praying the eucharistic prayer

Presiding ministers who are aware of themselves as leaders of prayer, who are comfortable with the ritual, reverent and attentive, invite the faithful into our great prayer of thanksgiving. The singing of the preface dialogue and all of the acclamations, and attention to posture and gesture, help form a people who are fully, consciously, actively engaged in eucharistic prayer.

7. Tabernacle is off-limits

Because the tabernacle is not a source for holy Communion, there is no need for anyone to approach it during the liturgy. If it is in view of the assembly, the sign of the Lord's presence is the sanctuary lamp. Additional candles are not lit. The focus of the eucharistic liturgy is the holy table, the altar. If the tabernacle is in proximity to the altar, it may properly be screened in order to move the focus forward to the altar table itself during the celebration.

8. Eucharistic ministers monitor the rite

Ministers of the body of the Lord take sufficient consecrated bread to their stations. If the supply is not sufficient, they may break hosts toward the end of the procession. If too much has been provided, they may give the last few communicants larger pieces of bread or more than one host. If the supply runs out, they look to other ministers for a supply. The tabernacle is turned to only if everyone runs out. Communicants may also receive of the precious blood alone if necessary.

9. Ministers return to the sacristy

The liturgy directs that the purification of the vessels may take place to the side or in the sacristy. In addition to consuming the remaining precious blood, the ministers may quietly consume whatever hosts remain, and cover the vessels to be cleansed immediately after Mass.

10. Ministers to the sick dismissed from Mass

Communion of the Sick extends the fruits of the Mass to those who, though apart from the Sunday assembly through illness, are nonetheless enfolded in the community's prayer and ministry. Assuring that their Communion is received directly from the altar enhances this understanding and gives public expression to an important part of the parish's life and ministry. The ministers to the sick are called forward, entrusted with the body of the Lord and asked to go directly to the sick to share word, sacrament and assurance of the community's prayer.

These ten commandments, with repeated practice over the course of a few months, will subtly transform the quality of celebration in a parish. The core structure and meaning of the eucharistic celebration will be available to worshipers in a new way. Our rites, celebrated with integrity and clarity, have the capacity to uplift our spirits and draw us more deeply into the mystery of Christ's presence. Trust the rites, trust the tradition. The benefits derived from following the church's pastoral plan for Communion more attentively far outweigh the investment of time and effort for change.

7

The Tradition Is the Sunday Eucharistic Assembly

Many faith communities in the world do not have a presbyter to celebrate the Sunday Eucharist with them on a regular basis. Some of these communities can gather for Eucharist only once a month, and in some places only a few times a year. Recognizing this phenomenon, the Congregation for Divine Worship issued the *Directory for Sunday Celebrations in the Absence of a Priest* (SCAP) in June 1988. The fundamental principle woven throughout this directory is to ensure "in the best way possible the weekly gathering of the faithful" and the Christian celebration of Sunday.

In this article, Patrick Malloy and John Leonard raised fundamental theological, ecclesial, pastoral, liturgical and ecumenical issues, among others, concerning Sunday celebrations in the absence of a presbyter. From 1994 to 2000 I served as director of the office of worship in the diocese of Great Falls-Billing, Montana. That diocese is the fifth largest (geographically) in the U.S. with a territory of over ninety-four thousand square miles with one hundred and sixteen faith communities served by approximately fifty presbyters. Under the capable pastoral leadership of Bishop Anthony M. Milone, the diocese has addressed the many issues surrounding SCAP—a reality faced by dozens of communities in this local church. During my time in Montana, Dr. Malloy visited the diocese on a number of occasions, and part of the fruit of his work was the publication of the video *Lay-Led Sunday Worship* (available from The Liturgical Press, Collegeville, MN).

Doctors Malloy and Leonard believe that the problem is not with liturgical praxis but with ministerial praxis. It is unlikely that we will see a change with phenomenon any time soon. Even though the SCAP ritual is laden with problems, it is the church's liturgy nonetheless. The church desires that the members of the body of Christ celebrate Sunday in the best possible way. This basic principle should also be applied to the keeping of the yearly Paschal Triduum. When Sunday and the Paschal Triduum are not celebrated we are not true to our identity as Catholic Christians

The church teaches that the community has a right to the Eucharist (as Schillebeeckx has argued so eloquently). Since the Second Vatican Council the church has spoken consistently about the Eucharist as the most perfect expression or manifestation of the church. We know that after almost forty years of celebrating the liturgy in the vernacular, both word and sacrament belong together. The tradition of the church from the earliest days is the *Assembly on Sunday for Eucharist*. We should keep these fundamental ecclesiological issues before us as we face the challenge of Sunday and Triduum celebrations in the absence of a presbyter.

A challenge is the search for a balance between liturgical principles and pastoral praxis. It will be interesting when the United States bishops debate all the issues surrounding the celebrations of both Sunday and the Paschal Triduum in the absence of a presbyter with courage, fortitude and patience. The long-range consequences of such gatherings should be explored. It could also be helpful, insightful and pastorally sensitive to seek the advice of local churches that have been faced with this dilemma, often for several years.

Each diocese grappling with these issues can provide excellent leadership, formation and training for competent liturgical presidency and preaching in the absence of an ordained minister. The local churches and the U.S. bishops could explore developing a ritual for celebrating the Paschal Triduum in the absence of a presbyter. This is to ensure that the faithful are not deprived of the yearly opportunity to renew their Christian life through participation in the celebration of the Easter Triduum. Likewise, there is a prime opportunity for fruitful catechesis of the assembly, the body of Christ, the church.

—Michael R. Prendergast

Sunday Eucharistic Liturgy or OSCAP

Patrick L Malloy and John K. Leonard

Sundays without a presbyter (SWAP) have arrived, at least in the form of a document, *Directory for Sunday Celebrations in the Absence of a Priest*. On the basis of that document an actual order of service was prepared, *Order for Sunday Celebrations in the Absence of a Priest* (OSCAP).

Is it correct to say, however, that this order is for times when the presbyter is absent? To be absent, as when one is said to be absent from class, or declared in the minutes of a meeting to have been absent at the last gathering, or to have stepped outside, say from a religious community on a leave of absence—all of these suggest that the condition is a fluke or is short-term. The expectation is that the person will come back. The student must come back or the truant officer will come calling; the committee member will soon return to the meetings or be replaced; the member of the community will declare an intention to return, or the community will declare that he or she has waited too long and may not return.

OSCAP is intended for parishes without a presbyter, not for parishes from which the presbyter is absent. OSCAP covers situations in which the presbyter is gone and will not return. There is a legal technicality that stipulates every Catholic parish have a presbyter as its pastor, but with ever-increasing regularity, there will be U.S. parishes whose presbyter is only on the books. A man who passes through only occasionally and who presides for the Sunday worship of a community, in some cases, but a few times a year, can hardly be said to exercise what we know as the "care of souls." The handwriting is on the wall, and OSCAP signals that we are making proximate preparations for a long eucharistic famine.

According to the *National Catholic Reporter*, between 1965 and 1985 the number of presbyters in the U.S. decreased by twenty percent, and according to the best statistical methods applied to an extensive body of data, we will be down another twenty percent by 2005. In forty years, we will have seen a forty percent decrease in the number of presbyters in the U.S. In some places, like New England, the drop will be even more severe: fifty-two percent. Closer to home, Dubuque will be down by seventy-three percent. All of this while the number of Catholics in the country is actually increasing. If things are looking up anywhere, it's in the South, but that's an illusion. Yet, in a few dioceses the number of presbyters will rise. But usually those are small dioceses where, for example, an increase from ten to twenty presbyters means a one hundred percent jump. In real numbers, however, it doesn't mean much. Or they're dioceses in prime sunbelt territory where the overall population increases so dramatically that the ratio of presbyters to parishioners will be pitifully low even if the actual number of presbyters rises. And let's not forget that presbyters, like the parishioners, retire south. Many of the presbyters who account for the upswing will also be retirees.

These projections are not the product of some Catholic-bashing number crunchers. This study was commissioned and supported by the National Conference of Catholic Bishops, which has received the report but hasn't yet made a public statement. What will we do? Part of the answer proposed is OSCAP.

Still, not all of the bishops approved OSCAP. Bishop William McManus, retired from South Bend–Fort Wayne, Indiana (who will publicly say now that since his retirement, he has nothing to lose and intends to speak his piece), and Bishop Raymond Lucker of nearby New Ulm were the most vocal. McManus stated that OSCAP was "a monster that could destroy the Sunday Mass tradition." I think Bishop McManus is right.

I don't mean to say that I think that the presuppositions and aims of the bishops are entirely askew. In the document *Gathered in Steadfast Faith*, which serves as the introduction to OSCAP, the bishops spell out at least these six unquestionable aims of the new rite:

1. to highlight the primacy of Sunday;

2. to keep alive the connection of Sunday with Eucharist;

3. to keep intact the immemorial observance of the Lord's day;

4. to celebrate the variety of the modes of Christ's presence, particularly in the assembly and the word;

5. to recognize the "royal priesthood" of the faithful;

6. to assure orthopraxis and orthodoxy in a type of service that is indeed celebrated and will continue to be celebrated whether the bishops approve it or not.

These aims are beyond criticism. Other people besides the bishops have added their own reasons for supporting this document and its order of service:

> 1. to provide opportunities for the faithful to learn other services besides the Eucharist: Liturgy of the Hours, services of the word;
>
> 2 to help people appreciate their presbyters and the Eucharist ("Absence makes the heart grow fonder");
>
> 3. to make the best of a bad situation.

These aims deserve less respect than those adduced by the bishops, but these, too, have some merit.

I choose not to go into detail on any of these nine reasons, because I believe that, taken together, they still do not measure up to the far more serious reasons against OSCAP. These reasons suggest, in the long run, that Sunday Communion services will undermine the sacramental assembly, the eucharistic liturgy, the source and summit from which and toward which our Christian life is oriented (*Constitution on the Sacred Liturgy* 10). We are about to abort, well short of term, the long-awaited offspring of post-conciliar liturgical renewal.

What is that offspring? It is, of course, the return of the liturgy to the entire people of God. No aim of the renewal has been more theoretically central nor more practically sought than the re-appropriation of the liturgy by the entire church, by all of us who are one in Christ. But this project is far from complete. The stranglehold of the system that treated the liturgy as a "separate" work—assented to by God's people, closely followed by God's people, perhaps even understood by God's people, but not done by God's people—has been hard to break. All the documents our liturgists can crank out, all the translations our linguistic scholars can render, all the instruments our musicians can squeeze into a choir loft, cannot instantly change long-held perceptions, especially those that touch upon ultimate realities and structures of power. The question of whose liturgy it is gets at the really-real and at power (a redundancy, I know).

Then why did the bishops approve OSCAP? The relative ease with which OSCAP passed through the Conference of Bishops and the seeming enthusiasm with which it is being received by God's people show how strongly gripped we still are by the old notion that the Eucharist is the work only of the presbyter. We continue to live with the notion that the *sacrifice* belongs to the presbyter and the *sacrament* belongs to us, not as actors but as passive recipients.

A worst-case scenario will show how OSCAP, rather than fighting against this errant view, will actually reinforce it. Imagine a rural area with many far-flung parishes and very few presbyters. The upper midwest is a good place to start looking. In not too many years, it will not be unusual for a "circuit-rider" presbyter to come to a parish mid-week to check in and "say Mass" (with assistants or without), to produce consecrated communion wafers for the week or weeks ahead, and to be on his way. Without a doubt, the consecration will be valid. No doubt, the Communion of the people on the following Sunday will be valid. Once again, however, the old dichotomy will have been reinforced: the Eucharist will have been the presbyter's; the Communion will have been ours. He will have "made it." We will have received it.

The situation will be worse than it ever was before. In a previous age, it is true that notions of liturgical efficacy centered almost exclusively on the presbyter with little regard for the laity. In the practical realm, the presbyter of a former day was not a sacrament-producing magician, whose work in the community was little more than the confection of communion wafers. He was also the one who baptized our babies, gave report cards to our children, witnessed the marriages of our young people, visited our sick, buried our dead, and, if he was a good presbyter, was in many senses one of us—sharing our lives in ordinary and concrete ways. It is true that the presbyter had sacramental "power," but it was a power imbedded in human relationships and in service. There was at least some chance of seeing that liturgy and life were of a piece, and that ritual was not mere hocus-pocus. In today's priestless parish, where a sister is the pastoral administrator, the one who baptizes, the one who witnesses marriages, the one who stands with us at the graves of our parents...the presbyter becomes, to put it bluntly, a sacrament machine. The power has come loose from its roots in service and community.

The Eucharist is not about power. It is not about an empowered few performing a sacred rite on behalf of a powerless multitude. Rather, Eucharist is an act of Christ, an expression of the entire Christ, and thus it is an expression of the church that is his body. Through us, Christ gives thanks to the Father. Through our assembling and our hearing and our eating and drinking, Christ gives himself to us. Through our going forth, Christ gives himself again to the world. The church is the body of Christ. To view the Eucharist outside the context of the entire church inevitably will lead to a fixation on "priestly power," and that is missing the point.

That does not mean that the body of Christ is a chaotic anarchy. It is an ordered body and when we assemble, ideally we assemble in our orders. The presbyterate is an indispensable order of the church and there can be no valid Eucharist without it. But the presbyterate is an order within the church. It is not a category apart from it. The impending implementation of OSCAP, which in some dioceses will become the normative Sunday service, betrays a lingering operative assumption that, indeed, the presbyterate and the rest of the body, including the ministries of service and charity, are not organically linked. This is clericalism: the radical juxtaposition of groups within the church on the basis of supposed power. OSCAP is as clerical in its assumptions as the documents of the Second Vatican Council are communitarian in theirs.

There is more than clericalism at stake here. Communion services give the impression that the prayer of the community and the eucharistic food have nothing to do with one another. How long now have we been saying that the Liturgy of the Word and the various rites and ceremonies of the Mass are not just devotional exercises to get us ready to receive Communion but are inherently linked to it? How long have we been saying that the Eucharist is not a thing (i.e., a consecrated host) but a great action: giving thanks to the Father, remembering the Son, calling upon the Spirit, sharing the meal of heaven's reign? In these OSCAP services, the Liturgy of the Word looks like nothing but a preparatory devotional exercise, and the elements of thanksgiving and *anamnesis*, although present in the rite, are studiously and rightly shown to have nothing to do with the eucharistic food, because they are pronounced before the ciborium is brought into view. In these services, "Eucharist" is not something we do, it is something we eat. "Eucharist means Communion" means that we will have lost important gains we've made in the Second Vatican Council.

Some commentators see another danger: that the people won't realize these services aren't Mass and will be content with this stop-gap measure. Their evidence is that many people already call communion services "Mass," as in "I like Sister's Mass better than Father's" or, in dioceses that have presiding by committee, "Max and Evelyn will be doing the 10:00 Mass tomorrow." I think that these commentators are wrong. People know that it isn't Mass; they just don't know any word for services except "Mass." But I do agree from what I've seen in some of the workshops I've been doing around the country that people do like these services at least as well as Mass and are in no hurry to have the presbyter come around. That should come as no surprise: the lay

presiders, perhaps because they're new at it, may prepare more diligently and preside more gracefully than their clerical counterparts.
Common sense also suggests that people would rather pray under the
leadership of a well-known, well-loved, ever-present lay pastoral
administrator than under the leadership of the person who's listed in
the Catholic directory as their pastor but who lives seventy-five miles
away and gets in to visit once a month. Whatever the reason, we will
end up with assemblies that are not sacramental, strictly speaking, but
are perfectly content with not being sacramental. They will be content
with it because, once again, they've learned through the years that
their part in the liturgy is to receive the sacrament, not to make it. The
food is sacramental. The assembly is not.

From earliest Christian times, the church gathered on the Lord's
Day to celebrate the Eucharist: not to eat it but to celebrate it. Now,
two thousand years later, the Lord's Day celebration of the Eucharist is
about to become an exception in many places, places where
Catholicism has deep roots. My fear is that it won't come as a shock,
because we've done so well to prepare ourselves for it. By going to
Mass on Saturday, we have weaned ourselves away from the notion
that Sunday is the indispensable day of Christian assembly. By distributing communion out of the tabernacle rather than from the table
about which the people have gathered, we have perpetuated the dis-
junction between sacrifice and sacrament. By denying ourselves the
eucharistic cup even after permission for it has been given, we have
reinforced the symbolic snooze into which we have fallen and readied
ourselves to live the Christian life, hardly ever experiencing the fullness
of the signs of our redemption.

We have the old saw: if it ain't broke, don't fix it. A corollary may
go like this: fix what's broken, not something else. Twenty-five years
ago, it was determined that the liturgy was broke and we began fixing
it. The problems I just mentioned were among the areas we tackled
and, I think, we were just now on the verge of seeing what was really
wrong and deciding what we have to do to fix it. Today, the church is
hearing very funny noises coming from another part of our ecclesial
machine: ministry. Rearranging the parts in the liturgy won't help that,
and it may well cause the liturgy to come to a grinding, gear-stripping,
smoke-belching stop. The ministry is broke. Let's fix it and leave the
liturgy alone.

What is so bad and so good about Communion services?

We rejoice that lay people are being asked to exercise their common priesthood in serving the prayer life of their communities. However, we must ask if the communion service should be one of the services led by lay people. We may regret later some underlying implications of this service. In the words of Archbishop Rembert Weakland,

> If [the substitution of Communion services for the eucharistic liturgy] were to last for many years—even a generation—I do not see how the Catholic identity could be maintained. We would become a different kind of church that would not be based on gathering around the eucharistic sacrifice...The difficulty is that we are creating a new tradition that is devotional and not communal and that could easily distort the nature of the theology of the sacraments.

What is this thing we call Eucharist?

The Eucharist is not a thing but a way of life that is ritualized in a traditional fourfold action: taking what we have been given, thanking and blessing God for it, breaking it apart in service and hearing it with one another. In the Communion service, we do not ritualize the central mystery of what it means to be Christian—that is the purpose of liturgy. If the Communion services become regular substitutes for the eucharistic liturgy, what would happen to the link between the worship we offer as the church and the worship of our lives?

Eucharist $\neq$ a thing

Eucharist $=$ Sacrament of Christ, an action,
a ritual celebration of the
Christian way of life:
- taking all we have been given
- blessing/thanking God
- breaking/pouring out self in service
- sharing self as a "living sacrifice"

Aren't the eucharistic liturgy and Communion services the same?

From the time Jesus took bread, blessed it, broke it and shared it with his disciples, this fourfold action has been essential to the Eucharist in Christian tradition. In a Communion service, there is only one of these, and it is separated in space and time from the other three. Recent ecumenical dialogue comes to impressive agreement on this: Eucharist includes not only the eating but also thanksgiving to the Father, *anamnesis* of the Son, *epiclesis* of the Spirit and the banquet of God's reign, all integrally linked to one another. In Communion services there is only eating. Thanksgiving in the form of a litany or hymn is not connected with the eucharistic food because the ciborium is brought out only after words of thanks have been pronounced. These services give the impression that the prayer of the community and the eucharistic food have nothing to do with one another.

Eucharistic Liturgy	≠	Communion Service
Taking		No
Blessing		No
Breaking/Pouring		No
Sharing		Yes
Eucharist (Thanksgiving) to the Father		Maybe
Anamnesis (Memorial) to the Son		No
Epiclesis (Invocation) of the Spirit		No
Banquet of God's reign		Yes
Sacramentally linked		No
Constant Tradition:		Sunday = Eucharist + Assembly

Yes, but aren't we making a "mountain out of a mole hill" on this?

Communion services may reinforce an incomplete understanding of eucharistic Communion. Only recently have we begun to move away from an individualistic communion piety—something that happens between Jesus and me, with little or no connection to the community gathered to worship in Jesus Christ. Sometimes other things get confused. Nevertheless, the eucharistic celebration is always in the context of the church gathered for prayer. In the communal celebration Christ manifests his presence under the form of eucharistic bread and wine, offering himself to us in the meal. In that meal we are united with him and one another.

If you wish to understand the body of Christ, listen to the apostle as he says to the faithful, "You are the body of Christ and his members." Your mystery has been placed before you on the Lord's table. You receive what you are. You reply "Amen" to that which you are and, by replying, you consent. For you hear "The body of Christ," and you reply "Amen." Therefore be a member of the body of Christ so that your "Amen" may be true.

St. Augustine (Sermon 272)

So what if offering the sacrifice and receiving Communion are separate?

When people regularly receive Communion at a time or place separate from the celebration in which the hosts are consecrated, they may gradually pick up mistaken notions: they may assume, for example, that the eucharistic prayer actually belongs to the presbyter. They could think that it is his work, assented to by lay people, followed closely by lay people, understood by lay people, but not done by them together with the presbyter. According to this notion, the presbyter works over the people and separate from the people in offering the sacrifice (an action that for some reason is believed to happen during the eucharistic prayer). Lay people only received the sacrament (Communion).

One can distinguish theoretically between "sacrifice" and "sacrament" in the Eucharist, but in practice and in experience the two must be integral, inseparable. This was the main point of the eucharistic reforms of the Second Vatican Council: each demands the other. The *anamnesis* of Christ's sacrifice in the Eucharist demands participation in the Communion meal of the new covenant established in Christ's blood, and vice versa. *Sacrifice* and *Communion both* refer to the entire ensemble of ritual words and actions constituted by the fourfold action that we Christians perform in obedience to Christ's command (*"Do this"*) as the *anamnesis* of his saving deeds (*"in memory of me"*). The separation of the two was repudiated in Vatican II, but it still has a stranglehold on our hearts, minds and experience. We were just beginning to realize the return of the whole liturgy to the whole people of God and now Communion services reappear. We are back to separating the offering of the sacrifice from the reception of Communion.

Isn't the presbyter the one with the power to consecrate?

Closely connected with the separation between sacrifice and Communion is the resulting overemphasis on the presbyter's power to consecrate. In so-called "priestless parishes," where someone else actually does the pastoral ministry, an ordained presbyter comes in to preside for Mass and consecrate enough hosts for x number of Communion services. The power to consecrate has been torn from its roots in service and community—leadership in the liturgy is separated from leadership in life.

The Eucharist is not about power. It is not about an empowered *few* performing a sacred rite on behalf of a powerless multitude. Rather, the Eucharist is an action of Christ, an expression of the entire Christ, an expression of the church, the body of Christ. To view the Eucharist as an act that can take place by a few who stand outside the context of the entire church leads to a fixation on the presbyteral power.

Does this imply that the presbyterate is dispensable? Absolutely not. The church is an ordered body, and when we assemble, ideally we assemble in our orders, i.e., with all the gifts and ministries needed and given for the building up of the body of Christ. But the presbyterate is an order of ministry, an order of service, within the church. It is not apart from the church.

What can we learn from this liturgical and ministerial problem?

It is true that we do not have enough presbyters for every community to celebrate the Eucharist every Sunday, or every day. However, could the rush to Communion services as the only alternative be a missed opportunity to rediscover the fuller liturgical life of the church? We learn many unexpected things from a crisis. Might we consider that other form of liturgical prayer known as the Liturgy of the Hours? Perhaps, if we celebrate Morning or Evening Prayer when we cannot celebrate the Eucharist, we will learn to discover, respect and treasure the many ways Christ is present in the very gathering of people in his name. We may discover Christ more powerfully in the psalms and other Scripture readings. We may find the Lord more directly in other members of the body. In the prayers we voice with Christ our head, we may identify more clearly with the needs of the entire world. The Eucharist is the apex, the source and summit of all Christian liturgy and all Christian life. But it is not the only liturgy. The Eucharist is the apex but not the totality of worship. Maybe the current crisis can lead us to rediscover the riches of the daily hours of prayer. Perhaps those hours in turn will prepare us to celebrate better the Sunday Eucharist.

Do Communion services reflect a liturgical problem or a ministerial one?

The answer, of course, is *both*. But let's not confuse them. Could Communion services give the impression that there really is no ministerial crisis at all? Might they enable people to conclude that everything is all right? Maybe we don't need ordained leaders in our communities as long as there is one ordained person who can consecrate enough hosts occasionally. Could the substitution of Communion services for the eucharistic liturgy become an easy habit? Perhaps a fast from Communion will help us realize the importance of the Eucharist for our lives, even as we wait in prayerful hope and serious reflection for the Spirit to lead us beyond this ministerial crisis. Can Communion services be a liturgical Band-Aid for a non-liturgical problem?

As we continue to pray to the Father "Thy will be done," we can put our gifts and talents at the service of our community worship. There are serious problems with Communion services but, if the local bishop decides to permit them, it is vitally important to lead them properly, with reverence and hospitality.

PART 5

Appendix

Today's Liturgy Celebrates
Twenty-Five Years

Jon Reddy

For the past twenty-five years, *Today's Liturgy* magazine has spent its time and efforts providing a quality liturgical publication to its growing number of subscribers. TL, now a seventy-two-page quarterly periodical, wasn't always what it is today. Its success and growth over the years have been a combination of good ideas and the ability to work with limited resources, say officials at its parent company Oregon Catholic Press.

Randall DeBruyn, the current executive editor of Worship Publications at OCP, was the second editor of TL, taking over the task of broadening the publication's scope from then-publisher, Owen Alstott. During his tenure, 1981 to 1984, DeBruyn watched the publication change title and size. Originally titled "Notes," TL was a simple newsletter, mailed out to subscribers and churches, offering liturgical suggestions for music.

First published monthly in 1976, the newsletter format adhered to a simple formula: offering subscribers two pages per Sunday worship. The left side of the document was a list of suggestions for music, the right side a planning worksheet for pastors and liturgy planners. After 1978, the publication became a quarterly, highlighting each of the Catholic Church's seasons: Easter/Pentecost, Advent/Christmas, Lent/Holy Week and Ordinary Time. Its name was changed to "Today's Liturgy Notes." "We immediately received letters from people who were delighted with the format of suggestions and planning pages," recalls DeBruyn. "The planner was so easy to prepare, it was popular right away." The publication was becoming a successful tool for churches, but its growth was prohibited by a limited amount of staff and resources.

Originally a very small operation, with less than one million subscribers, TL now goes out to every Catholic Church in the United

States and to a long list of dedicated subscribers. DeBruyn and Alstott did a great deal of refining of the publication, going over letters of thanks, praise and criticism about TL. After going through the responses, the pair decided to enlarge the publication by adding articles of interest and introducing a letter-from-the-editor section. "We started off by reprinting articles from other magazines, like the *American Organist* and *Hymn Society,* giving people access to information and liturgical ideas and tools they may never have known were even out there," said DeBruyn. Under DeBruyn, the publication expanded from a small typewritten leaflet to a two-color, up-to-twenty page booklet on newsprint. "We didn't have a lot of time or resources to put into the publishing of articles; the primary purpose of the publication at that point was not so much a magazine but a liturgy preparation aid," said DeBruyn.

Until 1984 and the hiring of Bari Colombari, TL was mainly a two-person operation: DeBruyn and Alstott. When Colombari became editor of TL, he was also working in a local Portland parish and was a frequent customer of OCP, dropping by the office to order music. Then called the "Chancery" (now the Archdiocesan Pastoral Center), the company shared a building with the Archdiocese of Portland's administrative staff. OCP's production equipment also shared their office space, including the composing room, dark room and the printing and binding area. The office areas were very crowded, and some of the employees actually shared phone extensions. One employee's first desk was inside a walk-in vault/safe. While in the old building, the company had a mainframe computer for the accounting, subscriptions and payroll. They also had one computer for generating letters and documents.

Before the company moved to its current location in Northeast Portland in 1986, it began using its first desktop computers, beginning with word processing programs. When DeBruyn began working at OCP, he shared an office with Archdiocese of Portland Priest Father Edmond Bliven, and the offices became increasingly crowded as OCP's publications grew in popularity. In 1984, when Colombari came on board, the warehouse and shipping departments were off-site, called the "Annex." Coincidentally, the Annex was located adjacent to OCP's current facility, near Providence Medical Center. "All of our editorial work was done on paper with typewriters," said Colombari. "Music editing was done on staff paper with pencils and tape; sort of the antiquated roots of the current 'cut and paste' craze in computer lingo."

Colombari, then also the professional projects coordinator and assistant editor of OCP's *Music Issue*, was editor of TL from 1984 to 1986. He says the articles, suggestions, notices of events and innovations in publications have frequently contributed greatly to the church. Under Colombari, the publication was in its most compact size, 5.25 inches by 5.5 inches. The number of pages was determined by the number of feasts covered. The periodical still only printed articles that were reprints from other magazines, "hopefully spreading the information to people who were unable to subscribe to other journals," says Colombari.

TL now features its original elements of music suggestions and liturgy preparation sheets, along with regular features from Elaine Rendler, Paul Covino, Thomas Tomaszek and David Nastal. "Our close work with Dr. Rendler proved invaluable," said Colombari. "Both the work she provided [columns and music suggestions], and also her valued counsel."

John Limb, current publisher of OCP, became editor of TL in 1986, enlarging its size and concentrating on presenting it in a magazine format with quarterly issues. Under Limb came the first issue with an article by Rendler, and subsequent issues that included expanded planning pages, letters to the editor and a clinicians' directory. "From the beginning, I believed in the importance of customer feedback. It was my goal to ensure that *Today's Liturgy* was responsive to the demands of good liturgy while being flexible enough to meet the unique needs of thousands of subscribers," Limb said.

In 1989, Larry Curran came on board as editor of TL for three years. During that time, the magazine featured a liturgical calendar insert. Under Dr. James Wilde, editor from 1992 to 2000, TL began offering octavo inserts, announcements on other OCP products, a "composer profile" feature and more extensive articles. Under Wilde, the publication solidified its current releases—Advent, Christmas, Epiphany • Lent, Triduum, Easter • Ordinary Time 1 and Ordinary Time 2—and grew to its current seventy-two-page length.

Oregon Catholic Press

Today's Liturgy's versatility over the years can be traced to the unique makeup of Oregon Catholic Press. "We're not-for-profit, tied to an archdiocese, with staff and composers who have worked or are working in the trenches," said Colombari.

The success of TL is due in great part to the success of its parent company, Oregon Catholic Press. OCP had its beginnings more than seventy-five years ago. In the early 1920s, the Ku Klux Klan was rampant in Oregon and the persecution of Catholics was one of its main goals. Archbishop Alexander Christie established the Catholic Truth Society of Oregon—the original name of Oregon Catholic Press.

The Society's purpose was to provide Catholics and non-Catholics alike with information about the church and the activities of its educational and charitable institutions. Within two years, the Society was distributing two hundred fifty thousand pamphlets to twenty-five states, the Philippine Islands and parts of Canada. It established a lecture program and began sponsoring a weekly radio broadcast in 1925. The Society became a corporation early in 1928 and borrowed the funds to acquire the *Catholic Sentinel*, the diocesan newspaper for the state of Oregon. Oregon Catholic Press continues publishing the *Catholic Sentinel*, one of the most successful and award-winning diocesan newspapers in the country.

In 1934, the Catholic Truth Society began publishing *My Sunday Missal*, a small, inexpensive "pamphlet-missal" with each Sunday's liturgy printed in English. By the early 1940s, *My Sunday Missal* was being distributed to parishes throughout the United States.

In 1974, the format of the missal was modified to include a better, broader selection of music and its name was changed to *Today's Missal*. The missal gained popularity in 1977 with the initial publication of its companion piece, the annual *Music Issue*. "The things that make our missal program successful are our music and the variety of publications we have," said DeBruyn.

In 1980, the Catholic Truth Society changed its name to Oregon Catholic Press, and the next two decades saw continued growth and accomplishment. Oregon Catholic Press introduced several other missal programs in both English and Spanish. OCP also began publishing its own collections of liturgical music.

In 1982, Oregon Catholic Press published *Cánticos,* its first hymnal to address the needs of Spanish-speaking assemblies. OCP has since published another Spanish-language hymnal, *Flor y Canto* (both are now available in second editions), a children's hymnal (*Rise Up and Sing,* available in first and second editions), a hymnal combining traditional and contemporary music (*Journeysongs*) and a hymnbook for young adults (*Spirit & Song*).

In 1994, OCP acquired the music and products of North American Liturgy Resources (NALR). Included in this acquisition was *Glory & Praise,* the most popular Catholic hymnal ever published. In 1997, OCP published an expanded, updated version known as *Glory & Praise, 2nd Edition* which included, for the first time, many popular songs published by Oregon Catholic Press.

Oregon Catholic Press continued its rapid growth in 1998 by acquiring Pastoral Press, originally the book publishing division of the National Association of Pastoral Musicians (NPM). The addition of Pastoral Press products helps OCP stay true to its mission of service by making it easier for customers to obtain books by well-known composers and authors.

Oregon Catholic Press has grown in other ways as well. Recently, OCP became the exclusive distributor of FDLC (Federation of Diocesan Liturgical Commission) literature and publications, expanded its non-English offerings to include a Vietnamese hymnal, *Chung Lời Tán Tụng: United In Faith & Song,* and other Vietnamese-language products, and refined its popular *Unidos en Cristo,* a side-by-side bilingual (Spanish/English) worship resource.

In addition to its partnership with various international distributors, OCP has expanded its convenience to customers through its innovative website (www.ocp.org), which was completely revised this year to offer several new features including multimedia composer interviews, streaming audio of featured songs (updated monthly), online liturgy preparation aids such as Liturgy. com and improved ordering capabilities.

To date, Oregon Catholic Press administers thousands of copyrights, has published hundreds of collections of music and more than one thousand octavos, and has produced numerous hymnals, periodicals, books, software and videotapes. Currently, almost two-thirds of the parishes in the United States subscribe to one of OCP's missal programs. Besides its publishing efforts, Oregon Catholic Press facilitates over four hundred workshops each year in parishes and dioceses across the United States. OCP also exhibits its products and services at many conventions and trade shows.

Oregon Catholic Press has grown and evolved in many different ways since its modest beginnings in 1922. However, one thing has not changed—OCP's commitment to service. This commitment is the foundation and driving force behind OCP's success, say OCP staffers. "The people are the greatest part of Oregon Catholic Press," says

DeBruyn. "Their commitment to the church and to OCP's mission is amazing."

The Future of OCP and TL

In 1984, OCP had 34 employees and worked out of an archdiocesan pastoral center. Now OCP has 170 employees, and TL has expanded along with the company. With the help of a full-time marketing and creative services department, the publication has grown in both its content and appearance. "The elements that made it so successful originally are still there, such as the liturgy preparation aid element of the magazine," says DeBruyn. "It was the thing that set us apart from other publications."

Current editor Michael Prendergast, a liturgy specialist, says that his focus will continue to be making the publication stronger by offering a wide variety of quality editorial content to support TL's strong liturgy preparation foundation. "The front half of TL now gives it a unique voice in addition to giving subscribers the basic elements of liturgy planning," says Prendergast. "I see my job as strengthening that."

Authors

Most Reverend Victor H. Balke, a native of Meppen, Illinois, has served as the ordinary of Crookston, Minnesota, since 1976. He is currently serving as a member of the Administrative Board of the United States Conference of Catholic Bishops and is a consultant to the Committee on Home Missions, which he chaired from 1995 to 1998.

Dr. Glenn CJ Byer is a native of Busby, Alberta, Canada, and is managing editor of Pastoral Press, the book division of Oregon Catholic Press. He holds a doctorate in Sacred Liturgy from San Anselmo (Rome).

Paul Covino is Associate Chaplain and Director of Liturgy, The College of the Holy Cross, Worcester, Massachusetts, and Program Coordinator, The Georgetown Center for Liturgy, Washington, D.C. He is editor of the wedding workbook *Celebrating Marriage* (Pastoral Press) and columnist for *Today's Liturgy*.

Deacon Owen F. Cummings is Regents' Professor of Theology at Mount Angel Seminary in Oregon and visiting lecturer at the Liturgical Institute, University of St. Mary of the Lake, Mundelein, Illinois. He is a Doctor of Divinity from the University of Dublin, Trinity College. Dr. Cummings is author of *Mystical Women, Mystical Body* (Pastoral Press).

Alan F. Detscher, presbyter of the Diocese of Bridgeport and archpriest of the Diocese of St. Maron (Maronites), has a doctorate in Sacred Theology from San Anselmo (Rome). He served as Executive Director of the Secretariat for the Liturgy of the United States Conference of Catholic Bishops from 1994 to 1996.

James A. Field, a presbyter of the Archdiocese of Boston, is the former Director of the Office for Worship and past board member of the Federation of Diocesan Liturgical Commissions.

Antonio Alcalde Fernández, author and composer, serves as pastor for the Church of the Good Shepherd and is professor of languages and letters for the Seminary of Madrid. There he facilitates courses, seminars and workshops on liturgical symbolism and pastoral music. He is liturgical consultant and coordinator for the Episcopal Commission of Spain.

Virgil C. Funk, a presbyter of the diocese of Arlington, Virginia, is President Emeritus, National Association of Pastoral Musicians.

Dr. Jeremy Gallet, SP, is a member of the Sisters of Providence of Saint Mary of the Woods, Indiana. Sister Jeremy is the Director of the Office of Worship for the Archdiocese of Portland in Oregon. She holds a Ph.D. in Liturgy and the Arts from the Graduate Theological Union in Berkeley, California.

Dr. Linda L. Gaupin, CDP, Ph.D, is a member of the Congregation of Divine Providence, was the associate director of the Secretariat for the Liturgy of the United States Conference of Catholic Bishops from 1991 to 1994 and is Director of Religious Education for the Diocese of Orlando, Florida. She has a Ph.D. in Religious Studies from the Catholic University of America.

Clara Dina Hinojosa completed a Master of Arts degree in Liturgical Studies from St. John's University, Collegeville, Minnesota. Employed by the Diocese of Kansas City-St. Joseph, she is a staff member of the Center for Pastoral Life & Ministry, an office committed to lay ministry formation and dedicated to modeling and promoting collaborative ministry within the chancery and diocese.

Edward J. Hislop is a presbyter of the Diocese of Helena, Montana, and served as chair of the board of the Federation of Diocesan Liturgical Commissions from 1996 to 1999. Fr. Hislop holds an M.A. in Liturgical Studies from the University of Notre Dame, Indiana.

Jan Michael Joncas is a presbyter of the Archdiocese of St. Paul and Minneapolis, composer of liturgical music, presenter of workshops internationally, professor of theology at the University of St. Thomas in St. Paul, Minnesota, and a member of the Liturgical Studies faculty of the Department of Theology at the University of Notre Dame, Indiana. Fr. Joncas holds a doctorate in Sacred Liturgy from the Pontificio Instituto Liturgico (Rome).

Dr. Corinna Laughlin is liturgy associate at the Liturgy and Music Office of Seattle's St. James Cathedral. She holds a Ph.D. in English from the University of Washington. Her previous publications have dealt with topics in eighteenth-century British and American literature.

John K. Leonard is associate professor and chair of the Religious Studies Department at Edgewood College in Madison, Wisconsin. He has a doctorate in Liturgical Studies from the University of Notre Dame, Indiana.

Patrick L. Malloy, a priest of the Episcopal Diocese of Bethlehem, Pennsylvania, is a member of the Standing Commission for Liturgy and Music of the Episcopal Church and rector of Grace Episcopal church in Allentown, Pennslyvania. He holds has a doctorate in Liturgical Studies from the University of Notre Dame, Indiana.

Dr. Dolores Martinez is currently the Director of the Office of Worship for the Archdiocese of San Antonio where she has served for over eight years. Her previous experience includes ministry as a liturgist and music director at both the parish and diocesan levels for the church in Texas.

Michael P. Mernagh, a native of Canada, is the director of liturgical music at St. Meinrad School of Theology in southern Indiana. He holds an M.A. in Theology with a concentration in liturgy from St. John's University in Collegeville, Minnesota.

Michael R. Prendergast is liturgy specialist and editor of *Today's Liturgy* and *Prayer of the Faithful* at Oregon Catholic Press in Portland, Oregon. He is the author of *Music in the Liturgy for Small Parishes,* a video published by The Liturgical Press of Collegeville, Minnesota. Michael holds a Masters Degree in Theological Studies from Mt. Angel Seminary, St. Benedict, Oregon, and an M.A. in Liturgical Studies from St. John's University, Collegeville, Minnesota.

Mary Jo Quinn, SCL, a Sister of Charity of Leavenworth Kansas, is director of music and liturgy at the Nativity of Mary Parish in Independence, Missouri. Mary Jo served on the board of directors of the National Association of Pastoral Musicians (NPM) from 1995 to 2001. Mary Jo holds a Master of Liturgical Music from St. Joseph College in Rensselaer, Indiana.

Jon Reddy is a reporter for the *Catholic Sentinel,* the newspaper of the Archdiocese of Portland in Oregon. A native of Portland, he holds a B.A. in journalism from Gonzaga University, Spokane, Washington.

Dr. Elaine Rendler is a teacher, author, choir director, composer and pastoral liturgist. Elaine works with parishes and dioceses throughout the country to further the cause of liturgical renewal. Her quarterly column appears in *Today's Liturgy*. Elaine is the director of pastoral music at Bellarmine Chapel at George Mason University in Fairfax, Virginia, as well as director of the Georgetown Chorale, a 90-member singing group that combines community service with music while performing the classics of choral literature. Elaine holds a Doctor of Musical Arts degree in organ performance from the Catholic University of America, Washington, D.C.

She is the author of *In the Midst of the Assembly* (9664PQ), *This is the Day* (10106PQ), *Keyboard Praise, Volume 1* (9081PQ), *Volume 2* (9735PQ), and double CD (11061PQ). Elaine also served as a co-editor of Pastoral Press's *Celebrating Marriage—Preparing the Wedding Liturgy: A Workbook for Engaged Couples* (6095PQ).

H. Richard Rutherford, CSC, a Holy Cross priest, is an associate professor of theology at the University of Portland. He is the author of *The Death of a Christian*. Father Rutherford holds a doctorate in Liturgical Theology from the Catholic University of Nijmegen (Netherlands).

Philip J. Sandstrom, S.T.D., presbyter of the Archdiocese of New York, is currently vicar for the English-speaking people in the Cathedral Parish of Brussels, Belgium.

Dr. James Savage has been director of music at St. James Cathedral since 1981. He has led the cathedral choir on concert tours to Russia, Italy, France and Spain. His doctoral studies were at the universities of Tubingen and Washington. He is on the Steering Committee of the Conference of Roman Catholic Cathedral Musicians and serves on the Council of the National Association of Pastoral Musicians, which named him Pastoral Musician of the Year in 2002.

Eugene Walsh, SS, S.T.D. (1911–1989) was a preacher, teacher, theologian and writer who spent most of his life in seminary work. In the wake of Vatican II, his passionate love of people, his commitment to life-giving liturgical celebration and his compassion for humaneness caught fire with the priestly people of God. His legacy of written material still speaks truth today.